The Color of Pure

A Story of Life, Love, and Sexual Purity, Rated PG-13

By L.J. Bleed

The Color of Pure
A Story of Life, Love, and Sexual Purity,
Rated PG-13

Cover design by Cathy Helms,
www.avalongraphics.org.

Published by LJB Communications, LLC
in the United States of America

ISBN: 978-0-9888322-2-0
First Paperback Edition: February, 2013

Contents

Dedicated to my sisters of present and future generations, from a prodigal with sexual scars. May you fall in love and learn to fight.

Soli Deo Gloria

"Why does your teacher eat with tax collectors and 'sinners?'" On hearing this, Jesus said, "It is not the healthy who need a doctor, but the sick. But go and learn what this means: 'I desire mercy, not sacrifice.' For I have not come to call the righteous, but sinners."

The Great Physician, Matthew 9:11-13

Prologue

I AM the WORD . . . I LOVE YOU . . . I CHOOSE YOU . . .

I AM YOUR FATHER . . . YOU ARE MY CHILD . . . EVEN THE DARKNESS WILL NOT BE DARK TO ME.

Did she hear this inside of her? No. This time was different. New little nubs on the side of her head burned when she sensed the words. She flicked her tiny hand against one of them and laughed.

YOU ARE FEARFULLY AND WONDERFULLY MADE.

Oh, the pretty music!

Beautiful harmonies soothed and excited her. She smiled and waited for her favorite crescendo, then somersaulted. *Whee! That was fun.*

I HAVE LOVED YOU WITH AN EVERLASTING LOVE.

The warm fluid encased her being.

She sucked her thumb. Smiling, she closed her eyes and drifted back to her dream. Her tiny heart felt safe and at peace. Praise radiated from her inner core.

I LOVE YOU, CHLOE.

Chapter 1

Chloe Rahab Hudson remembered them from in utero. But, can a person have memories from before she was born? Let alone remember colors no one else can see?

She breathed in the salty Pacific air, sashaying from pose to pose for the camera. The frigid waves cascaded her ankles, as the warm California sun penetrated her skin. A soft breeze tossed her hair, tickling her taut shoulders, far better than any well-placed studio fan.

Every click of Geena's camera filled Chloe with suspense, and that odd feeling that scientists dub *déjà vu*, a sensation that she'd experienced something, that by most given realities, she simply couldn't have.

Which one of my déjà vu colors will I see a glimpse of next? Dust? Veranda? Peekadilly?

"Chloe, you look fabulous. The camera loves you," said Geena, motioning her assistant to tilt the reflection screen slightly. "Let's get one in direct sunlight now to show off that beautiful skin!" Geena changed her angle and sighed. "Wow, skin with a natural touch of cinnamon and a hint of honey. *You* are gorgeous."

Getting paid to do this? What could be better? Maybe dust, veranda, and peekadilly were her secret modeling good-luck charms! *I was made to be a model. Why does Mom keep pushing the artist thing?*

"I heard you just had a birthday," said Geena. "So, let's see your famous-15 pose." Geena took a large step backward and changed her angle.

So far, fifteen hadn't been so grand. Suddenly everyone in the whole world expected Chloe to know what she wanted to be when she grew up, what she was "working toward," and blah, blah, blah. *But today is enlightening. Today seals the deal. I shall be a model. I'm telling Mom ix-nay on the art-nay.*

Though today was her first *paying* gig, Chloe had been modeling for her mother's camera, and seeing glimpses of her secret colors, for as long as she could remember. Mom was a professional photographer on the top of the freelance food chain. Her business, SDG Photography, consistently landed her major assignments in California, around the country, and even worldwide.

When Mom was on photo furlough, she carefully recorded every stage of Chloe's life. Some pictures were the goofy kind that all moms take, like Chloe balancing a book on her head or dressing up like a princess. Others were more calendar-like, with the help of props and backgrounds in Mom's home-based studio, in their beachfront bungalow, just a short walk down the beach.

Dust! A glimpse of dust hovered in the air until veranda appeared. Dust was short for Dusty, the name of her would-be, beloved pet dog which, unfortunately, she never got because of Mom's allergies and travel schedule.

The next two camera clicks brought dust again and again, and then veranda.

Veranda! Veranda was Chloe's favorite and the first color she officially named. When she and Mom traveled to Austria for the "Ski Resorts in Europe" spread, they stayed in a luxurious, five-star hotel with an entire wall of windows. Just outside, a beautiful veranda faced the Swiss Alps, reminiscent of a postcard.

"Hold on a sec, Chloe," said Geena, adjusting the lens on her camera. "I need a couple of minutes here. Just relax for a few."

Speckles of colorful beach towels dotted the sand. Moonlit Beach had just opened to the public at 10 a.m. A small group of tourists formed an audience on the waterfront, a few taking pictures of Chloe on their own, like amateur paparazzi.

Was Mom there? Chloe scanned the group, hoping to see a tall blonde. No Mom.

A twenty-something mother struggled to push a stroller with wailing contents on the wet sand. The baby's cry magnified, sounding like a revving engine. The young mom plucked a bundle of pale yellow into her arms and began rocking it, changing the wails to coos and gurgles.

The cry reminded Chloe of several of Mom's stories about herself. Or were they memories? Memories are tricky. How do you know if you are actually remembering something, or if you're just remembering a story someone told you about yourself?

When I was six weeks old, I remember a photo shoot in Mom's studio. I sat snuggled in my car seat, lined with a white furry blanket, on top of the round glass table, in front of a black background. "Say, 'Jesus Loves Me,' Sweet Baby," Mom said to me in a loving, playful voice. I cooed and smiled for the first three or four shots, the way I did when I watched my favorite Baby Einstein video. But then I screamed. When I was two, I could finally explain why I was so frustrated. "'Cause I like the pretty colors and they go bye-bye." When I was four, I received my first pack of 64 Crayons, the kind with the cool sharpener. I flipped open the cover and did a quick scan for dust, veranda, and peekadilly, and then a slow, careful re-scan. "Where are the other three colors?" I asked.

THE TALK, at age eight, was probably my biggest revelation. After the initial shock that my mother actually did THAT to have me, I started thinking . . . I remember when I saw my déjà vu colors for the very first time. Mom showed me a book of how babies develop and change weekly when they're inside their mom's tummies. How could any of that be familiar to me? But it was. It was at week 16 of development that I remember being aware of my déjà vu colors, there with me, in my small, dark space.

None of Chloe's friends could remember anything before kindergarten. And colors that don't exist on this earth?

"I don't see why not," Mom said. "Maybe your colors are a special gift from God." Later, though, Mom seemed a little upset and said it might be best to keep the colors a secret. Chloe tried lots of times to describe them to Mom, but it was like trying to describe a rainbow to a blind person.

Peppy wasn't much help either. AKA Mr. Pepperton, Chloe's private art instructor, Peppy was a high-strung, scrawny guy who looked like Norman

Rockwell in his self portrait. Chloe tried hundreds of times to duplicate her *déjà vu* colors with the acrylics on her artist's palette, but each attempt left a mess of dark brown or black that invited a Peppy scolding not to waste paint. When Chloe asked him if he knew anything about colors from a different dimension or colors farther down on the light spectrum, he just looked at her like she was a freak. Especially after she'd asked the third time. That's when he got out his Pantone Matching System set and said, "If they aren't on here, they don't exist. Got it?"

"Got it?" Geena said to her assistant. "Okay, Chloe. Sorry for the break. We're good to go again."

A warm feeling swept over Chloe as she watched the young mom now bouncing a pudgy-cute baby on her hip. *Someday I want to be a mom and have six kids with Mr. Right.*

"Keep the motion going, Chloe," Geena said, looking both shocked and delighted. "Oh, I can't believe this! You're a natural." Geena ferociously clicked her camera like she was operating a machine gun.

Peekadilly! Finally.

The color itself wasn't pleasing, but Chloe loved the name she chose for it: a combination of her favorite game as a baby (Peek-A-Boo) and Dilly: the name of her best-friend-Felecia's favorite sandwich, the most disgusting combination *ever* (peanut butter and dill pickle). They argued over whether it was actually a word, and Chloe won because it wasn't in the dictionary, and it didn't work on spell check.

"Great, Chloe. Okay, now let's see a few army poses, since this is Camo-N-Cute wear." With a flick of two fingers, Geena motioned her assistant to move quicker, slightly frustrated, as though she was missing masterpiece photos awaiting their moment in time.

Chloe laughed as she brought her arms together and clasped her hands to make a gun out of her index fingers.

"Yes, Chloe, you're a fighter!" Geena swished in the water around Chloe, clicking her camera as fast as possible from every angle. "Okay, that's a wrap. Awesome job. Oh, I can't wait to see these. I'll have the proofs online for you later today. Lisa--I mean your mom--has the password. Where is she, anyway?"

A pang of disappointment pinched Chloe's heart. "I'm not sure. I thought she'd be here."

"Seems odd that she would miss your first official photo op," said Geena. "What's up?"

Chloe feigned a half-smile behind her concern. "She's had a lot of appointments lately." *A lot of secret appointments.* "Geena, thanks for getting me this job. You know how much I want to be a model."

"I thought you wanted to be a world-famous artist."

"Yes, that, too. I guess I'm not really sure what I'm supposed to be." *I mean, really, how should I know? I'm only 15.*

"Well, if you do land on modeling, your sense of surprise and fun will take you far. You should try out for *Our Next Top Model*." Geena took a towel and wiped some saltwater off her camera before putting it in the case.

Our Next Top Model? Of course. Mom has connections in New York. It's meant to be. But Mom's not big on the whole modeling thing, not the way she is about my going to the School of the Art Institute of Chicago. Chloe pulled a T-shirt from her duffle bag and pulled it over her head. *But modeling has to be what I was made for. Why else would I see colors, special colors, every time a camera flashes?*

"Want a ride home?" said Geena.

"No, I'll walk, but thanks anyway."

* * *

Chloe grabbed a shiny red apple from the wire basket on the granite breakfast island and took a crunchy bite. A cool breeze ballooned through the large window above the stainless steel sink overlooking the ocean. She looked beyond the palm tree in the backyard to the crisp blue sky, puffed with clouds. Could today get any better? *Well, yes. Maybe if my best friend had been there to see the first moment of my official career, or at least left me a note saying where she was.*

On her last bite, she threw the core into the disposal and reached for the switch. There, Mom's ring holder, in the shape of a soaring eagle, with wings spread, sat patriotically. Mom's gaudy, fake diamond ring dangled around its neck, choking it, just as it had done to Chloe's attempts at matchmaking for her mom throughout the years.

A pang of disgust ran through Chloe's veins. She hated that ring. Its size alone, 1 1/2 carats of internally-flawless-diamond-whatever-that-means, screamed to a multitude of interested men, "Don't ask me out, because I'm already married!" and "Don't even *think* about becoming Chloe's dad!" That ring was a lie. Mom wasn't married, but she wore that stinking ring on her left finger as though she was.

Plenty of men noticed Mom and tried to talk to her. Then, they seemed to forget about how beautiful she was, and instead admired her intelligence, kindness, and zest for life. But that darn diamond ring squelched every fire of a romance before it could even get started. Until lately. Why wasn't Mom wearing it anymore?

The faint scent of Rhododendron wafted through the kitchen, mixing with the salty air and wooing Chloe outdoors toward the beach.

Reluctantly, she looked toward the living room at her art easel. Her self portrait entitled "Mocha" was due to Peppy tomorrow, and at this point, still portrayed her as alien-like. *Definitely needs a makeover*, she thought, walking through the openness of the bungalow toward her canvas. *Like Mom did to this place.*

Before-and-after pictures in the hallway off the foyer testified to Mom's uncanny ability to see potential in anything, and anyone, for that matter. In the case of their beach bungalow, she'd bought it for next-to-nothing on a fluke auction and then fashioned it into something that looked straight out of *Architectural Digest.*

Chloe settled in front of her canvas and picked up a brush just as the phone rang. She reached for the cordless on the computer desk and answered. "Hello, Hudson residence."

On the other end of the line, a sweet Indian voice spilled out. "Hullo, this is Dahlia from Dahlia's Bridal. We have all of your alterations completed. You can pick up your dress any time. We are open each night until 6 p.m."

Bridal? Chloe froze, her paintbrush slipping through her fingers.

"Hullo?"

"What were the alterations for again?" said Chloe.

"Your wedding dress, Dear." The woman laughed. "I don't have many brides forget about their dress. You won't forget to pick it up, will you?"

"No, of course not. Thanks so much." Chloe clicked the phone, her heart racing.

A wave of excitement went through her. A wedding dress? Secret appointments? Lots of errands? Could Mom have a secret lover? How exciting! *Is my dream finally coming true?*

Chloe had dreamed of romance for her mom, *forever*. Getting a dad out of the deal wouldn't be so bad, either. But wait. Married? Unless she'd missed something significant, no man was currently in the picture. Could Mom be in love with someone that her own daughter didn't know about? *Wouldn't she tell me?*

Still deep in thought, Chloe returned the cordless phone to the computer desk. She paused. The computer.

Maybe Mom had a mysterious, romantic Internet relationship? Of course. It all made sense. Why else would she be spending so much time online lately?

Chloe closed her eyes and pictured Mom with Mr. Wonderful. *At this very moment, they're probably enjoying a romantic beach picnic, feeding each other fresh fruit, drinking champagne, and reading Song of Songs, as he gently caresses her long blonde hair.*

Giddiness simmered inside her as she typed her password into the computer. Now, what was she looking for? Would Mom ever go to a chat room? Chloe's French-manicured fingernail tapped the keys to the Favorites Box, where she looked at recent search history: Foreverweddings.com, Anjou Fine Chocolates, and Dodge Monuments were the most recent entries.

Anjou Fine Chocolates! They made the sweetest wedding party favors--petite wedding cakes made from white or milk chocolate, in a molded clear-plastic dome, with a tiny satin ribbon around the base. They would be perfect. She and Mom were looking at them in the catalog last week, as they each munched a tiny pear chocolate from her annual one-pound birthday box from Uncle Gary in Indiana. Uncle Gary. He would for sure come out for the wedding. When could it be?

Chloe heard the muffled sound of the garage door opening. *Mom's home.* She hit the "X" at the top of the screen. *Be nonchalant.*

"Hey, Chlo, I'm home," Mom said, arms loaded with shopping bags, a large white box with UPS tape around it, and a CoffeeCups hot drink. She walked to the island and emptied her arms. "How was the photo shoot? Isn't that the coolest line? You get to keep the swimsuit, don't you?"

Chloe brimmed and a smile filled her face. "Mom, it was *so* awesome. Geena said I did really great." Chloe went for one of the bags, but Mom nonchalantly took it from her hands.

"I'm sure you did. How could you go wrong?" Mom paused, and looked deep into Chloe's eyes. Stroking her hair, she said, "You're such a beautiful girl. I love you, Chloe."

Was that a tinge of sadness in Mom's eyes? Or was she just tired? She seemed to be tired a lot lately. Wait. *She's probably sad that it won't just be the two of us anymore. It's okay, Mom, because the three of us will live happily ever after! I'm sure I'll love your Mr. Wonderful.* "I love you, too," said Chloe, with a hug. "I'm your Mocha, right?"

"Sweet and strong," said Mom.

"With a shot of stubborn." Chloe and Mom laughed.

"Well, Miss Mocha, tomorrow it's you and me. Day trip to Oceanside," said Mom, with a gleam in her eye. I have some things to talk about with you."

Of course, you do.

* * *

From the passenger's seat of Mom's VW convertible bug, Chloe absorbed the fresh breeze into her pores and inhaled the sea-salt scent, as Mom zoomed up the Pacific Coast Highway. Classical music blared from the radio. Chloe smiled big. Was there anything better than spending the whole day with Mom? *Shopping, lunch out, mani's and pedi's . . . and then wedding plans!*

Mom turned off at an unfamiliar exit and drove to the front gate of the Camp Joseph H. Pendleton Marine Base. She shifted the stick into neutral and searched her oversized Coach purse for her wallet. "We're here for the 9 a.m. group tour," she said, handing her driver's license to the Marine at his post.

Chloe scrunched her face. Really? Visiting a military base was not exactly what she had in mind for Girl's Day Out to learn about romantic-and-impending wedding. Confused, she stared at the twenty-something Marine who reminded her of a *Toy Story* soldier, minus the green face.

He turned to her and said, "And yours, Ma'am?"

Cool. He thinks I'm older. "Oh, I'm only 15, but I'll be getting my learner's permit soon," she said.

"How long does the tour last?" Mom asked.

"It's over at 11 a.m., Ma'am," he said, stately.

Impatience flew through Chloe's body. You're kidding. Two hours? When would they shop and walk the beach and drink mochas? Not to mention the fact that a Marine base was about the most *un-*

romantic place ever to learn about a new dad and discuss wedding plans.

Unless . . . .

Is Mom dating a Marine? Maybe Mr. Wonderful will pop up on the tour?

Not so.

After an ever-so-boring tour of duty--without *any* surprises, and learning more about the Marines than one person needed to know in a lifetime, Mom drove up the coast to Crystal Cove State Park.

Our picnic landscape looked like it could have won first place in a *Field and Stream* photo contest---dotted with white and sandy areas, amidst wild grasses and small yellow flowers. Mom spread an oversized throw and mounted it with the picnic basket and cooler on opposite corners. Within moments, a mini spread of two large salads, key lime cookies, and two bottles of Perrier water lay beautifully displayed in front of them. The light scent of salty sea air mixed with Mom's perfume as a warm breeze came off the waves, below in the distance.

A feeling of warmth and serenity penetrated Chloe's soul. She closed her eyes, letting the sun soak into her skin. Mom knew what she loved. Except for the little Marine tour blunder. What had that been about?

"I'll pray for us," Mom said, closing her eyes and looking toward the sky. "Our Father and Creator, we thank you for being our Savior and Great Physician, our Closest Companion, Provider and Protector, and the Lover of Our Souls. We love you and long for you."

Mom's standard prayer. Chloe knew it by heart. Some kids say, "Now I lay me down to sleep," or the Lord's Prayer, but this prayer she remembered even from when Mom tucked her into her crib as a baby. Yet, sometime in the last few years, the prayer started to make Chloe cringe. Closest Companion? *But Mom is alone.* Father? *Puhleese. I don't have one.* If God was so great, why hadn't he sent some earthly schlep before now to marry her mom, and be her dad, and take her to the Homeschool Purity Ball when she was ten?

"Chlo, I want to talk to you about something really important today." Mom reached into the side pocket of her sundress and pulled out her diamond ring, holding it up in the air, gazing at it, and then putting it on her left hand as if she were thinking, *We've been through a lot together.*

Of course. She wouldn't need that ring from H-E-double-toothpicks to scare off suitors any more. Mom and Mr. Wonderful probably had picked out a new engagement ring together. Wonder if it's pearl? Pearls are *so* romantic. Much more than gaudy cubic zirconiums. Mom's ring had kind of ruined diamonds for Chloe. *Mr. Right will someday give me a pearl engagement ring.* Excitedly, Chloe waited for Mom to place the ring on her finger, but she didn't.

"Your purity is a beautiful treasure, Chloe." Mom reached for the cooler. Opening it, she turned back toward Chloe and said, "Close your eyes."

Chloe felt a wrapped gift box being placed in her hands.

"Okay, open it," Mom said.

On the top of the dark brown box were the words D'Anjou Fine Chocolates ornately written in metallic gold. A stretchy gold ribbon diagonally secured the top to the bottom.

I love D'Anjou! Chloe carefully removed the ribbon, and twisted it two times around her wrist, making it into a bracelet. Her eyes looked bright as she removed the lid and saw a member of her favorite food group. Chocolate always made her smile. And get zits. But who cared? "Oh, it's so pretty."

Inside, a heart-shaped box, entirely made of dark chocolate, was topped with a delicate white chocolate ribbon, coated with shimmery pearlescent dust. Tucked next to it was a white iridescent envelope.

The good manners Mom had drilled into Chloe's head reminded her to open the card first. She pulled out a piece of stationary that matched the envelope. The words "Fighting Psalms" were printed neatly at the top in Mom's handwriting. Underneath, several Bible passages were listed.

Chloe bristled slightly inside. *Another dose of Mom's words of wisdom, Bible-Style. Why did everything have to involve God, the Bible, and religion? Well, at least there's chocolate with it.*

Chloe carefully plucked the chocolate heart, still cool to the touch, from the box. What kind of treasure could be inside? With a sense of anticipation, she slowly lifted the lid to find . . .

Army guys.

Army guys?

A handful of tiny army guys made from white, dark, and milk chocolate sat barricaded in the bottom of their chocolate foxhole.

"Chloe, love is a battlefield," Mom said with a serious look on her face. "And you have an Enemy." Mom stared at Chloe, waiting for her response.

Mom's Mr. Wonderful *must* be a Marine. "An Enemy?" Chloe said, with a small touch of sass. She picked up a white soldier and bit off his machine gun.

"Chlo, it's no secret that I didn't treasure my purity when I was your age."

Yep. It didn't take a Nancy Drew to figure that one out. The biggest clue was the story of my dad. But, "He did not know you," doesn't really qualify as a story. Stories have details, and beginnings and endings. The "story" I heard of my dad was more like the beginning of a dysfunctional haiku or the title of a country western song. A ditty where dear ol' dad supplies the sperm and splits.

A pulsating curiosity went through Chloe's body. *Maybe Mom was finally going to fill in the sketchy details of her sordid past?* She sat silently, pondering her mother's words. Then an epiphany struck her. Maybe *dad* was the new, mysterious boyfriend! Maybe he'd been searching for Mom and Chloe all these years to no avail. And then, the great and powerful Internet rescued and reunited him with the two women he loved and cherished most in the world.

Mom's face looked intense. "Nobody ever told me that my purity was a gift to protect. A *gift*, Chloe." Chloe lowered the cookie she was about to put in her mouth. "If only . . . ." Staring a dull stare toward the ocean, Mom said, "You have to do more than just treasure it. You have to guard it, even *fight* to protect it."

As if on cue, to make her point even stronger, a military helicopter flew over, probably from Camp Pendleton.

Not surprising. Mom was in cahoots with the Big Guy Upstairs. She was the epitome of what the religious crowd calls a prayer warrior. And she got results.

Having a prayer warrior for a mom actually came in quite handy. Every time there was a problem, Chloe deferred to Mom, who would either fix it or pray about it. Usually both.

"Chloe, you can't fight on your own, and what you crave can't be filled with any human relationship. You have a God-sized hole in your heart that *only* Christ can fill--nobody else--not a dad, not me, not a guy. I *know*. I tried to fill my emptiness with sex, but I was never satisfied."

"Not this again." Chloe rolled her eyes. "Mom. I can't even *talk* to a guy. And I don't have too many calling me, asking me for sex, thank you very much."

"I know, but you spend a lot of time fantasizing, and thoughts lead to actions. You might think you know yourself, but trust me, you don't. Every teen girl will be tested, because purity is a spiritual battle," said Mom. "You have to know what you're fighting against. Sin doesn't always look like a snake."

Chloe squirmed. She looked around the grassy landscape surrounding the picnic site, hoping there were no snake props in Mom's little story lesson.

"Especially sexual sin," Mom said candidly. "It's seductive and deceptive." Mom's eyes looked beyond Chloe's, like she was in some sort of weird trance. "But, it's a lie," she said slowly. "It promises to make you feel loved . . . and special . . . and accepted, but the whole time it's trying to kill . . . and steal . . . and destroy you." Mom paused, pushing back from Chloe and looking deep into her eyes again with a sense of urgency. "Chloe, each one of us was born with a sinful, selfish heart that wants to fulfill our own cravings. But sex is supposed to be an intimate *gift*. The world is full of deceptive philosophies, groups with agendas for you, people who want to justify their own sin . . . seductive advertising. The world constantly tells you that anything and everything is normal and natural, but that's a lie, Chloe."

Chloe looked at her watch to check the time.

"Sin is something you have to *kill,* not explore," continued Mom. "God loves you and has a plan and a purpose for your life, but so do Satan and his demons. They hate you and they want to wreck your life and your future. They'll use your own sin and confusion, and the world, to take you down any way they can, and sexual sin is one of their most popular tools because it works on so many people."

Chloe glazed over as Mom started to sound like Charlie Brown's teacher. *When is she going to get to the wedding stuff already?*

" . . . and so, here, I want you to have it." Mom slipped her diamond ring off her finger. It had become wobbly during the past few months. She held it up in the air in front of them. "I want you to wear it as a purity ring, as a reminder to keep your mind--and your body--and your heart *pure* for Christ and to remember that He is your Rock. He won't ever leave you. He'll fight *for* you, and He'll enable you to conquer your spiritual enemies."

For just a split second, Chloe thought she saw a tiny sparkle of veranda glistening in the diamond. Then, it was a fleck of dust, as Mom reached for Chloe's right hand, cupping her ring finger.

A thin, but sturdy gold band held the solitaire diamond, about the size of a pencil eraser. Mom squeezed the ring on Chloe's finger, pushing it down until it abruptly stopped above Chloe's knuckle. She tried again.

Chloe took over, pushing it too, but it was like Cinderella's stepsister trying to squeeze her size tens into Cindy's dainty glass fives. 'Tis a sorrowful day when one realizes her hands look like a bouquet of corn dogs. *I guess I'll never be a hand model.* "Do you think my fingers are fat?"

Mom looked at her hand. Hesitantly, "I've never noticed." She paused, staring. "So what. We'll just have to get the ring sized," she said. "Your fingers look fine. Don't worry about it."

Did my mother just confirm that my hands look like Porky Pig's?

"Chloe, you are a beautiful girl, fearfully and wonderfully made, *exactly* the way you are. We all have something we don't like about ourselves. Don't let your enemy use it against you. Don't believe lies."

"Okay," Chloe said, partially unconvinced. Chloe took the ring off her inflated phalange and held it in the late afternoon sun, twirling it ever so slightly. *Dust!* She angled it the other direction. There was veranda! And the tiniest twist brought peekadilly. With each turn and twirl of the gem, dust, veranda and peekadilly stared back at her. Or was she imagining it? *This is amazing!*

A rush of excitement coursed through her veins. To think that her *déjà vu* colors had been hiding in this ring, 24/7, for her gazing! Chloe thought of all the times she had tried to recreate them with her acrylics--all the flash photography pictures she had taken of her face when she was naming them--all of her intrigue in seeing them when she had her picture taken. And all of the frustrating times she had tried to describe the colors to Mom, who just couldn't visualize them. All of that, when she could have just looked at her *déjà vu* colors in Mom's annoying ring any old time she wanted? She turned to her mom with noticeable excitement. "Do you see them? My *déjà vu* colors are in the diamond!" Smiling, Chloe handed it to her. "Did you know they were in there?"

Mom peered closely at the ring, twirling it. "No. I didn't know," she said, stunned. A puzzled, but pleasant look filled her face. "I wonder if this means something."

"What? What does it mean?"

"I'm not sure," said Mom, seeming to shrug it off. "Maybe someday when I get to heaven, I'll see what your colors look like." She smiled at Chloe. "In the meantime, we'll get it sized."

"Thank you, Mom. I'll wear it all the time."

"You're welcome, my Sweet Mocha," said Mom, her eyes moist. "Be careful with it. I had it insured for---"

"Insured?" Chloe laughed. "Do people insure cubic zirconiums?"

Mom shook her head with a pleasant smirk. "Chloe," she sighed. "It's an internally flawless, signature cut, grade D diamond. It's worth about $50,000."

Shocked--like someone who buys a piece of junk at a garage sale and later finds out it's a museum treasure--Chloe stared at the ring, stunned. This ring she had despised all of her life, suddenly held new promise. Funny how something can be utterly meaningless to you one day, and the next, you realize it's infinitely valuable.

* * *

Patience was not Chloe's virtue. Did Mom take her ring to the slowest jeweler on the face of the planet? When was Mr. Wonderful going to make his debut? And when was Mom going to call her contact in New York about getting her a shot at being on *Our Next Top Model?*

Chloe dragged her favorite lounger from the sandy area behind the white picket fence at the bottom of the Hudson's stone stairway, through a maze of tourists polka-dotting the beach. The hot July sun drenched her skin, warming it. She smoothed her brightly-colored beach towel over the lounger, kicked off her flip-flops, and unbuttoned her coverup. Settling in, she pulled a manila envelope and sketch pad from her beach bag.

She held the envelope in her hand. Was she ready for this? Enclosed was Pepperton's evaluation of her self portrait. Nervously, she untied the red string from the clasp, closed her eyes and pulled out two pages. How many points would she get out of ten? Peppy always wrote the number in green. She peered down at the paper, opening one eye at a time to see a . . . big, fat, green six. A six? You're kidding. *See, Mom. There's no way I'm getting into the Art Institute of the Museum of Art of Chicago.*

Pushing her sunglasses up, she sighed heavily as she swallowed the five points of Pepperton humiliation.

One. I think you've used too much orange for your skin tone. It makes you look like a white person with a spray tan instead of an African-American with honey-brown skin.

Two. Aren't your eyes deep brown? Why did you paint them black?

Three. As I recall, your hair goes approximately two inches below your shoulders and is jet black. You portrayed it shoulder length and brownish black. You should have added a highlight to designate shine.

Four. Good work on your proportioning. Your height appears to be on scale. (Aren't you about 5'11" tall?)

Five. Your fingers are actually larger than you painted them.

"Your painting is coming along. Keep trying. Please see attached for your next assignment." Sincerely, Charlie Pepperton.

Chloe bristled. Ugh. *This must be confirmation that I'm supposed to be a model.*

She flipped to the assignment sheet and read, "An outdoor landscape." Tapping her pencil on her sketch pad, she looked around. Plenty of inspiration here.

A heavy blue band divided the horizon from the aqua-colored water. Shining brightly, the California sun delighted a slew of tan-seeking tourists.Vivacious waves crashed on the beach in rhythmic motion.

Just past the umbrella closest to her, a mom unpacked a wagon full of sand castle supplies, beach towels, and a car seat cupping an infant. Following behind her like ducklings, trotted five happy-go-lucky kids of stair-step ages.

Chloe watched the woman, admiring her.

Would she finally get the siblings she always wanted if Mom got married? *Someday I'm having lots of kids with Mr. Right. Oh, Note to self: Remind Mom to pray that I have three girls and three boys.* The beach mom alternated between lathering white bodies with sun screen and meeting requests for juice boxes and sand castle buckets.

A warm feeling went through Chloe. She closed her eyes for a moment and breathed in and out a few times. *Okay. Landscape. My beautiful beach.* Making a broad stroke with her pencil, she formed the horizon on her sketch pad. Next some clouds. She continued, alternating between her sketch pad and the beautiful landscape. Then, she did a double take.

A small red head bobbed in the water. Two arms flailed.

Chloe watched for two more seconds. Panicked, she looked at the mother of six and counted at rapid-fire speed. The mom looked completely unaware of any concern as she blew up a pair of floaties.

A rush of adrenaline coursed through Chloe's veins. Her sketch pad flew to sand, as she bolted toward the shore. Salty and cold, the water stung her legs as she scooped the toddler into her arms. "Help! I need help!" she yelled, struggling back toward the beach, patting his back. Cupping the back of the boy's head with her hand, she carefully lowered his limp body to the wet sand.

A lifeguard running full-speed met her at the scene, readying himself to perform CPR. Within moments, a small group of people had gathered around.

In the distance, Chloe heard muffled cries."Jonathon! Where's Jonathon?"

A woman, who looked frightened, poked her head through the circle of spectators. "Oh, no!" she said, pushing Chloe out of the way. She crouched next to the boy, placing her hand on his arm. "Mommy's here, Honey. Mommy's here."

The lifeguard pumped the boy's chest and began CPR. Jonathon's body lay limp and lifeless. Finally, small streams of water spurted from the mouth of his pale face. He looked around at the adult faces hovered over him and began to cry.

His mother kissed his forehead. "Thank God, you're okay," she said through tears. Turning to the lifeguard, she said, "Thank you. Thank you for saving my baby's life."

"You're welcome," he said and then turned to Chloe. "But she's the real hero."

Hero? Let's not be dramatic here. Chloe received the woman's hug. "I just did what anybody would . . . ."

Mr. Lifeguard interrupted, "Ma'am, I'm gonna call 911. I think I may have broken one of his ribs during CPR." He pulled a walkie talkie from the pocket of his red swim trunks and retreated from the circle.

Smaller doses of adrenaline still pumped through Chloe as she looked over at the lifeguard, tan and muscular, performing his beachly duties of saving lives. *He must be new. I would have remembered him.* Chloe felt someone hugging her leg. She looked down.

There stood a girl who looked to be about four. "Thank you for saving Johnny," she said, tugging tightly, her blonde corkscrew curls pressing against Chloe's wet legs. "He's my brutter."

Had Chloe ever seen a cuter girl? She bent down, gently grasping the girl's arms, and looked into her bright blue eyes that looked like Mom's. "I bet you're a nice big sister, aren't you?"

The girl nodded shyly, then responded to her mother's call by the ambulance, trotting away.

"Good job," said Mr. Hottie Lifeguard to Chloe. "I'm Brian."

Chloe's nerves began to fray and her heart pounded out of her chest. What should she say? *Think! Say something!* Had she ever actually talked to a guy she found attractive? Come to think of it, had she ever really met someone this cute? Home-school group? Nope. Boys at church? Nope. Not that she really had that many guys in her world. Mom's and her world consisted mostly of female friends, clients, and Uncle Gary. Except in the romances that frequently played through her mind. Chloe cleared her dry throat. “Um. Hi.”

“What’s your name?”

A drop of sweat formed on Chloe’s forehead. *Think of something!* “It’s--It’s Chloe Hudson.” *Brilliant.*

“Were you the one modeling at Moonlit Beach a couple of weeks ago?” Hottie did a safety scan of the beach. “I thought she looked like you.”

Forcing herself out of paralyzed position, Chloe dusted some sand off her leg. “Yes. That was me,” she said in a monotone voice. *Is he looking at my hands?*

Brian smiled, showing the bright white teeth that perfectly matched the whites of his eyes. “How old are you?”

I wonder how many white strips those took? “Fourteen. I mean, 15. I just turned 15.”

“Fifteen? Oh. I thought you were older than that.” He flashed one more smile her way. “Well, I need to get back to my post. Have a great day, Chloe.” He trotted away, the string of his whistle bouncing off his bronze six-pack.

A voice inside of Chloe chastised her with each squish of her toes in the wet sand. *Why am I so shy around guys?* Whenever she played these scenes out in her mind, she was bubbly and outgoing and flirtatious, but in real life, she was more like a wet dishcloth. *I feel like a social idiot.*

* * *

The next morning, Chloe sat in front of her easel, listening to Pachelbel’s Canon in D pour artist inspiration through her ipod. She sipped her green tea and looked out the large picture window facing the backyard. At the edge of the green grassy turf their palm tree reached toward the beach, the blueness of the Pacific peeking through the background. Should she put a seagull in her beach scene? A rainbow? Wouldn't it be cool if she could make a rainbow with her *déjà vu* colors?

An impatient feeling began bubbling inside of her. Wasn't it time for Mom to 'fess up and tell her all about her secret romance? *I mean we are best friends after all. And why is she so tired all the time? She used to get up at the crack of dawn and run with me on the beach every morning. Now she always sleeps in.* One would think a bride would be bouncing out of bed each day in anticipation of wonderful wedding orchestrations. Maybe she goes out at night for a secret rendezvous with him?

Chloe pressed her paintbrush to her practice canvas and doodled a sun. Sipping the last of her tea from her heart-shaped mug, she strolled to the kitchen for a refill.

The answering machine sat next to the coffee pot, blinking at her, so she obliged.

A weird, nasally voice spilled out of the recorder. "Lisa Hudson. Hey, Baby. Velvet Lemon here. So good to hear from you. I misplaced your cell number, but I still had this one in my files. Wow. Like wow. Can't believe it. You're actually selling that place? And going back to Indiana? Where is that, anyway? Listen, Sunshine. I have a smartphone full of clients who would kill for a place like yours. Beach front property doesn't come along every day. And with that interior design you've done, I'm sure we can get top dollar for it. Okay. Call me again and give me your cell. Don't forget. I'm the Lemon that makes you lemonade. 645-8888."

Chloe didn't move. Shock laced her veins. Wait. She must have heard it wrong. Selling this place? Indiana?

Her mind spinning, she pushed the replay button. Is Mr. Wonderful from Indiana? No way. That would be the most perfectly unromantic ending to what is supposed to be the most perfectly happily-ever-after story. Mr. Wonderfuls do *not* live in Indiana. It's okay for uncles to live there, but not future fathers or husbands-of-my-mom, thank you very much.

With a pang of nausea, a chill went down Chloe's spine and her arms got speckled with goose bumps. How could she be cold when it was 75 and sunny out? She heard Mom's slippers scuffling on the tile in the foyer, coming closer.

Mom was bundled in her fluffy white terrycloth robe, rubbing her sleepy eyes. "Good Morning, Mocha," she said, lightly kissing Chloe's cheek.

Chloe stared at Mom. When had she started to look so old?

Her once-bright blue eyes were dull atop dark circles. Her long blonde hair hung in stringy spaghetti-like strands, with a few clumps missing. When did she get so thin? Did she just look so bad because she didn't have make-up on yet?

Hesitantly, Chloe said, "You have a message on the machine." She watched Mom pour herself a cup of green tea and push the button on the recorder.

"Lisa. Hey, Baby. Velvet Lemon here." Mom pushed the button again, making zest of Velvet's words.

A sad and worried expression came across her face as she met Chloe's gaze. "Chlo, I have some things to tell you."

"Are you marrying someone from Indiana?"

Mom looked confused. She touched her bony hand to Chloe's arm. "Oh, look at you. You're freezing. Let me get you a blanket." She went to the quilt rack by the hearth and held open a zebra throw, inviting Chloe in. She went to the sofa, sat, and patted it. "We have some things to talk about."

Chloe let the satin lining envelope her skin. She looked into her mom's tired eyes. "Is it true?"

"Chloe, I wanted to get the ring back before I told you." Her tone was pensive. Mom leaned over to the small table next to the sofa, opened its drawer and took out a small, white satin box that she placed in Chloe's lap. She took both of Chloe's hands, lightly squeezed them and faced her. "It's big, Mocha." She paused and swallowed hard. "You *have* to remember that God will never leave you, and He loves you intimately. He has a great plan and purpose for your life, Chloe."

And a one-way ticket to Indiana.

Mom forced a faint smile. "I'm praying the ring will help you remember those things." She popped open the lid and took out the ring. Both the diamond and the gold band shone more brilliantly than ever.

Chloe stared down at the hands embracing hers, noticing that Mom was now wearing a simple, gold band on her wedding finger. "When are you getting married? Is the wedding going to be in Indiana?"

"No." Mom took a deep breath. "I'm marrying someone from heaven." Mom's tone was serious, yet eerily happy. "Chloe, I'm going to be a bride. I'm going to have the day that I've always dreamed of--the day when I'll finally meet my One and Only, my Jesus Christ." Her words were slow and deliberate.

A mixture of stun and confusion filled Chloe's mind. She laughed nervously, as she looked at Mom's frail body. A dull hollowness, with a shot of slow shock, penetrated her heart, as the meaning of her mother's words found definition. "Are . . . you sick?" she stammered.

Compassionately, Mom rubbed Chloe's arm. "I've only known for a short time." She spoke slowly and deliberately, as if to give Chloe time to process her words. "It's cancer."

Cancer? Does any other word in the English language have such power to make one feel stabbed in the heart? Cancer is one word, yet it's a saga in just six letters. Six letters that carry life-changing DNA and mutated futures. And when you hear that word, you know your compassion for cancer's victim should immediately kick in, but, instead, you find yourself, as selfish and guilty as it sounds, thinking of your own life without your loved one.

Chloe's mind flashed to the image of a tsunami hitting a brick wall. Mom and cancer in the same sentence? This changed everything. The only world Chloe knew was with this woman, who wasn't just her Mom and mentor and confidant. She also was her best friend--the only one who knew about her secret colors, the one she depended on, the one she *needed.*

Wait! God always answers Mom's prayers. With new hope, she turned to Mom and said, "Why don't you pray for God to heal you? He always gives you everything you want."

"Chloe, God *did* heal me, and He rescued you. He ordained my days before I was even born. Remember that part of Psalm 139? 'All the days ordained for me were written in your book before one of them came to be.'"

Chloe knew Psalm 139 by heart because Mom used to recite it to her on their morning beach runs.

Beyond thinking of it as a neat poem, Chloe had never cared much about what it said.

"It's my time, Chloe, and I can't wait to see Him face to face." Mom stared into the space in front of her, as though she was daydreaming. "It's truly a blessing that He's given us some time to make plans."

How sweet of Him. "Can't they do chemo or something?" Chloe asked, hoping.

"It's stage 4. And now there's another kind of cancer, too. I will fight it, Chloe, for your sake. But, I'm ready to go. I *want* to go." The two of them held each other in a strong embrace for several minutes, until Chloe broke.

And then Mom broke, too. Finally, she wiped her eyes into the sleeve of her robe. "Let me see your hand, Sweetheart." Mom took Chloe's right hand. Gently, she pushed the *déjà vu* rock over Chloe's knuckle to the base of her hand. Now, it fit perfectly.

Chloe stared down at the ring. "Thank you, again, Mom." She held her hand out in front of them, modeling the ring in a Vanna-like way. *It takes the attention away from my fat fingers. Or does it add to it?*

Facing her mother again, Chloe leaned in to hug her and stopped short. And then stared at Mom's chest.

She rubbed her eyes and looked again. Was she having some sort of break with reality?

In the middle of Mom's chest, atop her white terrycloth robe, lay a bright white heart, about the size of a grapefruit. It shone brilliantly, and its color was pure white with beams of light protruding from its edges. It made Mom "glow," sort of hurting Chloe's eyes to look at it directly. The glow spotlighted Mom's face, giving her a healthiness that Chloe liked.

But the new mysterious heart wasn't the only thing Chloe saw.

A thin outline, the color of dust, traced the entire perimeter of Mom's frail body, like chalk on a victim at a crime scene. The band of saturated dust was about two-thirds of an inch wide and clung to Mom's body.

"Chlo, what's wrong?" Mom looked alarmed. "You look as if you just saw a ghost."

"There's a . . . ." Chloe stammered. "You have a . . . ." She stopped herself, then hesitated. Oh, no. She wasn't turning into one of those granola-eating-tree-hugging-California nuts who could see auras on people, was she? Hopefully she was imagining this. Hopefully, this whole conversation with her Mom was just a big nightmare she'd wake up from.

"Chloe, are you okay?" asked Mom. "I know this is a lot to take in."

Doesn't Mom already have enough to worry about right now? *I think I'll just ignore this weird little paranormal thing for the time being.*

"Uncle Gary will take good care of you," Mom continued.

"Is he moving out here?"

"No. Think about it, Chloe. He has the farm and his taxidermy business. It's a huge responsibility. His life is in Indiana." Mom put her thumb under Chloe's chin and looked deep into her eyes.

Wow, that thing is bright. "I love Gary, but couldn't I live with Geena, here? I could go to Creighton High and keep modeling and . . . ."

"No way," Mom interrupted. "I want you with Gary. He's a believer and a great guy, Chloe. He loves you almost as much as I do." Mom smiled.

"Maybe he'll let you use your matchmaking abilities on him."

The two laughed softly.

Another wave of sadness cascaded over Chloe as she thought about Uncle Gary losing his sister. Who would he call every week or send Anjou Chocolates to frequently? *Wonder why he never got married?*

Mom looped her arm around Chloe, pulling her close. They sat in silence for a long time.

Finally, Chloe broke the embrace and sniffled. She and Mom both wiped under their eyes.

"Okay, I have a really important question for you," said Mom, acting borderline giddy.

Chloe stared at her Mom, trying to process this sudden shift in demeanor. *Maybe dust and bright white have made her delusional?*

Mom skipped to the hall closet and returned with a gray garment bag. She hung it from the brass hook in the kitchen and beckoned Chloe over. Slowly, she unzipped the bag, revealing something satin and shimmery white. Carefully, she pulled out a full-length Vera Wang wedding gown, fashioned with intricate pearl work on the bodice. "It's my wedding dress." A glow masked the paleness of her face, and a smile filled it. "For when I meet my One and Only. Chloe, will you be my maid-of-honor?"

For your funeral? You're kidding.

* * *

Chloe awoke to the sound of tourists on the beach. She sat up and rubbed her eyes. *Ugh. What is this new feeling?* She hurt deep inside her soul in a way she had never experienced. Numbness consumed her, like the feeling a person gets the split-second *after* she hits her funny bone, right before the *real* pain starts. *How will I do life without Mom?*

Sunlight streamed through the mini-blinds of her bedroom window, inviting her over. She got up and peeked out.

The sun was fully up.

She scanned the gray Pacific Ocean, feeling small.

Above the water, a pelican swooped down, over and over, trying to grab a fish, and finally succeeding.

Poor ordained fish. *It's such a blessing that He's given us some time to make plans.* Chloe thought of Mom's words and bristled, looking back at the pelican. *I'm sure Mr. Fish was ever so grateful for the opportunity to plan being breakfast. Not.*

The rhythmic sound of the waves pulled at her. The beach was her haven, and today she needed it more than ever.

Chloe threw on her running clothes and sat on the edge of her bed to tie her tennis shoes. The new guest on her finger got in the way. She wasn't used to wearing a ring. She pulled it from her finger, holding it with both hands in front of her and gazing at it.

The ring will help you remember that you are never alone. God is intimately with you. Chloe stared at the ring and moved it around. *God is with me? Well, I hope so, because I have a few things to say to him today!*

Chloe twirled the diamond in the air, looking for glimpses of her *déjà vu* colors. *Nothing?* She walked over to the window and held it to the light. Still nothing. No traces, flecks, or glimpses of dust, veranda, or peekadilly today. Instead, flashes of blues, reds, and yellows glistened with each turn, but not her *déjà vu* colors. *This is good!* she thought.

Her heart began to pound faster with new hope. *Maybe Mom was fine! Maybe I just imagined her weird white heart and dust band. Maybe all of yesterday was just a bad dream.*

She and her curiosity tiptoed down the hall toward Mom's bedroom and cracked the door, peeking in.

The room was dark, except for the sunlight pushing through the curtains.

Mom slept, curled in a fetal position with her robe on and a heavy quilt covering her feet. Her bright white heart shone like the headlight of a train coming out of tunnel, projecting a heart onto the wall across from the bed.

A pang of anxiety poked Chloe. *I wasn't imagining the heart. Or the dust outline.* She took a step backward, pulling the door almost shut. She inhaled a gasp, suddenly needing some fresh air.

I can't wait to run! Run away from all of this.

After some quick bathroom business, Chloe washed her hands and glanced in the mirror.

The elevator of her heart went from floor 3 to floor 10, raising her blood pressure, as she stared at herself. *No. No way.*

There, on her chest was a veranda heart! Right smack in the middle, about six inches from the underside of her chin, lay a dull-deep-colored veranda heart, about four inches in diameter, with distinct edges. Chloe traced it with her finger while looking in the mirror and poked at it to see if she could feel it. No physical feeling per se, but it felt "heavy," and made her cringe.

Inside her stomach, nausea began to form. She suddenly felt claustrophobic, as though veranda was invading her personal space. *Is this what a panic attack feels like? I have to get out of here!*

Like a caged tiger breaking free, she ran toward the outdoors, letting the door of the lanai slam behind her.

She stood in the backyard, paralyzed, breathing deeply several times, trying to calm herself. *What should I worry about first? Mom? Déjà vu colored hearts? Indiana?* She closed her eyes, trying to block everything out except the crashing of the waves and the sun's rays on her face. *Breath deep. Breath deep. Fill. Empty. Fill. Empty.*

After much la maze for her lungs, Chloe sat on the grass and stretched out the muscles of her legs, visually absorbing every square inch of their perfectly-manicured lawn. The faint smell of orange blossoms filled her nostrils. She and Mom had planted the tree on Mother's Day when she was six. Last year, they got their first crop of three oranges, enough to make two tiny glasses of fresh-squeezed juice. After a few minutes of stretching, she strolled down the brickwork patio passed their palm tree en route to the sandy beach. If only palm trees from California could be moved to Indiana. *But I'd trade all of this if I could just keep Mom.*

Chloe walked toward the shoreline, zoning out everyone around her. She skipped warm-up niceties and broke into a full run. The words of Psalm 139 penetrated her mind, compliments of Mom's years of christening each morning run by reciting the first 18 verses. *O Lord, you have searched me and know me.* Would this silly poem come to her mind every time she ran? Today, she made a conscious effort to block it. *She* would be doing the talking today, thank you very much.

Anger seared her heart as wet sand flew behind her. *God, if you are really God, you wouldn't let this happen. I'm mad at you--and her, too! You two seem so happy with this new arrangement. What about me? For years Mom has talked about how You healed her and rescued me. Yeah, right. If you healed her, I wouldn't be an orphan moving to Indiana. And rescuing me? From what? My perfect life here in California, where I'm starting my dream of becoming a model and traveling the world with my best friend whom you've just zapped with cancer? Where I would have a mother to show me how to use a tampon when I finally get my period! Or be there to someday take pictures of me on prom night? Or walk me down the aisle at my wedding, when I marry Mr. Right? Or bake cookies for the six kids I want to have with Mr. Right? Thanks a lot, God. Thanks so much for rescuing me from that. Not.*

And that's not even all of it! She expects me to jump on her happy little maid-of-honor train. Weird. Chloe's own thought hit her like someone had elbowed her in the stomach. How many years had she dreamed of planning a wedding with her mom? First, they'd plan Mom's big day to Mr. Wonderful. Then, when Chloe grew up, they'd plan her big day to Mr. Right. It would be ultra special and memorable and romantic. But not like this.

Sorrow and pain collided within her. She countered it by running as fast as she could. The salt of her tears mixed with the salty mist coming off the water. She screamed inside for all of heaven to hear, pressing faster and farther. Her body and soul finally exhausted, she slowed to a trot and then a walk.

In the distance a yoga-group was gathering. Wearing black must have been a prerequisite for the class. Most of the students looked like twenty-something females, with the exception of a few granny-granola types, and a few men. Several students fanned their yoga mats on the sand, checking their space. Poured into a spandex jumpsuit, one overly buff-surfer type pulled his blond hair tightly back into a ponytail. Another woman, who should have been banned from wearing spandex, chose a colored stretch band from the instructor's selection and fanned her face with a Chinese paper fan.

Chloe stopped, as though she'd just walked into a brick wall. *Peekadilly hearts! Dust outlines!* She could hardly believe her eyes. *Peekadilly* hearts? She stared, trying to be inconspicuous, spanning the group in search of bright white hearts like Mom's. Or veranda hearts like hers.

Span . . . span . . . span. A couple of the students had *no* heart and *no* outline, just as everyone in the world had looked the day before. Some students had a peekadilly heart *and* a dust outline, while others only had the heart. The peekadilly hearts looked thick and saturated, exactly like her veranda heart, with no beams of light protruding from them, like Mom's. *But why aren't there any veranda hearts like mine?*

The instructor, whom Chloe guessed was a woman, had a bright dust outline and a heart that screamed peekadilly. Her tall, Amazon-like body was tan, muscular, and cut. Not the kind of girl you'd want to make mad in a back alley. Her facial features were more masculine than feminine and her blonde, shimmery head, Butch-style, matched her curly armpit hair. She stood with her elbows out and hands pressed together in front of her. With eyes closed, she raised her hands toward the sky above her. "Begin with a sun salutation and feel the energy!" she said in a low voice. Her dust outline followed each of her movements.

This is wild! Chloe plopped down on the gray sand, stretching while she stared. *First Mom, then me, now a bunch of people!* She looked around, her eyes peeled on the other beachcombers, some who looked like they'd been dunked in *déjà vu*, and a few others who glowed with a bright white heart.

A wave of panic shot through her as she looked up and down the beach. Her intriguing colors now stupefied her. *This is not the time in my life to be figuring out some weird supernatural thing! I have teensy-bit-bigger priorities right now. Like yelling at God. And being a good maid of honor. Weird.*

Chloe switched to a Hollywood stretch, bringing her right leg straight out in front of her, and curling her left leg in toward her inner thigh. Sand stuck to her moist legs. Grabbing her right tennis shoe and pulling gently, the new ring on her hand sparkled. This ring . . . Epiphany! *I didn't see my colors on people until I put the ring on yesterday! I'll just take the ring off, and then my sweet little dust, veranda, and peekadilly can jump right back into their little home. And if that doesn't work, I'll give this possessed ring back to Mom! But she would be so hurt. Okay, I just won't wear it! Well, I did kind of promise Mom that I'd wear it, but that was before I knew it came with the annoying déjà vu-deluxe add-on!*

Chloe felt hopeful as she took the ring from her hand.

"Now, everyone turn to the East," yelled the female Amazon. "Feel your power from within!" The instructor's words startled Chloe, causing her accidentally to drop the ring into the sand.

She quickly scanned the beach again, hoping it would be void of *déjà vu.* It wasn't.

Crap. Even with the ring off, her colors were still splattered on the population around her. *Mom has always called my colors a gift from God, but maybe they're a curse! Maybe they're God's cruel joke on me for not embracing Him! Seeing dust, veranda, and peekadilly my whole life when a camera flashed was neat. Seeing them inside Mom's ring was neat, too. But seeing my* déjà *vu colors in hearts and outlines on people? On ME? Creepy.*

A slow panic began to ooze inside of Chloe. What should she do with this new unwanted guest? Pack her suitcase for the nut house? See an eye doctor? Maybe talk to Geena? Yes. Good idea. No. Bad idea. Geena would probably send her to one of her flaky, aura-seeing-hippie friends or refer her to Oprah.com--Geena's answer to every question or problem in life.

Chloe weighed her choices, always landing back on her default setting in life: Run to Mom. Depend on her. Need her. Have her pray about it.

Chloe scooped a few handfuls of sand, letting it sift through her fingers until she found her ring again. She stared at it briefly, then positioned it back on its new home. She stood, dusted the sand off her legs, and then headed toward home, her mind racing.

Should I tell Mom? Would sharing this little revelation be like stealing attention from a bride on her big day? Would it make me a bad maid-of-honor?

Mom always said stealing attention from a bride was wrong, because there are only three days in a woman's life when she rightfully gets to be the center of attention: on the day she is born . . . on the day of her wedding . . . and at her . . . .

Chapter 2

Gary Hudson

It was August. A thick Indiana humidity hung in the air. Gary Hudson squished the butt of his cigarette in the ashtray of his white GMC pick-up truck and drained his coffee mug with one last gulp. He stepped out and walked down the corn row.

Two ears on every stalk. Could be a bumper crop. Hopefully, the corn prices would stay where they were, but who cared?

Gary had more important things on his mind. *The most important woman in my life will soon be gone, and the second-most-important woman in my life will soon be here.*

Gary exited the corn row and jumped across the small irrigation ditch. His Colts' T-shirt was drenched from the dew of the corn and clung to his tan, over-insulated chest. He looked at his watch:

10:30 a.m. *Better start mowing, whether it's dry enough or not.*

He drove about five minutes to the far west corner of the farm, back by the 25 acres in the government set-aside program that teemed with wildlife--deer, rabbit and muskrat this time of year. A small dirt path opened up to a clearing back in the woods. Gary lifted a push lawnmower from the back of the truck and walked it down the path.

A small plot of land, about 50 square feet, was surrounded by a short, shiny black iron fence that was new. On the gate at the entrance a sign read "Hudson Family Cemetery."

A large tree root had pushed up the flat gravestone of Bernice Hudson, 1835 - 1902. A few feet away stood a large stone engraved with a picture of a John Deere tractor and inscribed with the names "Miriam and Walter Hudson," and the simple words, "Rest in Peace."

Gary stood silently in front of the stone for several minutes with his eyes closed. He stooped and picked away a large cluster of small mushrooms from the stone and from a few others that had the same problem, then made quick work of the mowing. Minutes later, he headed for home, slowing his pickup by an oversized tin mailbox with large decal letters to check for mail. He turned onto a gravel driveway lined with mature oak trees and sped up to shave some time.

At the end of the drive stood a large white barn with the words Hudson Family Farm shingled into its green roof. Slightly to the north, a smaller and newer white shed, with a cooler attached, stood in the background.

Today, a black pick-up was parked close to it, waiting for Gary's return.

I can't do short notice today. Gary drove up and rolled down the window. "De Veen," he said, tipping his head slightly and turning the key to deaden the truck's engine. "What did you get today?" Gary stepped out of the truck and shook Harding De Veen's hand.

"It's a raccoon. Just a small job, but I haf the perfect place for it in the trophy room. It vill go next to the moose by the waterfall," said Harding De Veen, with a Dutch accent. He removed his glasses to wipe the sweat from his brow. "It's a hot one today, yah? I hoped you might get to it before long."

"Looks like it'll have to be next week," said Gary. "I'm heading out of town for California later today, but he'll keep in the cooler."

"California? What's your business there?"

"Going to visit my little sister and my niece, Chloe." Gary tapped a cigarette from a half-full pack and lit up. "It's Friday. Aren't you usually out of town on Friday?"

"Yah. I've rearranged appointments because Alice is getting some surgery today. Ty gets his driver's license next week, za day before school starts, but I'm driving him to the gym later to see his personal trainer."

"Is I.U. still looking at him?" said Gary.

"Yah. Davion Griffin said he'd sign him the first day he could. Ty will have to put some good points on the board dis year as a junior, but that shouldn't be hardt."

"Did you know Griffin is from here? He played at Jefferson when I was in high school. He was a friend of mine."

"Oh, sure. I know all about him. He haz been Ty's idol forever. When Ty was 10, he was always on the computer, following Griffin's career in the

NBA. When Griffin took the head coaching job at Indiana, Ty started sending him basketball footage of himself." De Veen laughed. "Zat was still back when we were in the olt country. You still keep in touch with Griffin?"

An unsettled feeling penetrated Gary. "No, we lost touch a long time ago." Gary glanced at his watch. "I've got to be somewhere at 1:00," he said, changing the subject. He took one last puff from his cigarette, threw the butt on the ground, and squished it with his foot. He grabbed the coon by all fours out of the back of De Veen's truck. "I'll give you a call next week, when this one's finished."

* * *

Gary pulled into the parking lot of D'Anjou Fine Chocolate at exactly 12:58. He stuffed the rest of his Big Mac into his mouth and slurped the last sip of his Super Size Coke. Checking his back pocket for his wallet, his work boot hit the pavement. He approached the large, ten-foot-tall-double-wooden doors, heavily shellacked and intricately carved with ornate pear designs and swirls. The scent of apricots wafted through the air, mixing with his musk-scent cologne.

Soft classical music piped throughout. The seating section had chocolate-brown walls, accented with bright white trim. Picture molding highlighted the framed, contemporary artwork throughout, except in the corner, where an oversized sofa surrounded a large, square coffee table.

Gary stood in front of the crystal clear case, looking at the hundreds of tiny chocolate masterpieces. He knew Lisa's and Chloe's favorites. Lisa loved Anjou's two signature pieces, a dark chocolate pear with a light green Anjou filling, and its companion, a milk chocolate pear with a dark red

Anjou filling. Chloe's favorites were a milk chocolate European heart, blended silky smooth with hazelnuts, and a milk chocolate rose, filled with liquid caramel. Gary wasn't sure what his favorite was. Maybe Anjou's version of the "turtle?"

Unlike most of the times he'd been here, today the Shoppe was dead. He could hear people talking and laughing behind a door adjacent to the register that read Corporate Office. Maybe he should stick his head in?

Through an open door at the far end of the front area, a large black woman with silver hair tucked into a hairnet came through, stirring a large cup of something. "Anybody help you yet, Child?" she said, pleasantly. She set her cup next to the register. The gold name tag on her white overcoat read "Marg" and "Kitchen Manager" written in cursive.

"No, not yet. I have a 1:00 appointment with Candice Jones," said Gary.

"Okay, Child, let me get somebody." Marg picked up the phone and hit a few buttons. "Attention, Miss Candy. There's a nice lookin' guy up here in the Shoppe who wants to see you," piped through the intercom, replacing the music momentarily. Turning back to Gary she asked, "You wanna a sample of somethin'?"

A warm blush went over Gary's face as he pondered her words *nice lookin' guy*. Last time someone called him *that* was about forty pounds and not-as-bald ago. "No, thanks, Ma'am."

The door of the office flung open and a skinny gentleman in a suit poked his head out like the tiny bird in a cuckoo clock. "Marg, we've talked about this," he said, pulling his head back in before she could respond.

"Sure thing, Mr. Namby," she said softly and sarcastically. Taking a sip from her cup, she leaned against the back counter and smiled at Gary while she waited. "That's Mr. Namby-Pamby," she whispered.

Moments later a young twenty-something woman came through the open doorway from the back.

"Well, now, it's about time there, Miss Candy," Marg bellowed.

"Thank you, Marg," Candice said with a smirk. She looked at Gary and stopped short for just a moment with an expression that said, "It's you." Her face blushed slightly as she nervously extended her hand. "Hi. I'm Candice Jones."

Gary's heart pounded a bit faster, as it always did when he talked to a woman his age. "I'm Gary Hudson." Candice looked familiar to him. He'd seen her throughout the years when he came in to buy Lisa and Chloe gifts.

Candice looked about an inch shorter than him, 5'7" or so, and had red hair tucked neatly under a black beret, with a single long tendril on each side framing her china doll face. Her pale skin brought extra brilliance to her bright green eyes and plum-colored lipstick. She wore a black turtleneck and slimming black pants with her gold name tag, and a gold apron with appliqué pears, apparently the traditional garb of an Anjou Shoppe employee.

"It's nice to meet you, Gary," Candice said, slipping into a business-like professionalism. "Let me grab my laptop and catalogs, and I'll meet you by the coffee bar over there."

Gary chose a bar stool in the center of the granite countertop, front and center of the flat screen TV mounted on the wall behind it. Cool. ESPN.

Candice arrived with some supplies, set them on the bar and then clicked off the TV. She went around to the opposite side and sat in the stool right next to Gary, slightly invading his comfortable personal space. "So, what can I help you with today, Gary?" she asked, emphasizing his name as if she were pleased to be using it.

A small wave of embarrassment went through Gary as he remembered Lisa's list in his back pocket. *Why didn't I copy it to a plain piece of paper?* He pulled out and unfolded an 8 1/2 x 11 piece of pink stationary, with lacy edges and butterflies. "I need to get some quotes on party favors," he said.

"Oh, you're having a big party! Is it your parents' 50th anniversary or a welcome-home celebration of some kind?" Candice asked, excited.

Gary paused, searching for the right words to describe the event but not finding any.

"How many guests will you be expecting?" Candice asked, filling in the silent gap.

"Well, we're not exactly sure," Gary said, with a slight wince. "Probably about four or five hundred."

Candice looked surprised . . . and disappointed. "Oh, this must be for a wedding then," she said slowly.

Gary felt a bead of sweat forming on his forehead, so he reached for a napkin on the coffee bar. "Sort of, I guess." He looked down at his pink guidelines and said, "Could you give me a quote on a four-piece box, with the two pears, the heart piece and the rose caramel?"

"Yes, of course," Candice said, in a matter-of-fact tone. She flipped through a catalog and fiddled a few moments on the laptop. "Do you need delivery?"

"Yes," Gary said, fixing his eyes blankly on the TV. "To Encinitas, California."

"What's the delivery date?"

Gary hesitated. "Do you need to know that now?"

Candice looked irritated. "Well, if it is during warm-weather season, we add ice bricks to the shipping boxes, and that costs more." She pulled out a calendar from a shipping catalog and laid it open in front of Gary. "Knowing when you want something delivered is kind of an important delivery detail."

A pit formed in Gary's stomach. He looked at the calendar. October? November? Who knows how long she has left? He hoped it wouldn't be until next spring or summer, for Chloe's sake, but then again, he hoped it would *never* be. "Look, I'm not sure. Just quote it with the ice bricks," said Gary, craving a cigarette. "And what's the lead time?"

"For an order that size, probably about a week." Candice took a calculator from the pocket of her apron. "There's a price break at 500, so let's do that. You're looking at about $8000 or so," appearing a bit shocked herself by the price. "She must be a special lady."

"She is," Gary said. A silent picture show of childhood memories, high school, and Chloe reeled through his head. "Thanks for the information. I'll be in touch."

"Thank you, Mr. Hudson," said Candice.

* * *

Evan Smith

The day was pleasantly and unseasonably cool for August in Indiana. The previous night's thunderstorm answered the thick humidity of the past week with a welcomed inch of rain.

Free throw 199. Just need one more. Evan Smith breathed deeply. He closed his eyes, envisioning the shot as the over-time-game-breaker. He shot the ball. Swish. The crowd went wild! Smiling, he grabbed the ball on the first bounce, dribbled out and then back toward the hoop mounted on the side of his family's pole barn, ending his training session with an easy lay-up.

Daily quota met. Cool. Every day, since eighth grade, Evan had forced himself to do 200 sit-ups, push-ups, arm-curls, and successful free throws. Five miles was the quota for his daily run, during which he also met his goal of memorizing one new Bible verse. He picked up his watch at the edge of the concrete and checked the time: 8:00 a.m. Still time to pray by the pond, for a while at least.

At 10:00, the vacation Bible school kids were expecting him in his debut acting role as Goliath. His 6'3" svelte build was the closest body type that Miss Nancy could find and his sister, Grace, who was back from college for the summer, had volunteered him. He didn't mind. Evan loved kids. When he was 15, he went on his first mission trip to an orphanage in Nicaragua and fell in love with the kids there.

Evan grabbed the hand towel by his watch and wiped the sweat off of his face. He kicked off his basketball shoes and sweaty socks, then slid into a pair of slides.

The short dirt path through the woods to the pond was soft and squishy, but the air was fresh and clean. The path opened up to the Smith Family

Pond, a four-acre, spring-fed pond that had enticed Bud Smith, Evan's dad, to buy the property thirty years ago. The dock in the middle of the pond, which Evan and his dad had built, had a large slide and a diving board. Most of the pond's edge was left natural, dotted with patches of cattails, small bushes, and wildflowers, except for a large, manmade, white sandy beach.

Evan sat down at one of several picnic tables and looked out over the pond. Lots of memories here. *Of fishing with dad. Of ice skating parties and bonfires. My baptism when I was a kid. Of Katie . . . before . . . .*

Evan looked around and then started his prayer. No eyes closed or hands folded. That's why he loved praying in this place. No formalities needed--just him and God.

"God, You are good and loving. All-powerful. You notice every detail of my life and You're in control. Please forgive me for yesterday with that jerk at the Y.

My buddies and I had reserved a court and when we told him and his buddies that it was ours, he said, "Screw you. We're here, so it's ours." Where is this guy from, anyway? I've never seen him around before. I'd remember someone who was that tall with some weird accent.

Anyway, God, I'm sorry for what I said back to him.

I got my SAT's in the mail yesterday. *2138.* Thanks for helping me.

I know you have a plan for me. Does it include basketball? Please show me your will.

Lord, I want to love you more. Help me be a good Goliath today."

Chapter 3

A taxi dropped Chloe and Mom off at the CoffeeCups parking lot. Mrs. Peabody of "Happy Ending Weddings" would be there at 4:00.

Mom ordered a grandé soy latte. Chloe ordered her favorite, a grandé white-chocolate mocha. She watched while a barista with a bright dust outline prepared it. *A dust outline like Mom's. What would a teen girl with tattoos and multiple piercings have in common with Mom?*

Mom pulled a table and extra chair up to a corner sofa. "Hey, Sweetie, I'll be right back," she said, laying her clipboard on the table and heading for the Ladies' Room.

Chloe fell into the corner of the sofa, eyeing Mom's clipboard. Mom had lists for everything, and each was stored in the file cabinet under the tab "Master Lists." For example, every trip to New York, Indiana, or Europe had its own list that detailed trip preparations, items to pack, and names and numbers of great restaurants, hotels, and tourist attractions.

A shot of curiosity streamed in Chloe's veins. She looked to see if Mom was out of sight and then flipped through the papers on the clipboard. The heading at the top of the first page said, Happy Ending Weddings. *What a stupid name,* she thought, glancing at the items Mom had carefully written on the list.

1) Invitations, 2) Programs--ask Chloe to design, 3) Eulogy and Bible verses, 4) Party Favors from Anjou Fine Chocolates, 5) Engraved Bible for each guest, 6) Flowers, 7) Photos for foyer table, 8) Music/Harpist 9) Interpretive Dancers to Pachelbel's Canon in D?

A bittersweet feeling, mostly bitter, went through Chloe. She flipped up the page and saw another list, more detailed, that completely filled the page with some of the items already crossed off.

1) ~~Call Gary~~, 2) ~~Give Chloe my ring~~, 3) ~~List House~~, 4) ~~Notify photography clients~~. Several more were still untouched. 5) Chloe's 16th birthday gift 6) Seaside Retirement Center, 7) Contact Dodge County Commissioners about plot, 8) Dodge Monuments, 9) Hope and Help Center donation . . . .

"Oh, jolly! You must be Lisa Hudson. I must say, you look a bit younger than I envisioned you."

Startled, Chloe looked up. A short, plump woman dressed in a bright yellow suit and a large white hat, started unpacking catalogs and samples from her briefcase. *Dust outline, too?*

"I'm Delores Peabody. You must be the giddy bride?"

"No, actually I am," said Mom, walking to the sofa. She extended her frail arm for a handshake and beamed a full smile. "I'm Lisa Hudson. Can I get you a coffee drink?"

"Oh, absolutely not! I don't dare drink my calories. It's how I keep my figure," said Mrs. Peabody in a thick English accent.

That figure? Who'd want to keep that? Chloe wondered.

Mrs. Peabody looked Mom up and down. "Dear, do you feel okay? You look a bit---"

"Can we get started?" Chloe interrupted.

"Well, ladies. You've called the best. I've done weddings that have been in the top bridal magazines. Now, Dearie, the first thing I need to know is the date that you and your *special man* have picked for your big day! I'm booked quite far out, you know, but perhaps you'll be lucky."

"Well," Mom hesitated. For the first time ever, she suddenly seemed to notice for herself the awkwardness of planning this event. "The wedding I have in mind is something a little different."

Mrs. Peabody's face turned beet red, as if she had just caught herself in the worst of wedding faux pas. "Oh, yes. I'm sorry, dear. I do *those* kind of weddings, too."

"So you've done funerals that are like weddings?" Mom asked.

Mrs. Peabody stared at Mom, with a horrified look on her face. "A funeral that's a wedding?" she asked sarcastically. After a long pause and what appeared to be steam coming from under her hat, Mrs. Peabody said, "No, I meant we do weddings that have two brides or two grooms, or a female groom or male bride, but we *don't* do *funeral* weddings. That would be preposterous!" Mrs. Peabody began to laugh and looked at Chloe. "And I suppose you're her Maid of Honor?"

A rush of anger went through Chloe's body. *How dare this bowl of jelly make fun of my mom.* Chloe's own thought chided her. Hadn't she been reacting to Mom's wedding plans in the same way, only silently and less British? She turned to Mom and smiled, then hurled a smirk at Mrs. Peabody. In the best British accent Chloe could muster, she said, "Mom, I don't think we need Mrs. Peabody's services, because I *am* your Maid of Honor, and I want you to have the most beautiful day of your life."

Mom looked at Chloe with a new sparkle in her eye.

"Well then, Ladies," said Mrs. Peabody curtly. "Good day."

* * *

The Lemon realtor was right. Within two weeks of listing their house, Mom had three buyers in a bidding war. Once a closing date was set, every day was a blur of life sermons, wedding plans, packed boxes addressed to Indiana, and colors that couldn't take a hint.

Yuck. Enough with the déjà vu already! Chloe thought. Dust outlines, peekadilly hearts, and her one-and-lonely veranda heart annoyed her. Even the shape was irritating. Hard to believe *hearts* would ever irritate a die-hard romantic like Chloe, but they did!

And the mystery of why some people had hearts and outlines, and some didn't? There probably was a reason, but Chloe didn't want to know.

She decided it was time for these once-loved-colors to pack their little bags and go back up yonder to the big *déjà vu* crayon box in the sky. Shouldn't you be able to give a gift back, if you didn't want it anymore? She still hadn't told Mom about them and decided if she did, Mom would get all religious-y on her, and who wanted that right now? And, since these clueless colors apparently weren't going to play nice, Chloe's new strategy would be to ignore them. (But, that's sort of like trying not to notice the oversized zit on the tip of your nose, while hearing the song *Rudolph the Red-Nosed Reindeer* in your head.)

An assisted-living apartment at the Seaside Retirement Center became "home" when the Hudson bungalow sold. Chloe and Mom drove away from their heavenly home on the beach in Mom's VW Bug. *That* was a hard day. Chloe was mad at the world, but what really made her mad was that Mom *wasn't* mad.

In fact, Mom was insanely joyful, especially for someone whose body was deteriorating by the day. She'd mumble odd things like, "I praise you, Father. I thank you for what you are doing in my life. I love you." And she must have been going for the most-popular-person-on-your-deathbed award, because every morning she had tons of visitors--friends, business contacts, nurses, and new acquaintances from Seaside who checked in on her, just to say, "Hi."

Chloe would try to focus on her home-schooling on the computer in the living room, while half-way listening to all the cackling, stories, and praying in the other room.

Every afternoon when Mom napped, Chloe went to the apartment commons and got to know some of the elderly residents at Seaside. Bingo and bunko ruined her resolution of ignoring her colors. Seeing *déjà vu* on folks two generations older than her was too tempting not to sleuth.

Why did Mr. Tipton, the eighty-five-year-old-techie, have a bold and bright peekadilly heart? He thought of himself as quite the ladies' man, shuffling through the recreation center, looking for senior gals who were interested in his latest techno gadgets. Where did he get them? He always said he had "connections on the outside," as if he was some sort of jail inmate. Most of his time was spent either surfing the Internet or snow skiing on the wii. And who did he text all the time? More than once, he had lost his technology privileges for inappropriate acts. Like the time he pinched sweet little Mrs. Harper in the butt! Apparently pervs come in all ages. Or do they become pervs when they are young and just lose their filter?

On Thanksgiving Day, it was an unseasonal 80 degrees. "Chloe, let's go to the pier today," said Mom.

Chloe was shocked. "Really?" She looked at Mom bundled in sweat pants, a turtleneck, and a thick sweater.

Mom's face was pale, but filled with a smile and illuminated by the bright white protruding from her *déjà vu* heart.

"Are you sure you're up for that?" said Chloe.

"Absolutely," Mom said. "I really want to go to the pier with you, one last . . . ." She stopped herself, then continued. "Nobody will be there today. We'll have it all to ourselves."

The Seaside bus dropped Chloe and Mom off at the entrance to Moonlit Beach. Chloe helped Mom into her wheelchair and pushed her toward the pier. Isolated--just as they had hoped.

A late-morning haze now covered the hot sun, making the air feel like a thick, heavy covering. The salty air blended with Mom's perfume, sending a familiar pang of emotion through Chloe. Lately, moments of despair would ebb and flow, becoming as predictable as the waves breaking on the beach.

At the end of the pier, Mom said with a big smile, "Let's dangle our feet the way we used to."

A surge of happiness went through Chloe. How many times throughout the years had they sat here? Chloe helped Mom from the wheelchair and slowly eased her down, then sat next to her. She slipped off her flip-flops and tossed them on the weathered wooden planks behind her. Mom looped her arm around Chloe's waist, as they looked out over the blue-gray ocean in silence.

Chloe felt nervous. *This would be the perfect time to tell Mom about my colors. Should I?* She swallowed hard, and waited a moment for a burst of confidence. "Mom, I have something I've been *dying* to tell you," she blurted. Chloe paused, trying to rephrase with better word choice." I mean . . . well, it's about my colors."

Mom closed her eyes and opened her palms to the sky. "Praises," she said softly. "Chloe, I've always prayed that God would give you a special gift. And He did! He gave you your colors. Think of how intimate that is. Only you and God know about your colors."

Chloe's eyes got moist. "And you." Chloe paused, then asked, "What am I going to do without you?"

Mom's eyes were now moist, too. "Sweetheart, you're going to get up each day and depend on God, trusting Him one day at a time. This has always been my prayer for you." With a gentle plead in her eyes, Mom looked at Chloe. "Do you *know* Him? Chloe, you can't depend on Him, if you don't have a personal relationship with Him."

"I thought your biggest prayer for me was purity?"

"It's kind of the same thing, Mocha. God created you, Chloe Rahab Hudson, for a love relationship with Him. When you give your purity to Him as a gift--your whole heart, your mind, and your body--you'll understand the meaning of your life. But He's a gentleman. He won't force a relationship with you. He'll wait to be wanted."

"I don't get what that has to do with sex."

"Because most women want to know 'Who am I?' and they yearn for intimacy. They want to be loved, and they sometimes think sex is the answer. Chloe, *Christ* is the answer. If you depend on *anything* or *anyone* other than Christ, you'll make bad choices that come with consequences--some of them lifelong. But you can't depend on Christ if you don't know Him. And you can't know Him, or have a relationship with Him, if you ignore Him day after day."

Chloe sat silently as the word "depend" penetrated her mind. Who did she depend on? If she were honest with herself, the answer would be her *mom*--totally and completely--even though she always complained about how her life was so sheltered and how she needed more independence and how public school would be *so* much more exciting than her boring-old-home-school.

"Do you *know* Him, Chloe? Do you depend on Him?" Mom continued staring at Chloe, waiting for a response.

"I guess so." Chloe said, with a slight sense of guilt.

Mom forced a half-smile and gave Chloe a side hug. "I think He has a *big* purpose for your life. I felt that even before you were born."

Chloe's face scrunched, and she rolled her eyes. "You act like I'm going to save the world or something."

"No, Jesus is the only one who did that." Mom turned her head toward the ocean, deep in thought. "But, Chloe, you never know. Every life is sacred. Every life has a purpose."

"I thought mine was to be a model," said Chloe. "But that's not going to happen in Indiana." Chloe searched Mom's eyes for sympathy, not finding any.

"Are you spending time in the Word?" Mom asked, looking genuinely hurt and worried. "If you want to know what you were created for, you have to ask your Creator. Have you prayed about it?"

"I don't know," said Chloe, pausing. "Not really, I guess."

"Don't you get it?" Mom looked more emotional than Chloe was used to. "The whole God-thing isn't about religion or rules. It's about having a *relationship* with your Creator, where you listen to Him and talk to Him." Mom's eyes were intense. "And fall in love with Him."

Anger mixed with annoyance inside of Chloe. "I'm not like you. I don't want to be a nun," said Chloe sharply.

Mom started to laugh, lightening the moment. "I think you have to be Catholic to be a nun." She put her hand on Chloe's leg. "Being single was God's plan for me. Maybe it won't be for you. But whether you're single or married, the only way to your Happily-Ever-After is if Christ is at the center of your life."

Feeling a slight sense of nun-relief, Chloe stared over the water. "Well, what if I pick wrong? What if I get married when I'm supposed to be single? And how am I supposed to know what I should be when I grow up?"

"That's why *every day* you ask the One who knows you better than you know yourself--the One who knew you before you were born, who sees *you* each and every day, and the One who has written each of your tomorrows. He holds all the answers to your life."

Chloe felt a recently-familiar stirring inside of her.

I LOVE YOU, CHLOE. I'M WAITING FOR YOU.

Chloe felt Mom's hand rubbing her back. She turned to her Mom. "You're waiting for me?"

Mom looked back at her, confused. "Waiting for you? What do you mean?"

"Didn't you just say you're waiting for me?"

"No."

I know I just heard her say that, thought Chloe.

"What I said was to abide in Him, pray, and read His Word," said Mom. "And discover your gifts. God gives people gifts and talents for their good and His glory. But there again, you have to ask the Giver of the gift what it is meant for."

Chloe perked up. "Like my colors?"

"Absolutely. I've always thought your colors were a special gift, like Samson's hair or Esther's beauty. Somehow, God is going to use your colors for His Kingdom! I just know it, Chloe."

A sober feeling came across Chloe, like the kind a soldier must get when he's commissioned for a top-secret, important mission. "Haven't you always thought I should be an artist, because of my colors?"

"I think it's good to develop your interests and talents, but you still have to ask God what His purpose for them is."

"Something's happened with my colors lately," Chloe blurted, with a sense of urgency.

"What is it?" Mom said.

Chloe looked at her Mom's bright white heart, wondering if angels glisten like that. "When I put your ring on, I started seeing my colors on people . . . well, *some* people."

Silence.

Mom sat completely still and listened intently.

"Anyhow," Chloe stammered. "Some people have peekadilly-colored hearts on their chests."

"Hearts?" said Mom. Her eyes got bigger, and she looked as if she were swallowing a heaping helping of questions, resisting the urge to ask them.

"Yes," said Chloe. "And you have a bright white heart with sunbeams shooting from it." Chloe traced the edges of the heart on her mother's chest, further describing the color bright white, a much easier task than describing dust, veranda, or peekadilly had ever been. Chloe smiled, gazing at Mom's *déjà vu* heart with a sense of wonder, similar to when she first saw the *Mona Lisa.* "It's really beautiful," she said.

Mom absorbed Chloe's words for what seemed several minutes. She turned and looked at Chloe. "And have you seen any other colored hearts on people?"

Like veranda? Chloe stared straight ahead, carefully avoiding eye contact with Mom. A cross between shame and concealment hiccuped inside of her, causing her to blush. *I wish I had a bright white heart like her, instead of this thing. But I'm not admitting it. And besides, it probably means nothing.*

Or if it does mean something, it's probably not important. My veranda is my little secret. I'll tell Mom when I figure it out, but until then, no one needs to know.

"Um . . . no. Nope. Um, the only hearts I've seen on people are either peekadilly or bright white," said Chloe, as she continued staring at the ocean. *She asked 'on people,' not on me,* Chloe rationalized. After a few moments of silence, she looked back at Mom.

Mom was in deep thought with her eyes closed. She pondered several minutes and then her eyes opened and widened, as if she had just won the epiphany-of-the-year-award. "Chloe, this is so exciting! It's just like my One and Only to give you this."

Is she having another delusional-bride-syndrome attack? Chloe thought.

"Pure." Mom stared at Chloe, as though she was waiting for Chloe's epiphany moment to join hers. "Maybe your colors have something to do with sin and forgiveness," Mom said, smiling big.

Chloe's epiphany apparently had another commitment.

"Chloe, when I met Christ, and confessed and repented of my sin, He forgave me and healed me. He covered my sin. He covered my peekadilly heart with bright white! When He looks at me--at my heart--He sees me as forgiven and pure."

Bright white means pure? It made sense. Mom was the purest person Chloe had ever known.

"Chloe, don't you see how great this is? If you can see who has a peekadilly heart, you can see who to pray for and who to share Christ with."

Okay, now she's got me being an evangelist instead of a nun. "Well, why do you think some people don't have either colored heart? And why do some people have a dust outline all around their body?"

"What do you mean?" Mom said, her bubbly demeanor turning more serious.

"Well, some people have a thin outline of dust traced around their body." Chloe hoped her mom didn't think she was crazy. "It's not an aura," she quickly added. "Like what Geena talks about. It's not that. This is a deep solid-colored line of dust."

Mom looked genuinely puzzled. "How big is it?"

Chloe reached her hand toward Mom's body, positioning her fingers on Mom's dust outline. "I'd say about 2/3 of an inch."

Mom looked shocked, and slightly panicked. "You mean you see a dust outline on *me*?"

Chloe nodded.

"Dust? Who else has dust? Have you seen anybody else with dust?"

Mom seemed a tad obsessed with the word dust. "Well, Geena has dust." Chloe paused. "And that wedding planner had dust, but everybody else has just been random." Chloe studied Mom who now looked fully mystified. "Oh, there was this yoga instructor that had it too."

A dull haze came over Mom's face as she slightly scrunched it, staring out over the water. "Chloe, was that yoga instructor a she or a he?"

"A she. Well, at least I think," said Chloe, smirking.

After several minutes of silence and blank stare, Mom's face exhibited a rapid fire succession of expressions--first confusion, then epiphany, then I-wasn't-planning-to-tell-you-that-Chloe, then sadness. She sat silently, looking over the sea.

"Chloe, I might need to tell you some things that were being saved for eternity."

A pulsating curiosity went through Chloe's body. Maybe Mom was going to come clean about dear ol' dad after all! Or maybe she had even *darker* secrets? Secrets hidden in my middle name? *Rahab.* Seriously, how many women name their daughters after a prostitute? *Thank goodness it's my middle name and not my first,* Chloe thought, as her eyes landed on an old rope dangling around a post of the pier.

For the first decade of my life, I happily signed my name, Chloe Rahab Hudson, to all my artwork and papers, next to my cute little signature stick person. Then, one day, Felicia, Little-Miss-Bible-Know-It-All, comes over and looks at one of my paintings. She stares at my name and puts her hand over her mouth, snickering. "Rahab, the Prostitute?" she asks. I don't know what to say, because I don't know what a prostitute is. I go skipping to ask Mom, wondering if it means a beauty queen or something. So, Mom reads me the story of Rahab from Joshua 2 and does a little story lesson with a rope from our garage, telling me how Rahab let the spies down the Jericho wall and saved herself and her family.

"Is there more to the story about my middle name?" Chloe asked hesitantly.

Mom started to laugh and patted Chloe's knee. "No. It's just like I told you. I chose Rahab as your middle name because she became a *great* mom. She was the grandmother of King David, and even in Jesus' genealogy. Rahab is a great example of how God is a God-of-second-chances, and that your past doesn't dictate your future once He is at the center of your life." Mom smiled. "Chloe, in case you're wondering, I was not a prostitute. But even if I had been, Christ can change anybody. There isn't a sin that God won't forgive, except rejecting Him."

"Well, then, what do you think dust means?" said Chloe.

"I need to pray about this," Mom said, scooting back on the dock and then motioning Chloe to help her up. "I'll let you know."

* * *

Seaside Retirement Home was beautifully decorated for Christmas. Chloe finished her semester of home-school and had three weeks off. At the request of the recreation director, she chaired the annual Popcorn Stringers Society and was amazed at how quickly five little old ladies could string popcorn, in spite of their arthritic hands and poor eyesight. The group met several times, making plenty of strands to adorn the Recreation Room's 10-foot spruce tree.

In appreciation for Chloe's leadership, the ladies arranged a gift for Chloe and Mom. A week before Christmas, a four-foot live Christmas tree, decorated with white-lights, strands of popcorn, and several small candy canes was delivered to the apartment. Chloe put it next to the hearth, where it looked very sweet.

One morning Chloe awoke with an urge to run. How long had it been? Long enough to forget where her tennis shoes were. She tiptoed through the darkness of the apartment to the kitchenette and flipped on the track lighting to check the closet.

A small bouquet of white roses, stems cut short, sat snug in a small silver vase on the countertop. A petal pink envelope addressed to "My Sweet Mocha" was propped against it.

Roses. My favorite. When did Mom leave these? Maybe last night, when I was watching *It's A Wonderful Life*? Mom had connections on the outside, too.

Chloe held up the envelope. It appeared to have several pages inside. The back flap was scalloped with a delicate edge that looked like lace, interwoven with tiny butterflies. She picked up the vase and inhaled the clean and fresh aroma.

Running could wait. This couldn't.

Chloe brewed a single cup of green tea and placed it, and her bouquet, on the end table in the living room. She grabbed a throw from the quilt rack, snuggled into the chair next to the fireplace and hit the remote to start the fire. She sat there a moment, sipping her tea.

Anticipation went through her, then a sense of surreal. She stared at the envelope for a long time. What could it say? When you know the most important person in your world is not going to be there much longer, everything she gives you becomes a keepsake.

Mom had written her lots of letters throughout the years because she knew how much Chloe loved them. Surely Mr. Right would someday send her letters, because letters are so romantic!

Chloe carefully opened the envelope. She tugged at the folded contents and pulled out a small stack of light pink stationary with scalloped edges and tiny white butterflies that appeared to be fluttering around its contents. She took a deep breath and began to read.

My Dearest Chloe,

For the past week, I've been thinking and praying about your colors. After our conversation at the pier, I began asking God, again, to show me what to share with you. Part of my story is in this letter, and part is saved for eternity.

Sweetie, I have a past that you know nothing about. Throughout your life, I've been like a yo-yo, with "up" being "tell her" and "down" being "no, wait." Ever since my diagnosis, I've thought about it even more. And now even more, because I believe your colors might have special meanings linked to my past.

It's hard to know what details to include and how much to share. Will my story help you? Or hurt you? Will you hold it against me? I hope you will not. I hope you will see how Christ rescued us and healed me, and then used the scars of my past for His glory.

As I've told you, I've always prayed that God would give you a special discernment in the area of sexual purity, and I think your *déjà vu* colors may be the answer to that prayer. (You will have to ask God about this . . . I don't know for sure.)

You know how I always had appointments on Tuesday nights? I know you assumed they were with my customers, but they weren't. They were with young girls and women at the crisis pregnancy center downtown. Chloe, God used my emotional scars to help them, just as He used a special friend to help me many years ago.

That's often how He works. He heals the wound, but leaves the scar.[1] Even though there's pain when a wound is being healed into a scar, there's beauty in the suffering, because it's then that we realize we can't heal ourselves and how much we need Him. And when the Great Physician has healed us, He often uses us, and our scars, to tell others about Him. (Like the woman at the well in John 4.)

Our scars remind us of how merciful He is, because the wounds, though painful, don't kill us, and often they are the very thing that lead us to Him. Even Jesus still has scars on his hands and feet! They remind us that He loved us so much He died for us, of His healing and freedom, and His victory over sin and death.

Chloe, the girl I was when I was 15 is far different from you. She was not sweet and strong, like my Mocha. She was distilled-stubborn-concentrate, but also broken and lost and empty. She felt totally unloved, even though she probably wasn't.

Like you, I longed for the attention and embrace of an earthly father. All through my childhood, I wanted my dad, your Grandpa Hudson, to love me, but he always seemed to love Gary more. Maybe it was because they were both guys and liked farming and hunting and guy stuff. I craved his love and affection, until I figured out how to get that kind of attention somewhere else. (Now I know that I was really craving intimacy with Christ.)

The summer after eighth grade, I blossomed. I had always been the ugly one--the scrawny farm girl whose mom made her clothes. But then I got contacts and my braces came off. My body changed from toothpick-like to curvaceous. Suddenly, I was getting all the attention I dreamed of and craved. I tried to talk to my mom about it, but the focus of the conversation was always,"Just be safe."

Finally, one night, I gave away my precious gift of virginity to a guy who told me he loved me. He said I was the only girl for him. It all happened so quick. Part of me thought there would be time to stop, but there wasn't. The next day I felt horrible. And the next. The more I regretted it, the more it started consuming my mind. Then I tried to comfort my regret with more sex, because I craved that momentary feeling of being loved and embraced by a guy. After a few weeks, he moved on to someone else, and so did I. In fact, I moved on to a lot of other guys.

When I was the same age that you are now, I got pregnant. I didn't even know for a few months, because my period was always so random. I was terrified. I didn't know what to do, or who to turn to. I didn't know who the dad was. The only person I knew to go to was my mom.

On March 22, Grandma Hudson drove me to North Bend, Indiana, where I had an abortion. Even to this very day, I wonder what your sister or brother would have been like. I've ached for that little one. Maybe she would have been the first female president, or he would have been the one to find a cure for cancer. Maybe she would have been the mom of a great evangelist. Or maybe he or she would have done something totally insignificant by the world's standards, yet extremely important in God's eyes.

Soon after, Grandma Hudson took me to the gynecologist and put me on the pill. Chloe, I was such a mess. I felt like a machine gun had let go on my heart. The only way I knew how to cope was to keep looking for love, but after awhile, almost all the guys had taken their turn.

I guess the bright side was that I started doing photography. I think I found it therapeutic, because it made me take the focus off of me, and my mess-of-a-life, and put it on whoever or whatever I was photographing. When I met Christ, He trumped photography a million times over! ☺

Chloe, He changed me and forgave me . . . and healed me. He gave me hope. Not instantly, but with time, and through His Word and the wise counsel of my friend. And He rescued you! That's when I made Him the love of my life, my Savior and Great Physician, my Closest Companion, and my Provider and Protector.

I took a marriage vow, and promised to save my purity, from that day forward, for Christ. The gold band that I'm wearing now was my wedding ring. (Not the diamond I gave you. I bought that years later, when my photography business became profitable, and when it started getting awkward every time a man asked me out.) God gave me a new hope and a future that included being your mom! He showed me His plan and purpose for my life. My new life with Christ has been the most precious and beautiful relationship I have ever known.

Now maybe you understand why I've always "preached" purity to you (as you often put it). Honey, if you remain pure, you'll never be confronted with a choice the way I was. Sex outside of God's plan puts choices in your path you don't want. Besides, you don't know if marriage is in God's plan for you. Maybe He will write a beautiful earthly love story for you, but maybe He will want your purity only for Himself, like me. If that's the case, you don't want to "arouse or awaken love" in your body (as the Word says in Song of Songs). Either way, Christ wants to be your first love, your One and Only.

Chloe, fall in love with Him. This remains my greatest prayer for you. You can't have an intimate relationship with Him until you accept what He did for you on the cross. You have to recognize your sin. He paid the penalty for all of it--the sin you were born with, and every sin you've done, and will do. He loved you so much that He died for you! (Is there anything more romantic than that?)

I've sheltered you your whole life, but soon you'll be on your own. (You'll have Gary, but you know what I mean.) If you reach out to God, He'll strengthen you and help you. And I think He may use your *déjà vu* colors to do this.

OK, so you're probably wondering how dust and bright white fit into this. Like I said on the pier, I believe bright white might represent purity. Jesus covered my sexual sin! (Chloe, He always forgives us and welcomes us back to fellowship with Him when we ask.) So, when God looks at me, He sees me as "pure" because my sin is covered with Christ.

But, even though Christ heals our wounds, there are still scars. He doesn't remove the consequences. Sin always has a consequence, and it always brings death of some sort, whether spiritual, emotional or physical. God restored my life, but I had to work through a lot of emotional pain and remorse, and there was a permanent consequence: My mom and I killed a baby--not just my baby, but one of my brothers or sisters in Christ. God had a plan and a purpose for that baby, and we only thought of ourselves. Perhaps a dust outline shows the consequences of having an abortion? My Sweet Mocha, if that is the case, please don't judge these women or girls. Pray for them! I know their struggle. I'm one of them. I know that apart from Christ I would have never healed.

Soon, I will meet this precious one whose life was taken. And we'll be with the Most Precious One, Jesus Christ, my Redeemer and Savior. We'll all be waiting for you, Chloe.

Love, Mom

PS: Until I met Christ, I hated my mom, because I blamed her for taking me for the abortion. But, Chloe, that wasn't fair. It was my own sinful choices that put me in the situation. Once Christ forgave me, I was able to forgive my mom (your Grandma Hudson). Unfortunately, I never got to tell her, because she and Grandpa Hudson were hit by the drunk driver on the New Year's Eve before I met Christ. I hope I see her, and my dad, in heaven.

Chloe was numb. Slowly, complete and total shock pulsated through her body. Then anger at Grandma Hudson. Disbelief. More shock. More questions. *Why hadn't I ever asked about Tuesday nights? I had a brother or a sister. Did Gary know about this?*

Chloe read the letter again, absorbing its words to her core.

Addicted to sex? Abortion? Craved male attention? These descriptions had never been in the same sentence, or galaxy for that matter, as Mom. Chloe dropped the letter in her lap. How can you know someone your whole life, yet not *really* know her? Does everybody have skeletons, this size, in her closet?

Chloe's empathy cut deep. Poor Mom. *And to think that she was my age!*

Dust! Does this really mean that the person had an abortion? Chloe fought the new sense of disdain she was feeling for the color she once loved. How could God give a gift like that? Dust was not information that she wanted to know about someone else. *Geena. Really?*

Please, don't judge these women. Please pray for them. I know their struggle. I'm one of them. I know that apart from Christ, I would have never healed. Mom's words reverberated through Chloe's head. No wonder Mom is such a Jesus freak.

* * *

Evan Smith

Stars dotted the indigo sky, illuminating the early morning and spotlighting the frozen Smith Pond. Beauty like this was the kind of stuff Christmas cards were made of.

Evan Smith cupped his mug of hot chocolate with his gloved hands and took a sip. He lowered the mug in front of him and sighed, forming a mist that collided with the cold air, as he sat on the cold bench. He breathed deeply, inhaling the freshness of the morning. He loved mornings, especially Christmas morning. The break from basketball practice today would be good, too.

Once Evan decided he wasn't playing ball in college, he made the mistake of telling the coach. Since the mention, he wasn't getting as much playing time.

Whatever, he thought. *It's okay.* "Thanks for the years I've played," he prayed. "They've been good. Maybe someday when I'm a dad, I'll coach one of my kids' teams."

A sense of closure settled in him, interrupted by a thought of anticipation. *Next year at this time, I'll have a semester of college under my belt.*

Evan took another sip from his mug, smiled, and looked toward the sky. "God, Thank you for guiding me. And thank you for sending your Son. I love you, O Lord, my strength."

℞

Chapter 4

Chloe felt a heaviness in her soul and body, and anxiety laced her veins. What was this feeling of hopelessness? Depression? Grief? *It must be grief,* thought Chloe. Though Mom was physically still alive, she was already gone. So, when are you actually supposed to grieve?

A rotation of respite nurses cared for Mom 24/7. All were pleasant women who tended to Mom's comfort every ten minutes or so, but quietly faded into the scenery, not speaking much with Chloe.

Mom fell in and out of consciousness, and she didn't talk very much, but her eyes were intense--like she was fighting to hang on. She looked at Chloe with a longing in her eyes, like she was peering into her soul and still praying fervently.

I LOVE YOU, CHLOE. I'M WAITING FOR YOU, Chloe sensed in her spirit. Were these her mother's words? Or her Father's? Lately, the words had been coming with greater clarity and more frequently. Each sensation brought a welcomed momentary shot of peace, but then a rebuke from a hateful internal thought.

You don't recognize that voice. Did God really say that? If God really loved you, he wouldn't let your mom die, would he?

I LOVE YOU, CHLOE. I AM WITH YOU. YOU'RE MY CHILD.

Chloe sat by the edge of Mom's bed, staring at her. "I love you, Mom," she whispered, as she took Mom's hand in hers.

Mom weakly rubbed Chloe's diamond ring with her bony thumb and pressed a smile. Mom, though frail and in pain, seemed to have a peace, love and lightheartedness emanating from her bright white *déjà vu* heart.

Veranda wasn't as kind to Chloe. It felt dark . . . and evil . . . and hopeless--like a 100-pound valentine from an enemy, hoisted on her chest and weighing her down. And eerily offended by Mom's bright white heart.

A feeling of claustrophobia overcame Chloe and her heart pounded. *I have to get out of here! Someone, please, rescue me!*

Barefoot, she ran out of the apartment, down the hall, and through the door under the exit sign. Like an inmate breaking out of prison and being chased by a veranda warden, she tried really hard to run fast, but her legs felt shackled.

The beach waited. Her haven.

Finally.

She broke into a full run as the words of Psalm 139 flooded her mind, as if her Mom were jogging next to her and saying them in an audible voice. *Oh,*

Lord, You have searched me and know me . . . . every word came crystal clear to her recall, as she sprinted down the beach, wet sand flying behind from her footsteps.

She ran and ran until her body was exhausted. Finally, she slowed to a walk, wanting to rest and be alone.

Just beyond the end of the sand was a secluded spot, a small cave on a bluff surrounded by tall wild grasses.

A warmth and security filled her heart as she dropped to the sand. She poked her head out of the covey and did a privacy check. *Good. I'm alone. Except for this veranda heart. If only I could yank it from my chest and throw it to the bottom of the ocean.*

I LOVE YOU, CHLOE, she sensed again.

"Who are you?" she finally asked out loud.

I'M YOUR FATHER . . . YOUR CREATOR . . . YOUR SAVIOR . . . .

Was this an audible voice? Or did she hear this in her head? *I know I am not imagining this.*

CHLOE, I KNIT YOU TOGETHER IN YOUR MOTHER'S WOMB. I ORDAINED ALL THE DAYS OF YOUR LIFE. YOU ARE FEARFULLY AND WONDERFULLY MADE, AND I HAVE A PURPOSE FOR YOU.

A strong sense of *déjà vu* overcame her. Did she remember these words from before she was born?

Silence. And a sense of awe left her speechless.

CHLOE, DO YOU ACCEPT WHAT I DID FOR YOU ON THE CROSS? I TOOK YOUR PENALTY. I LOVED YOU SO MUCH THAT I DIED FOR YOU. AND I ROSE FROM THE GRAVE THREE DAYS LATER. I'M ALIVE. I WANT YOU TO SPEND

ETERNITY WITH ME, AND I WANT TO GIVE YOU AN ABUNDANT LIFE HERE AND NOW.

Silence.

WILL YOU ACCEPT ME AS YOUR FATHER?

Silence.

WILL YOU ACCEPT WHAT JESUS DID FOR YOU ON THE CROSS?

Silence.

WILL YOU ALLOW MY HOLY SPIRIT TO INHABIT YOUR HEART?

"My heart?" said Chloe. "My heart is stained with veranda."

ADMIT YOUR SIN, AND REPENT, AND CHRIST WILL COVER IT WITH RIGHTEOUSNESS.

"But, I don't have any sin. I'm a good person."

YOUR HEART IS STAINED WITH VERANDA, CHLOE. DO YOU SEE YOUR SIN?

"But I've never drank or had sex or stolen anything. And I don't smoke either."

IT IS NOT THE HEALTHY WHO NEED A DOCTOR, BUT THE SICK. FOR I HAVE NOT COME TO CALL THE RIGHTEOUS, BUT SINNERS.

More silence.

"And I do a lot of nice things, like helping people."

MY SALVATION IS A GIFT THAT CAN'T BE EARNED OR BOUGHT.

"Well, I'm not the only one with a veranda heart." *Wait. I guess I am the only one with a veranda heart.* "I mean, I'm not the only one with sin."

BUT CHLOE, YOU'RE RESPONSIBLE FOR <u>YOUR</u> SIN.

Pondering.

Stirring in her heart.

And then . . . clarity, realization of disease, and Jesus hanging on a veranda-stained cross.

Entitlement. Stubbornness. Pride. Control. "Lord, please forgive me for all of my sin. Forgive me for being a know-it-all, for thinking the world revolves around me instead of You, for feeling sorry for myself, for judging people and not forgiving them, and most of all . . . for rejecting You. I'm sorry, Lord. I repent. I'll go a different direction. Please cover my sin and change me."

I FORGIVE YOU AND LOVE YOU. I'VE BEEN WAITING FOR YOU, MY CHILD.

Chloe's heart pounded inside her chest. Slowly and quietly, she bowed her head wondering . . . .

It's gone!

Her veranda heart had melted away. Now, in it's place, a new bright white heart had taken up residence! Chloe's new heart was clean, with crisp edges---but no sunbeams.

CHLOE, I LONG FOR YOUR COMPANIONSHIP. I WANT INTIMACY WITH YOU, WHERE WE SPEND OUR DAYS TOGETHER, IN CLOSENESS AND CONVERSATION.

Silence. And a sense of awe left her speechless.

I AM THE LOVER OF YOUR SOUL. WILL YOU ACCEPT MY LOVE AND LOVE ME BACK?

Silence. And a sense of relief . . . and peace . . . and infinity . . . a closeness she had never known. A presence of God the Father, Jesus the Son, and the Holy Spirit.

DO YOU ACCEPT ME AS YOUR ONE AND ONLY?

"I," whispered Chloe. "I do."

And suddenly, in the sunny, broad California daylight, Chloe sensed the darkness lift, and she walked into the Light.

* * *

"Mom," Chloe whispered with excitement. She took her mother's hand, caressing it gently.

Mom lay there, unresponsive.

Chloe's heart bubbled with tenderness. She kissed her mother's cheek, then lightly caressed it with her hand. She leaned in close, and whispered in Mom's ear. "I made Him my One and Only!" She pulled back, hoping to see some sort of response. She touched her new bright white heart like she was saying the Pledge of Allegiance, then brought her hand, purity ring sparkling, to Mom's bright white heart heart with bursting sunbeams of light.

If only I'd told her sooner. Chloe closed her eyes, imagining what her Mom's response would have been in earlier days. Mom would have said something like, "This calls for a celebration!" or "We're going to party over this," or "Praises." Chloe visualized her mother's arms engulfing her in a hug. She crossed her arms in front of herself, tugging and squeezing her hands into her arms, imagining Mom's warmth.

"Oh, my," said the respite nurse from her chair in the corner.

Chloe opened her eyes and saw the nurse quickly joining her at Mom's bedside.

They both stood, staring in amazement.

Mom was sitting up in her bed, with her face glowing as bright as her bright white *déjà vu* heart. Her eyes were wide open, and a smile filled her face. "The Shepherd is coming," she whispered.

* * *

Chloe dusted a fuzz ball off her black dress. Would she be able to be a good maid-of-honor today? *Today is Mom's day. She wants it to be a celebration.*

The morning was crisp and clean. Chloe glanced beyond the church parking lot for a quick view of the ocean. In the distance, a flock of seagulls looked like doves to her. They glided and soared, like they were celebrating. The Pacific sky was dotted with a pale-yellow sun and speckled with fluffy white clouds.

At 8 a.m., Chloe and Gary walked up the large concrete steps leading to the grand entrance of the historic First Baptist Church of Encinitas. The guests were to arrive at 10.

"You ready for this?" asked Gary.

Sadness bubbled in Chloe. How can you ever be ready to put the final punctuation mark on your loved one's life? "Not really."

Gary pulled open the large walnut door and held it for Chloe.

Once inside, a woman with a kind expression greeted them. She was tastefully dressed in a black tailored suit, accented with a bright white *déjà vu* heart. "Hello, I'm Pamela Hale. I'm the church's new wedding coordinator." She extended her hand to Chloe. "You must be Lisa's daughter. I'm so sorry for your loss, Dear."

Chloe stared back at her with a blank expression. "Thank you," she said.

Gary stepped forward to introduce himself. "I'm Lisa's brother, Gary, from Indiana. Thanks for putting all of this together. Lisa told me a few weeks ago that she had really enjoyed working with you."

Mrs. Hale looked as though she was thinking about Mom and was genuinely touched by the thought. "She was the most-in-love-bride I've ever worked with," she said with a faint smile.

Chloe wasn't used to this new way of talking about Mom in the past tense. Would she ever be?

"Today will be beautiful--just as she planned," said Mrs. Hale. She pinned a white rose boutonniere on Gary's black suit and placed a white rose corsage, accented with Baby's Breath, on Chloe's wrist. "Why don't you both take some time alone with her?" She pointed to the front of the church where a closed casket stood, surrounded by a band of white roses fashioned into an arch to halo it. "I'll be downstairs, if you need anything."

Chloe looked around the foyer and turned to Gary. "Why don't you go first?"

"Sure. I'll take a few minutes," Gary said, touching his hand to Chloe's shoulder.

Chloe held up her left hand, admiring the corsage. As she looked closer, she saw several tiny white butterflies, ornately cut from pearlescent paper, subtly strewn through the white forest of roses. She took her diamond purity ring from her right-hand and placed it on her left hand. *For today, I'll wear my ring on my wedding finger, in honor of my Mom and our One and Only.*

I LOVE YOU, CHLOE, she heard in her spirit.

Chloe looked around the foyer, full of details with Mom's fingerprints.

A parade of photographs decorated two long, sprawling tables, flanking the large double doors. Each photo was professionally matted in an 11 x 14, black-ebony frame that popped against the white, matted satin table cloth beneath it. Several of the photos showed the progression of Chloe's childhood, and others were favorites of Mom's work.

Chloe began the photo journey by staring at a sepia of her as a naked baby on the beach.

I remember that day. My déjà *vu colors were there when the camera flashed, but then they vaporized, which made me really mad. After my temper tantrum, Mom calmed me and took me for a walk in the stroller.*

The next photo was Mom's first national-award-winning-still-life. She must have taken thirty or forty shots of that apple. *I remember watching the light show from my playpen in the studio.* Then, Mom threw the apple in the air, caught it, and took a big, crunchy bite. *I remember thinking that was so funny!* Afterward, Mom picked me up, bounced me on the side of her hip and said, "You're the apple of my eye, my Sweet Little Mocha."

Next, a picture of three-year old Chloe sitting in the backyard, with a double rainbow and the Pacific Ocean as a background.

Maybe Mom is seeing rainbows today? Heaven must have rainbows! *But not with my colors, because heaven will have no pain, no sin, no sadness.*

The next photo was of the J Brothers modeling their purity rings.

Would they be here today? Possibly. Mom used to stay connected with some of her clients. She had this magnetism that drew people to her. She acknowledged it, always saying that it wasn't her, but Christ shining *through* her. After the proofs were sent to the J family, Mom got an e-mail from their mom. *I had kind of hoped the two were arranging a marriage for yours truly! But since I didn't get to go to the photo shoot, how could Mrs. J see what a wonderful daughter-in-law I would make? Why did*

Mom have to pick <u>*that*</u> *trip to force herself to leave me for the first time? Gary and I had fun, but still.*

Chloe's eyes locked on the next photo. It was ten-year-old-her, with a mouthful of braces. *Did she have to include that one?*

The next frame housed a photo of Gary, one Chloe had never seen before. A much thinner, nice-looking guy, dressed in camouflage, kneeled next to an eight-point elk.

Chloe recognized the elk. It hung above Gary's fireplace in the farmhouse. Mom said it was his first taxidermy project. A seasoned taxidermist oversaw his work and said he was an incredible artist.

Artist? Art is painting and sketching, *not* making dead animals look alive.

One of Mom's photo shoots for a clothing designer came next. A teen girl stood on the rock of a bluff overlooking the ocean. Her slate gray T-shirt was imprinted with the words "removed our transgressions" with a large red heart beneath it, inscribed with "Psalm 103:12," the letters diagonally cascading down the lower rim of the heart. The girl's long, shiny blonde hair, straight and thick, reminded Chloe of Mom's hair before she got sick.

Mom and I had scouted the location the day before, looking for the perfect rock for the model to sit on. We spent an awesome day together. That was the day I wondered about doing some modeling myself, because maybe modeling was the purpose for my déjà *vu colors?*

The next rectangle held a photo of Grandma and Grandpa Hudson, standing in front of Gary's farmhouse. Chloe knew it well. It's home had been on a small pedestal table in the hallway for as long as Chloe could remember.

Chloe's heart beat faster as she picked up the frame, looking into the eyes of the grandmother she never knew. *How could she have done that?* Feeling a trickle of anger welling, she turned toward the last photo on the table.

Chloe felt a rush of embarrassment go through her.

It was a photo of herself from her modeling gig last summer. Her swimsuit certainly covered everything, not that there was much on top in need of covering. But she looked "bare." In all the thought she had given to modeling, she focused on how fun it would be to see her *déjà vu* colors, and be in front of the camera, and work in a glamorous industry. But she had never given much thought to the result of a photo shoot: an image of you, that everyone can stare at in detail, and draw mustaches on, and use as a pin-the-tail-on-the-donkey game, or as a tool for making fun of girls with fat fingers.

Ew.

Moving on . . . a large, round table perfectly filled an open space in the foyer. In the center, hundreds of small, gold D'Anjou Fine Chocolate boxes were neatly towered in the form of a wedding cake.

Chloe plucked the top box from the cake, being careful to not tumble the tower. She removed the small gold bow from the box, lifted the lid, and saw two small chocolate pears, a heart, and a rose. *My favorite and Mom's.* She closed the box again, carefully returning it to its summit.

A small waterfall lightly trickled in the center of another large, round table. Surrounding the base, hundreds of small, white leather-bound Bibles were neatly stacked. Each one was inscribed on the front, with gold letters in the lower, right-hand corner, with the words, "God's love letter to you."

A wave of emotion swept over Chloe as she took it all in. She looked through the glass windows of the sanctuary, toward the front, at her Mom's light pink casket. Gary wasn't there anymore. She stood at the back of the church, the long aisle before her.

Her heart bubbled, as she began her processional. She walked down the aisle, slowly and deliberately, evenly pacing her steps, walking the most gracious maid-of-honor procession that she could. She placed her hand on the casket, beautifully engraved with pearlescent butterflies and a verse from Revelation. *I love you, Mom.*

She stood there for a long time with her eyes closed until she heard people quietly entering the pews behind her. She turned and saw Gary sitting in the second row. She slipped into the spot next to him and felt his arm slip around her shoulder. Thank goodness for Gary. He had a good heart. *And a déjà vu heart. A strange* déjà *vu heart.*

Gary's heart was the first two-tone heart that Chloe had seen. The center of it was bright white, but the outside of it was peekadilly. And it didn't have any sunbeams shining from it. Weird.

By 9:45, all the seats were completely filled, and guests were standing in the aisles. Pastor Johnson sat in the choir area reviewing some notes. Mrs. Hale was directing the janitor to set up folding chairs in the aisles.

Beautiful harp melodies and the scent of roses filled the church.

Chloe stared at the brilliant colors in the stain-glassed window up front, then closed her eyes and listened intently to Pachelbel's Canon in D, waiting for the crescendo. So many memories . . . .

"Dearly Beloved . . . We are gathered together to celebrate the life, love, and legacy of Lisa Hudson," began Pastor Johnson.

After just a few-minutes-of-a-sermon, he said, "Lisa wanted my words to be short and sweet, with all the focus on Jesus Christ. Dear Friends, the Father and Creator loves you, died for you, and longs for you. He wants to be your Savior, Great Physician, your Closest Companion, Provider and Protector, and Lover of your Soul."

Then, an older couple, whom Chloe did not know, sang a beautiful song to the tune of "How Great Thou Art." The words, slow and deliberate, in two-part a cappella harmony spoke directly to Chloe's soul.

"O Mighty God,[2]when I behold the wonder, Of nature's beauty, wrought by words of Thine, And how Thou leadest all from realms up yonder, Sustaining earthly life in love benign."

Chloe closed her eyes and listened intently, absorbing each word.

"When I behold His Son to earth descending, To help and heal and teach distressed mankind; When evil flees and death in fear is bending; Before the glory of the Lord divine."

When I behold His Son . . . Mom is beholding Him right now.

"When, crushed by guilt of sin, before Him kneeling, I plead for mercy and for grace and peace, I feel His balm and, all my bruises healing, He saves my soul and sets my heart at ease."

I feel His balm, and all my bruises healing. Chloe felt the presence of God, encompassing her with comfort.

"When finally the mists of time have vanished, And I in truth my faith confirmed shall see, Upon the shores where earthly ills are banished, I enter, Lord, to dwell in peace with Thee."

Mom's dwelling in peace with her One and Only--with You, Lord. Thank you, God. Thank you for my mom's beautiful life.

Chloe felt her tender soul stir, then strengthen, then sing . . . *My Savior, God, to Thee. O Mighty God, how great You are.*

I LOVE YOU, CHLOE. I AM WITH YOU ALWAYS.

℞

Chapter 5

Chloe and Gary left early the next morning. Mom's VW was chock full of what was left in the apartment at Seaside Retirement Center.

Chloe woke up at the border of California and Nevada. She rubbed her eyes and tried to stretch her legs. She inhaled deeply and coughed. Yuck. Men in their thirties emanate weird and unwelcome smells. The temporary kind she could deal with. But the musty, polluting, lung blackening, sticks-on-you-and-your-clothes-smoke of Gary's cigarettes . . . *not.*

Chloe stared at Gary's two-tone heart. *Does peekadilly mean the person smokes?*

Gary squished the butt of his cigarette in the ashtray and cracked the window. "Morning, Chloe," he said. "You hungry?"

Chloe looked at the empty flower holder under the ashtray. For as long as Mom had driven her VB, she had always put a fresh flower in there. No flower today. *Just as well, I guess. The poor thing would have wilted from smoke inhalation.*

The familiar "pit" settled in Chloe's stomach. *Am I hungry?* Would these "pit" attacks always be part of her life, now that Mom was gone?

"Chloe?" Gary said.

Chloe fidgeted in her seat. "Yes. I guess I am kind of hungry."

Gary took the next exit and pulled into the parking lot of the only restaurant: Tiny's Diner. "This looks good," he said.

It does? To Chloe's recollection, the word "diner" was not in the title of any restaurant she and mom had ever eaten at.

Gary and Chloe had their pick of booths and tables. Tiny's Diner apparently wasn't too much of a hot spot. Gary slid into a booth and flipped over the coffee cup on its saucer sitting atop a paper placemat. "You a coffee drinker?" he asked, holding up her cup.

"No. But I'll have some green tea."

He flipped it over just in time for a large, hairy male arm to pour it full of coffee.

"Welcome to Tiny's. I'm Tiny himself. You travelin' through today?" he said, looking eager for conversation.

Chloe stared. *Dust. Bright dust. Big dust outline on Big Tiny.*

Tiny was anything but tiny. His rotund body reminded Chloe of an oompa-loompa from the chocolate factory. His large droopy arms dangled from a black T-shirt that hung over a pair of jeans. A dirty white apron, smeared with grease marks, held a name tag that proudly declared him "THE OWNER." All several hundred of Tiny-pounds were covered with a thick layer of dust.

Don't judge these women, Chloe. Pray for them. Chloe remembered Mom's words. *Dust might be an emotional scar from having an abortion.*

Dust on a man? Was Tiny once the dad of a baby who was aborted? He would have emotional scars, too, wouldn't he? Or was Mom's meaning wrong? Maybe dust has nothing to do with abortion.

Chloe stared at Tiny's chest. Sitting on top of it was a peekadilly heart. A bra would have been a good idea. *His chest is bigger than mine.*

Nevertheless, Tiny was definitely a tom, not a hen. His voice, hairy arms and beard confirmed it.

Wait. *Have I ever seen dust by itself? Isn't it usually accompanied by a peekadilly heart--or a bright white one, as in Mom's case?*

"Ahem, young lady," said Tiny. "Will you have the biscuits and gravy special too?"

Gravy? *My arteries say, "No thanks."* Chloe quickly glanced at her placemat. "I'll have some oatmeal, cantaloupe, and some green tea."

"We're out of oatmeal today, but we have grits."

"I'll just have the cantaloupe and green tea."

"We don't have cantaloupe and our tea is brown."

"What about the fresh fruit on the menu?"

"That means bananas."

Chloe sighed. "Okay, I'll have some toast and a banana."

"Comin' right up there, young lady," said Tiny, fading off to the kitchen where Chloe could hear him pop the toaster down.

* * *

Hundreds of miles through seven states. Chloe didn't feel like talking. Gary did. Across the state of Nevada, she pretended to a read a book, but couldn't concentrate above Gary's country music bellowing out twangy soap opera stories.

Gary threw several random topics into the conversation stratosphere, but Chloe let each one promptly disintegrate into thin air. By Utah, Gary looked like he was about to give up.

Little pangs of guilt started to poke at Chloe. After all, this guy had just rearranged his whole life to take his orphan-of-a-niece in. *The least I can do is not be mute. Okay, I'll talk.*

Now Gary was silent.

Chloe sat there, waiting to be inspired with a conversation starter. She waited some more, but still *nothing*. Her brain was like a deep cavern where no words wanted to go spelunking. Then she started to get nervous, then embarrassed about her nervousness. *Why can't I talk to people with Y chromosomes? This is my uncle--not some hottie lifeguard--for heaven's sakes!*

Besides, this could be a great time to play "100 Questions" with Gary. Maybe she could figure out why his *déjà vu* heart couldn't decide on bright white or peekadilly. Or why he's thirty-one and still not married. And if that went well, who knew? *Maybe even info about my biological father!*

Chloe took out a journal from her travel bag and pretended to doodle, waiting for another chance at verbal volleyball. First things first. On the top of a blank page, she wrote the words, "Findings of my *déjà vu* colors."

She wrote the word "veranda" and then made a dash mark. She tried hard to recall the details of how her One and Only turned her veranda-colored heart to bright white. And wondered why she only saw peekadilly and bright white hearts on other people. Why didn't she see any other veranda hearts? No matter. Her veranda heart was gone and she was glad.

Next . . . dust. *Why is it always an outline and not a heart?* Chloe thought. *I don't think it means the emotional pain caused by an abortion.*

Moving on. . . She flipped the page and jotted the word "peekadilly," and scribbled some notes. Nonchalantly, she peered at Gary's chest through her peripheral vision and made a few more notes. *Two toned déjà vu heart? I know Gary is a believer . . . so why is his bright white sharing space with peekadilly? What can peekadilly mean?*

Gary turned down the guy on the radio singing about his red Solo cup. "What are you writing there?"

Chloe stiffened, slightly startled. "Oh, I'm just thinking about the scenery and making some notes. Sometimes I look through here for inspiration on what I should paint."

"Do you ever do waterfalls, like what we saw at Yellowstone?"

"I haven't, but that sounds cool," said Chloe. "That trip that you took Mom and me on was really neat."

Gary took a pack of Marlboro's from his shirt pocket, tapped one out and lit up.

Agitation knocked on Chloe's internal door. "When did you start smoking?"

"Recently," Gary said, in a case-closed way.

"Well, do you know that a lot of girls don't like to kiss guys who smoke, because it gives them really bad breath?"

Gary turned and gave her a look, half smirk, half annoyance. "Really," he said, irritated. "I didn't know that."

"Well, you *do* like to kiss *women*, right?"

Gary gave her the look again, the annoyance factor in exponentials. “Chloe, you don’t need to try to fix me up like you always did your mom. But, just so you know, I do like women. I just haven’t met the right one yet. Not sure I ever will.”

Chloe jotted a note in her journal under “Peekadilly.”

“When is the last time you dated someone?”

“Several years,” said Gary, staring at the highway ahead of him and offering no extra details.

“Why don’t you use a cell phone?”

Gary paused. “I don’t need one. I have a phone out in the shed and one in the house. That’s all I need.”

“But you used to have one, didn’t you?”

Gary took a big puff of his cigarette and flicked the ashes out of the cracked window.

“Do you have a church that you attend?” asked Chloe.

Gary answered with silence.

Okay. Any time now. Impatience bubbled inside Chloe.

“Well, do you?”

“No.”

“Why not?”

Gary threw the butt of his cigarette in the ice of an old drive-thru cup. “Why do I get the feeling that I’m being interviewed?”

Chloe’s face blushed, feeling embarrassed. “Oh, sorry. What do you want to talk about?”

“I see my sister gave you her ring,” said Gary.

Chloe held her hand up in the air, admiring the ring. “Yep.” Would she ever tell Gary about her *déjà vu* colors? How they hid in Mom’s ring all these years and then jumped out in the form of outlines and hearts on people? Chloe listened to the words in her head and decided Gary would probably think she had a mental problem to match her speech impediment. *And, besides, Mom said it was probably best to keep my colors a secret--just between God and me.*

Gary pointed ahead in the distance, trying a new topic. “Look at those mountains. I wish we could take them back to Indiana with us. Someday, a long time from now, I want to be a park ranger at Rocky Mountain National Park. What about you? You going to college or to that art school in Chicago?”

The question again. *How am I supposed to know what to be when I grow up?* “I don’t know.”

“Well I’ve heard Jefferson High has a great art program.”

Podunk Indiana school has a great art program? “Oh . . . really?” said Chloe.

“I’ll take you over there next week to get you registered,” said Gary. “You’ll be just in time for second semester.”

Chloe’s heart skipped a beat. Registered? Isn’t it kind of soon for that? *Do I really want to go to public school?*

“Lisa--I mean, your mom, said that you always wanted to give public school a shot. You’ll love Jefferson High School.” said Gary.

It was true. During the past couple of years, Chloe talked about how public school sounded a lot more fun and glamorous than homeschool. *But did I really mean that?*

“That’ll be a good way to meet people, too. Jeff is my alma mater, you know,” said Gary, who was now sounding like an infomercial for Jefferson High School.

Maybe I'll like it. It's probably tiny and filled with lots of nice girls who want to be my friend and tons of cute guys who will ask me to prom. Chloe's demeanor brightened. "Is it pretty small?" she asked.

Gary looked surprised. "Nope," he said proudly. "It's one of the largest schools in the state. About 500 a class. That's why our sports teams are so good . . . and why they have all those good art classes."

Five hundred per class? Chloe gulped. "So, there's more than 2000 kids?"

"Yep. It' s a lot bigger now, than when your mom and I went there. But, I've heard it doesn't seem so big, once you know people. I can introduce you to one of my customer's sons. He knows a lot of people, even though they just came last year. He plays basketball. Did I ever tell you about the team when I was . . . ?"

Midway through Gary's glory-days, Chloe's stomach gurgled and her brain glazed over, zoning him out. "Is there a Christian school around?" she interrupted. "I haven't told you this, but I accepted Christ."

"You did? Did you tell your mom?" Gary said, with excitement. "That was the one thing she wanted most."

Gary's statement pricked Chloe's heart. *I guess that's why I resisted it. But why did I resist? Because the person I loved most in this world wanted that for me? Why was I so stubborn?* Chloe's rhetorical questions were laced with regret. "I did."

"Awesome," said Gary, smiling a sense of contentment. "There isn't any Christian school in Dodge, but you'll be fine at Jeff."

* * *

I LOVE YOU, CHLOE. I AM WITH YOU.

The previous night was a blur. Chloe had fallen asleep somewhere between Chicago and Dodge when an ice storm formed, adding several hours to the trip. She remembered a blast of cold air waking her momentarily, until she plopped into a warm bed, clothes still on.

Chloe sat up and rubbed her eyes, unsure of her surroundings. Was this Gary's farmhouse? She recognized the Colts quilt on her bed, but just about everything else looked different since her and Mom's visit two years ago. She got up and walked to a cedar plank ledge that overlooked the main area below.

Cool. It looked like a smaller version of the lodge at Yellowstone Park. Gary took Mom and her on a camping and hiking trip there when she was nine. She had loved the three nights they spent in the lodge, better than the four nights they'd spent in a tent.

The floor of the farmhouse's second level, which also was the ceiling of its first level, had been cut out, forming a loft that went three sides around the perimeter. The main wall, which used to be the wall of the sitting room and upstairs bedroom, was masked with real, tan-colored logs. The antique fireplace, covered with fieldstone, extended to the ceiling, sandwiched between two large picture windows that framed thick woods outside. Gary's elk above the mantel stared at her, lifelike.

Chloe sniffed, then inhaled. A pungent odor, with a hint of Pine Sol, filled her lungs.

One side of the loft was filled with boxes she and Mom had packed and sent last summer. Light from two windows shone from behind the boxes. Chloe walked over to the adjacent side, where Gary had formed a sitting area, with one window and a wooden desk that held what looked like a new laptop computer. On the desk was a stapler, a pencil holder, and a picture of Mom.

A wave of emotion hit Chloe as she picked up the picture and closed her eyes. *I love you, Mom.*

An open staircase, also made out of cedar logs, formed an L-shaped landing that descended into the living room, sparsely decorated with an aged, country-motif sofa, a solid green La-Z-Boy chair and a wooden coffee table.

Brrr. My feet are freezing. She walked back toward the bed and put on her tennis shoes that lay next to it.

The entire back wall appeared to have brand new drywall, completely dull-white, stark and bare, begging for a personality.

This is my new home. Chloe wondered if it would ever feel like home, because any place without Mom didn't feel like home.

A screen door slammed downstairs and footsteps walked across a creaky floor.

"Chloe? You up yet?" said Gary.

"Uh-huh. Be right down."

"How do you like what I've done with the place?" asked Gary, as she cornered the landing of the stairwell.

"Awesome," she said. And then she froze.

On top of the coffee table stood a small raccoon that looked paralyzed. Two of his paws were lifted in the air, like he'd been stun-gunned mid-stride.

Gary started to laugh. "How do you like it? I did one for a customer a while back and did this one for me." Gary poured himself a cup of coffee and took a sip. "You'll have to come out to the shed sometime and see how I do taxidermy."

"Sounds . . ." *G-ross!* Chloe caught herself. "Yes. I'll have to do that sometime."*Like when H-E Double toothpicks freezes over!*

"Did you see the canvas I left for you?"

"No."

"The back wall up there. I left it unfinished, so you can paint a picture of whatever you want." Gary's warm smile was highlighted, albeit dimly, by the whiteness and peekadilly of his *déjà vu* heart.

A warm feeling swept over Chloe. "That was really nice of you. Thank you, Gary." She brushed the sleeve of yesterday's outfit. "I need a shower," she said.

Gary pointed toward the bathroom. "Make yourself at home."

"Do we have to go anywhere today?"

"Nope. Just get settled in. Maybe start on your picture."

"Yes," said Chloe. Images of her California beach popped into her mind, but something inside of her said no. *Mountains and a waterfall. That's what I'll paint.*

* * *

I LOVE YOU, CHLOE. WOULD YOU LIKE TO SPEND TIME WITH ME?

Chloe checked her look in the passenger mirror as Gary pulled into a parking lot at Jefferson High School. He drove past several entrances, sharing a "best memory" story for each doorway. A sense of nostalgia hovered over him, as if he were getting ready to break out with the Jefferson fight song at any moment.

"We won state that year," Gary said.

"In what?" Chloe asked, trying to sound interested.

"Basketball. It's really big here."

"What position did you play?"

"Oh, I didn't play. I was the team manager," Gary said.

"You mean you played the bench?" Chloe teased.

"Ha. Ha," said Gary.

Chloe looked at Gary. Poor guy. If anybody had ever wanted to be an athlete, it was him. And if anyone was ever born with zero athletic ability, it was him, too. And height. Chloe could tell he felt self-conscious about the fact that she was a good 3 or 4 inches taller than he was.

Gary circled to the front of the building and parked the truck.

Jefferson High looked more like a small university than a high school. A large rectangular fountain sat in the middle of a courtyard area bordered on two sides with sets of doors, with the words "School Office" above one of them.

The pit that had been forming in Chloe's stomach turned into full-fledged nausea. *Why did I stick my size 11's in my mouth about going to public school?* She rummaged around the floor of Gary's pick-up, looking for an old fast-food bag, just-in-case. The last thing she wanted to do was use Mom's Coach purse for a barf bag.

A loud bell rang through the complex, and students started trickling through the courtyard and down the sidewalks around the building.

A group of about ten students, both girls and guys, walked in front of Gary's truck, en route to their next class.

Déjà vu hearts. And dust outlines. If only I'd brought my journal!

A couple holding hands, who seemed to be in their own little world, leaned on Gary's front bumper, apparently not realizing that Gary and Chloe were sitting just a few feet above their heads. They dropped their books on the sidewalk and pulled each other close, locking their mouths in a tight tongue wrap, coming up for air every few seconds. The boy rubbed his hands down the girl's arms and settled them on her butt. Their heads bobbed back and forth, like they were biting each other.

Each of their peekadilly hearts clung like velcro on their chests.

Chloe looked at Gary, who was noticeably flustered by the PDA hood ornament in front of them.

A rush of embarrassment went through Chloe, too, mixing with her nausea and making her face warm. She'd seen this kind of making out in PG-13 movies, but not in real-life, up close and personal. She continued her stare, concluding their encounter reminded her of a couple of hyenas picking at a fresh kill.

Yuck. Chloe's first kiss would be soft and tender. She may even save her first kiss for her wedding day, but she wasn't signing up for that level of purity yet. Mr. Right would look deep into her eyes, caressing her face gently with the back side of his index finger. Then, he'd caress her hair and tell her she was beautiful. *Oh, what would it be like?*

Another bell rang, causing the couple to scoop up their books and run through the crowded courtyard, parting ways through different entrances.

"Okay, then," said Gary. "Ready to do this?"

Chloe's stomach rolled. *Why am I even doing this? Shouldn't I just come clean and tell Gary that I want to continue with home schooling? Maybe I could start next fall? You know, give myself a chance to get more settled? And, Hello . . . I'm still grieving!*

Chloe reached for the McD's bag in her hand and used it. Hot drips streamed down her face. She fumbled through her purse again, searching for a tissue to wipe her mouth. "I don't want to go here," she blurted out.

Gary's expression was a mixture of stun and male awkwardness, like seeing a female having a "moment" was completely foreign to him. Add to that . . . Someone *not* wanting to go to his beloved Jefferson High School? That really stumped him. "Are you okay? Are you going to puke again?"

Wouldn't that make a great first impression? *Hi, I'm b-l-a-a-g-h.* Then they'd call the janitor over the PA system because some new kid puked in the foyer. *And I'd forever be labeled, The Puker.*

Chloe sniffled and wiped her nose with her sleeve. "Can you just go in and get some information that I can read at home?"

Gary looked disappointed, like a tour guide without any tourists. "Sure."

"Could you hurry?" Chloe said.

Minutes later, Gary returned and hurried home, cutting the normal 15-minute commute down to ten.

A sleek black Jaguar was waiting by the taxidermy shed when Chloe and Gary pulled in. A maroon leather penny loafer stepped out of the car attached to a classy, professional-looking man with no *déjà vu* heart. Tall. Good looking for his age.

"Harding De Veen," said Gary. "Good. I wanted you to meet him."

Harding De Veen rubbed his leather gloves together. His tailored wool trousers, a tiny plaid design, looked expensive and met his highly starched white shirt with a black leather belt. He buttoned his Ralph Lauren wool overcoat, tucking in his satin gray tie, then straightened his narrow glasses on his face.

Gary pulled up to him and rolled down the window. “Cold enough for you, De Veen?”

“I haven’t seen cold like this since the Olt Country,” he said, pulling off his glasses that were fogged up from the heat spilling out of Gary’s pick-up.

What kind of accent is that?

“This is my niece, Chloe, who I told you about,” said Gary. “Remember, from California?” Gary leaned back in his seat to clear the view between the two of them. “This is Dr. Harding De Veen. He’s one of the new docs for Dodge Regional Hospital.”

“Yes. My wife wanted to get back to the states and be closer to her parents in North Bend. It’s been a goodt move. Most of the teens call me Dr. D,” he said, extending his hand over Gary to Chloe in the passenger’s seat. “Or they call me Ty’s dad.”

Chloe reached over Gary, extending her hand, noticing some snot on her sleeve. Ew. “Nice to meet you,” she choked out insincerely.

A strong *déjà vu* feeling came over Chloe, and a sense of uneasiness gripped her heart. *Why does his voice sound familiar to me?*

“You have a goodt, strong handshake there, Young Lady,” said Dr. D.

Is that supposed to be an insult about the size of my fingers? Really? Even with my gloves on? “Thanks,” she murmured.

“Have you met Ty over at the school yet?”

Silence.

Another wave of nausea knocked on Chloe's stomach's door. She dodged out of the truck, running to the house.

"She's getting the flu or something," said Gary. "We just came from the high school. Chloe's probably gonna keep home-schooling this spring and maybe try Jefferson next fall."

"Oh, I see. I'll have to bring Ty over some time, so she can meet him. I have a feeling he's going to like her," said Dr. D, looking toward the house. "So, your message said you finished up my deer?"

"Yep. Turned out beautiful," said Gary. "You busy now? I could follow you back in my pick-up to your place."

"Superb," said De Veen.

℞

Chapter 6

I LOVE YOU, CHLOE. WOULD YOU LIKE TO SPEND TIME WITH ME?

Sure. I'll pencil you in for next week.

The Shoppe of D'Anjou Fine Chocolates was packed. The faint scent of pears wafted and classical music piped through the air. Tiny cupids subtly dotted the merchandising area, perched on velvet covered heart-shaped candy boxes displayed on mirrored shelves. The glass case sparkled above hundreds of chocolate masterpieces, including a seasonal piece--a red and white swirled heart of chocolate.

Chloe inhaled the smell of Anjou pears and studied the Shoppe's eclectic mix of classical and contemporary design elements. Very cool. She imagined what the lobby must be like on Valentine's Day, with all kinds of Romeo-types buying heart-shaped boxes of love for their girlfriends.

Chloe and Gary waited several minutes in the foyer as they watched the other line move steadily, servicing about three customers to each one in their line.

Chloe caught a glance of Gary, who didn't seem to mind the wait.

Gary craned his neck, scanning the group of workers behind the case, as if he was looking for someone in particular. He reached into his pocket and pulled out a form marked *Anjou Invoice*. "I need to pay this today," he said, unfolding it.

The 500 party favors for the funeral had turned out to be a good estimate. Mrs. Hale had given the leftovers to the activities director at the Seaside Retirement Community, who gratefully planned on using them as bingo prizes.

Behind the counter workers were packing chocolates into heart-shaped boxes. Two of them were older women without *déjà vu* hearts, and the other two, a guy and a girl, looked like twenty-somethings, both with peekadilly hearts. All four of them were laughing and really seemed to enjoy their jobs.

What a cool place to work. Maybe I could get a job here someday.

The line in front of Gary and Chloe finally disappeared, bringing them directly in front of the register.

"May I help you?" said a really short girl looking up at them. She was wearing the Anjou garb of a black apron with gold pears, a red shirt for Valentine's Day, a black beret, and . . . . The cashier began processing the invoice Gary handed to her, while Chloe stared.

Chloe's heart took an extra beat. A new outline she had never seen! Around the girl's entire body was a thick band of sparkly gold that encased the girl, including her peekadilly heart.

Sparkly gold was unique from all the other *déjà vu* colors because it had a texture. It looked like thousands of tiny granules of shiny gold, randomly melded together to form a thick and brilliant covering.

I wonder if the streets where Mom lives look like that? Or are they smooth? She stared, mouth open, eyes glued.

"Excuse me. Can I *help* you?" said the girl slowly and deliberately, as if she were talking to a kindergartner.

Gary jumped in, saving Chloe from the awkward moment. "I'll have a sundae."

Miss Sparkly Gold proceeded to interview Gary, asking him a series of detailed questions. "One scoop or two? Dark or milk chocolate dessert cup? Which two toppings? Almonds or pecans? Whipped cream?"

Mesmerized, Chloe studied this new, intriguing, beautiful *déjà vu* outline, which instantly moved into first place as being her favorite. Well, second. Bright white was still the most beautiful, but only if it had the sunbeams shooting from it. Not if it had peekadilly neighboring it, as Gary's heart did.

The world around her seemed to be moving in slow motion. Sparkly gold was inviting her to touch it.

Chloe felt like someone was drawing squiggly lines in her stomach, the same feeling she'd had many times as a kid when Mom said not to touch something, and it just made her want to touch it ten times more. In this moment it was just her and this new *déjà vu* friend, a beautiful visitor who kept inviting her to touch it.

Curiosity pulsated through her body. Anticipating what wonderful feeling would come from touching, Chloe reached out her arm, extending her fingers to its beauty . . . and touched the sparkly gold on the girl's head.

"What are you doing?" snapped the cashier. "Get your hands off of me," she said, muttering "freak" under her breath.

A manager came quickly to the situation. "What's going on here?"

"She touched my head," said the cashier, sarcastically.

Chloe zoned out. A hole inside of her began filling to the brim with embarrassment and overflowed, spilling out into every crevice of her body. Her face felt like a red-hot-cinnamon disc sprinkled with cayenne pepper. Snapping herself back to reality, she stammered, "Sorry. I'll have what he's having." Then she darted off to the bathroom, where she promptly decided she would *never* work at D'Anjou Fine Chocolates.

* * *

I WAITED FOR YOU, CHLOE.

Sorry. Something suddenly came up.

I LOVE YOU, CHLOE.

Why? I feel like such a loser.

* * *

Five years ago, Chet and Beverly Hicks moved from town to Rural Route 4. By day, Mr. Hicks sold insurance. By night, he raised a small herd of cows and kept rabbits, thus fulfilling his childhood farming dream.

The Hudson Farm was about 1/2 mile down the gravel road from the Hicks' Farm, making Gary their closest neighbor. But more than neighbors, they were friends. Gary spent every holiday with the

Hicks family--Thanksgiving, Christmas, and Easter--unless he was visiting his sister and niece in California.

Beverly Hicks was known for her down-home-down-right-delicious cooking. For the past three years her entries took Grand Champion in the County Fair Cook-Off, earning her the top prize of a year's supply of specialty butters and lard. Mrs. Hicks' cooking was more than a talent, it was her expression of love to her family and the world at large.

A few days after Chloe and Gary got home from California, Mrs. Hicks brought over a meal of pot roast, mashed potatoes and gravy, homemade bread, and cherry pie, made from scratch. When Chloe opened the porch door, Mrs. Hicks walked right in, setting the covered dishes on the counter. Warm and friendly, she expressed her sympathies to Chloe and said, "I'll have to introduce you to Mayble. She's about your age."

Mrs. Hicks had a bright white heart and a dust outline, just like Mom.

Around 5 p.m. on a Friday in late January, Gary drove his GMC truck through the snow up Hicks' lane. "Wonder what Beverly is cooking tonight?" he said to Chloe.

Chloe's goal for tonight's dinner at the Hicks' was simple. She wanted to be friends with Mayble Hicks. She needed a friend. One friend. Any friend! More than a milk commercial needs a mustache. Somebody who was into talking, shopping, boys, and sharing complaints about Indiana.

Gary pulled close to the shoveled sidewalk to let Chloe out.

I wish I'd brought a hostess gift, thought Chloe. *Mom always brought a hostess gift whenever we were invited to someone's house.* Chloe waited on the sidewalk and shivered from the cold. *Don't say anything stupid tonight!* she told herself. Fortunately, the Hicks' boys, by virtue of their ages, wouldn't pose a threat to her Y-Chromosome-communication disability.

Gary pulled into the turn-a-round and backed the truck so it faced outward--the prudent way to park in January in Indiana, in case a snowstorm hits.

Mrs. Hicks opened the door before they could knock. She wore an apron and a welcoming smile. "Gary, it's so good to see you again. And you too, Chloe." Mrs. Hicks shut the door behind them. "Come in where it's warm. Let me get your coats."

Upstairs, a baby was crying.

Mrs.Hicks turned behind her and yelled up the stairwell. "Mayble! The Hudsons are here. Bring down Louie with you."

Moments later a girl bounded down the steps holding a baby on her hip. Mayble was pudgy, abundantly blessed on top, and had long, light brown hair that hung in tight corkscrews. She was dressed in black from head to toe, about 5-foot-5-inches and went a little heavy on the eye make-up and the bright red lipstick. She handed Louie to her mom and turned to Chloe, looking surprised.

"You're black?" she said.

"*May*-ble!" yelled Mrs. Hicks, noticeably mortified.

"Oh, uh, sorry," Mayble stammered. "I just wasn't expecting . . . I mean, there aren't many people around here . . . well, anyway, I'm May." She looked at her mom and said *May* again, emphasizing her name was one syllable. "Nice to meet you, Chloe."

Black? *I'm not black, I'm honey-brown.* Chloe thought back to the countless times throughout childhood when people would assume her mom had adopted her.

Not that Chloe had anything against being black . . . it was just that every time she had to fill in her official race on a bubble questionnaire, she'd wind up mad about dear ol' absent dad.

"Nice to meet you too, Mayble," said Chloe.

May shot Chloe a dirty look.

I mean May! Chloe caught her mistake, but the moment for reprise had passed.

"Why don't we all head to the dining room," said Mrs. Hicks. "Dinner is already on the table."

The dining room table was full and set simply. It reminded Chloe of the Norman Rockwell Thanksgiving portrait, *Freedom from Want*, that she had written a paper on in fifth grade. And so did the meal, which consisted of a turkey with all of the fixings.

Gary was visibly excited about the spread.

Chet Hicks and the smaller Hickses introduced themselves. Timmy and Tommy were ten-year-old twins. Baby Louie sat in a car seat close to Mrs. Hicks's chair, looking content with the bottle May had just given him.

Mr. and Mrs. Hicks had matching *déjà vu*--dust outlines with bright white hearts. None of the Hicks children had any traces.

But tonight is not about déjà vu sleuthing!

Tonight, Chloe's efforts would be focused on appearing to be a *really* interesting person, the kind any teen girl would kill to have as a friend.

Mrs. Hicks directed the seat assignments. After everyone was settled, she said to Gary, "Would you mind saying the blessing?"

Chloe smirked. *I don't think Gary is really the praying type.*

"Be happy to," Gary said. "Lord, thanks for these great friends, this great food, for bringing Chloe here, and for the beautiful life you gave my sister. Thank you for making us new creations in Christ. Amen."

Sheepishly, Chloe opened her eyes and looked at Gary. *Did a tiny sunbeam just burst from the bright white core of his heart?*

The table was buzzing with dishes passing and spoons scooping.

"Chloe, can you start the gravy around?" said Mrs. Hicks.

"Sure." Chloe nervously reached for the gravy boat, accidentally jerking her arm and tipping it over.

The brown gravy oozed over the white tablecloth. Timmy and Tommy poked each other and started laughing.

"Oh, it's all right, Dear," said Mrs. Hicks, jumping into quick-clean-up mode, as though it was a routine part of a Hicks family meal.

Chloe's heart beat faster as her face changed from honey to auburn. She looked at May. *Did she just roll her eyes at me?*

"Chloe, I hear you are home-schooled," said Mr. Hicks. "How is that going for you, here in Indiana?"

I'm lonely. "It's fine, but I'll be starting at Jefferson next fall."

"What grade?" asked May.

Chloe paused to think. "Hopefully a junior. It kind of depends on if they take all of my homeschool credits." She tried to inject a smile in her sentence. "What year are you, *May*?" she said with an expression that was trying to say, "Can we start over?"

"I'm a sophomore," said May, standing up and putting her napkin on her half-eaten plate. "Sorry, everybody. I have to go to work." May leaned over and kissed her dad on the cheek.

"Bye, Princess," said Mr. Hicks, returning the kiss.

A warm sensation, mixed with a teaspoon of jealousy, went through Chloe's veins. May was so lucky to have a family--a mom, a dad, siblings, a baby Louie.

"Where do you work, May?" Gary asked, scooping his third helping of mashed potatoes.

"Anjou Fine Chocolates," said May.

Chloe stiffened. *Oh, no.* She probably knows Little Miss Sparkly Gold, who will tell her about the freaky black girl who touched her head.

"Nice to meet you, Chloe," said May. "Hey, are you on Facebook?"

Chloe felt like she had a big L on her forehead. "No, but I will be soon."

* * *

CHLOE, I THOUGHT OF YOU WHILE YOU WERE SLEEPING.

The first Friday in February brought with it five inches of fresh snow. Chloe woke up and looked out the window of her loft. Gray again. How do these sun-starved Hoosiers do "gray" for so many days out of the year? She leaned over the loft rail, looking for Gary. Gone again. Where did he go all of the time? Most likely, he was out in his taxidermy shed turning some little forest animal into "art."

She sat on the edge of her bed, pulling on an extra pair of socks, and looking at the half-painted mural on her wall.

The mountains were begging for pine trees.

Chloe really needed to get back to homeschooling. Today! All of January, she had waited for inspiration to hit her, and it never had. It never even showed up! *Mom always used to make it show up.*

After an internal debate between home school and pine trees, Chloe compromised. First, some pine trees for these poor naked mountains, then the whole afternoon for home school.

After a couple of hours and several hundred brush strokes, she craved some green tea.

Chloe looked out the kitchen window as she poured cold water into the coffee pot and stuck a tea bag in one of Gary's John Deere mugs.

A girl dressed like an Eskimo was trudging up the driveway, through a narrow path shoveled in the snow. She was carrying something wrapped in several dish towels. *May!*

Chloe opened the kitchen door leading to the porch and met her at the screen door, opening it for her.

"Hey, delivery from the Hickses," May said, handing Chloe a pan that was still warm. "It's blueberry coffee cake my mom made." May stomped the snow off her boots and took off her winter gear, tossing it on the floor of the porch in a pile, then walked into the kitchen as if she knew where she was going. "This is amazing," she said. "Last time I was here, the place still looked like an Amish farmhouse." May walked over to the fireplace and looked up, inspecting the loft. "Cool.

Still could use a woman's touch, though," she said, smiling.

Yay! *May must not have thought I was a total dork!* Chloe unwrapped the pan and inhaled the sweet scent of blueberries and cinnamon. "Want some green tea with this?" she said.

"No coffee cake for me," said May. "How many calories in the tea?"

"None."

"Then sure," said May, sitting at the kitchen table. "I'll have a large cup."

Chloe set her mug in front of May and poured a new cup for herself. She scooped a large square of coffee cake onto a plate and sat down too. "Why aren't you at school?"

"Snow day," said May, with a huge smile. "Hal-he-who-ha! I worked late last night, so I was so psyched when the 'rent shut my alarm off."

"So there are advantages to this arctic tundra," Chloe said, smiling.

"Yep. One less time riding that God-forsaken bus," said May. "I cannot even tell you how *lame* it is. It's filled with loud bratlings, and the bus driver smokes like a chimney. It's a little much for 6:30 in the morning."

"Why so early?"

"Because I'm one of the first ones on, and last ones off," said May with disdain. "I can't *wait* until next year, when I can drive."

"So, you don't have your license yet?"

"I do, but you can't drive at Jefferson until you're a junior, because there isn't enough parking." May sipped her tea. "Mmm. Where's the Unc?"

"Probably in his shed working on Bambi's cousin," Chloe said with a hint of sarcasm.

They both laughed.

"Yeah, I've seen Dr. D over here before. Have you met his infamous son?"

"No. What's his name again?"

"Didn't you see all the Ty paraphernalia at Jefferson High School? All those posters of him plastered everywhere?" said May, rolling her eyes. "I work on the yearbook and his mug was all over it last year."

May sat up straight and broke into news reporter mode, "And now, since poor Jefferson High School hasn't had a basketball star since the great Davion Griffin almost two decades ago, we are immeasurably fortunate to have the ever-so-popular, *amazing* immigrant, T-Y-The-Guy, who sailed the ocean blue from the far away Netherlands, to rescue our feeble and rural little--I mean big--high school, thus putting Jefferson on the hoops map, once again."

Chloe laughed. "I take it you don't like him?"

"Oh, I don't know," said May. "I don't really know him. He's a year older and attached to one of the cheerleaders."

"His dad dresses nice," said Chloe.

"Yeppers. Supposedly Dr. D and Ty *only* wear Ralph Lauren--*everything*. I guess it's hard to find stuff that fits when you're uber tall. Did you meet his wife?"

"No, why?"

May shrugged her shoulders. "Oh, never mind," she said smirking.

"Come on, what?"

"Well, she's just kind of . . . interesting," said May, changing the subject. "Do you do any sports?"

I would really like to know what is interesting . . . "No. Well, not really. I'm a runner, but not for sports or anything. I'm more into art."

"Cool. Jefferson has a bunch of art classes. I've done quite a few of them, because photography at Jeff is through the art department."

"My mom was a photographer," said Chloe. She speared the last bite of coffee cake from her plate, then squished the leftover crumbs into her fork and ate them.

"Sorry to hear about your mom. That must be hard," said May, awkwardly.

"You want to see some of her photos?" asked Chloe, bringing her plate to the sink.

May's eyes widened with delight. She followed Chloe up the steps to the loft and looked around. "This is really cool. I never knew Gary had this in him." May perused Chloe's photo gallery, which included all the pictures from Mom's funeral, from their beach bungalow, and a bunch Mom had framed for Chloe the previous fall. "She did a lot of work for some women's magazines in New York, but I'm not sure which ones."

May's mouth hung open. "You're kidding. That's my dream. I can't wait to graduate and get the heck out of here. I'm going to New York to do photography for a magazine like *Glamour* or *Cosmopolitan*." May walked over to Chloe's bed and flung herself on top of it. "What's that?" she said, staring at Chloe's mural as though she didn't "get" it.

What's there to get about a mountain, a waterfall, and some pine trees? "It's my painting," said Chloe. *Did she just make a face?*

"Oh," said May, pausing. "That's . . . good."

A rush of warmth flushed over Chloe's face. Was she a bad painter? Mom never said so, but what mother tells her daughter that she's lousy at something? Come to think of it, the only thing Mr.

Pepperton ever said, in all those years of art lessons, was, "It's coming along." And then he'd jump in his car, drive over the speed limit to the bank, and cash Mom's check that very same day!

A touch of anger festered within Chloe. *It's these stupid déjà vu colors. They're messing up my painting.*

May curled into a fetal position on Chloe's bed as she continued staring at the painting. "Blaaah. I've got the curse today."

"The curse?"

"You know? Riding the cotton pony."

Chloe looked blank.

"My p-e-r-i-o-d," said May sarcastically. "Seriously, how do women do this for thirty or forty years? Is yours bad?"

Chloe blushed again. *Mine?* "I haven't gotten it yet."

May looked shocked. "You're kidding. I got mine when I was ten. Is something wrong?" May gave Chloe the once-over. "Maybe you're too skinny."

A pang poked Chloe's heart. *Is something wrong with me? Am I too skinny? But I haven't lost any weight.*

"I don't know any girls who get it that late. You better get that checked out," said May. She put both hands on her stomach and rubbed it. "Uggh. I wish I could give you mine. I'm never going to need it anyway," she said. "I don't want to be the quintessential homemaker, with scads of kids, like my mom. I'm too much of a feminist to stay home and bake cookies for twenty years."

What's wrong with cookies? Chloe wondered. She looked across the loft at a large picture of her mom and dissected May's statement in her mind.

Quintessential homemaker? Feminist? Neither of those labels sounded good. But, scads of kids? That hit a nerve. While she didn't go around broadcasting it, her happily-ever-after included getting married to Mr. Right and having six kids with him. For as long as she could remember, she dreamed of a family--the kind that May had--with a nice mom, cute and lovable kids, and a dad who calls his daughter, "Princess." Sure, she wanted to go to college, maybe do some modeling, and maybe get a gig with the Remedial Painters of America Society, but most of all, she someday wanted to be a mother. Chloe wanted what Mom had, with two exceptions: a husband of the *earthly* sort and *lots* of earthlings. *And to do that, I need a period.*

After May solved a few world crises and gushed for a couple of hours about a guy named Jason, she helped Chloe set up a Facebook account and then noticed the time. "Jinkies. Got to get to Anjou."

"Do you like working there?"

"I love it. It's such a blast," said May. "Chloe, you should totally try to get a job there! Actually, Jason said some girl just quit and since you homeschool, you could work during the day."

Well, I could meet some more people and study Miss Sparkly Gold at the same time. "Maybe I will. It sounds like fun," said Chloe.

"Here's the hot tip," said May. "Memorize the catalog."

Cool. I'm good at remembering things.

* * *

I LOVE YOU, CHLOE. DO YOU WANT TO SPEND TIME WITH ME?

I'm really sorry, but I already have another date scheduled.

* * *

The world of Facebook fascinated Chloe. What could be wrong with it? Mom *was* overprotective. S*he would have eventually let me get a Facebook account, wouldn't she?*

Chloe glanced away from her computer screen and looked at Mom's picture. *Chloe, keeping some privacy is good for your love life. Don't take the mystery and discovery out of romance! A guy worth having likes to do the pursuing. The Neanderthal types might like to be chased--through texting and Facebook and calling--but not the nice guys.* Blah, blah, blah. Chloe had filed the discussion in her mental "Irrelevant" file. What could a Protestant nun know about this stuff?

Chloe flipped Mom's picture over again and stared into her beautiful blue eyes. But Mom *did* know about attracting guys, and romance, even though she was never *trying* to.

Chloe thought about all the men who had pursued Mom. Like Andrew Jones, who was, by all standards, the total package and a hottie to boot. As soon as Geena told him that Mom's ring was a decoy, and that she really wasn't married, Andrew was determined to date Mom. He pulled out all the stops and persisted longer than any of the other poor schleps that had tried to woo her. Poor Andrew. *I had high hopes for him.*

A slight pang of guilt went through Chloe. She felt as if Mom was staring at her. *Will Mom be upset with me up there if I do Facebook?* Chloe stared back at the photo. *Mom, I promise I won't turn into a stalker or post too much info about myself.*

Chloe's home page screamed to her attention that she only had *one* friend. One friend! She thought of every person from California she knew and sent each a friend request.

Mr. Tipton, the techie from Seaside Retirement Home, must have been online as usual, because he responded right away. He wrote on Chloe's wall: "I see you've gone high-tech. We all miss you." Chloe stared at his photo. *No peekadilly heart. So photos don't show déjà vu colors.* She pulled her journal from her desk and made a quick notation.

Chloe went to the D'Anjou Fine Chocolates page and "liked" it, then clicked on the link for Anjou's website. She clicked on the "Products" tab and printed the ten-page product manual.

Next, she clicked on "Employees" and scanned through, searching for May. About a hundred Anjou workers were pictured, each designated as a Shoppe, kitchen, or office employee.

Chloe searched for May, but instead stumbled upon . . . *I know that face.*

It was Miss Sparkly Gold, holding up her favorite candy piece for the camera and smiling. Minus her sparkly gold outline.

Chloe continued her scan, hoping to see some pics of May.

A girl who strikingly resembled May smiled from the screen, as she held a giant chocolate penny in front of her. Was this May? She looked like May, except she was a much larger version of May. Much. Fifty pounds? Seventy pounds?

Since there was only one employee named Jason, Chloe wondered if he was May's boyfriend. Jason looked like a nice guy. *May deserves a nice guy. I wonder how old he is? Maybe he home schools, too, since he works during the day? Maybe he has a nice friend for me, so May and I can go on double dates?*

Chloe exited from the website, then gathered the Anjou papers from the printer and stapled them. She went to her bed and plopped down, daydreaming about what chocolates she would want Mr. Right to send her someday.

℞

Chapter 7

"Aren't you coming in?" asked Chloe.

Gary pulled up to the double doors of D'Anjou Fine Chocolates at 7:00 a.m. and idled the engine.

"I'll be back in just a few. I need to get some smokes," said Gary.

Inhaling her frustration, Chloe jumped out of Gary's pick-up truck and slammed the door. *I bet I smell like smoke. Yuck.* She smoothed her black skirt and fixed the collar of her blouse, lifting it from her winter coat and folding it over its black wool. She opened the doors and entered the quiet Shoppe.

Anjou was decorated for Saint Patrick's Day with clovers and tiny leprechauns. A bright-green-four-leaf clover chocolate was prominently featured as the seasonal item.

"May I help you?" asked a redhead, with a smile and no *déjà vu* heart.

Chloe's nerves began to tease her, but she silenced them and walked to the register. She swallowed hard. "Hello. I'd like a one-scoop sundae made with your luxuriously creamy vanilla blend, in a silky milk chocolate cup, with two of your five gourmet toppings--the tart wild boysenberry and the crispy peanut butter--topped with roasted pecan halves and dairy-fresh whipped cream, please," said Chloe. "And I'd also like your two products that contain gluten, the biscotti and your chocolate-covered pretzels."

The redhead smiled. "We don't get that order very often, at least not with that level of eloquence."

A rush of excitement went through Chloe. *She just called me eloquent!* "Hi. I'm Chloe Hudson. I've been eating your chocolate since I was a little kid. I've memorized every ounce of your catalog," she said, trying to sound as sweet as possible. "I really want to work here. Are you taking applications?"

"Don't you have school today?"

"I home-school," said Chloe. "I'm 15 1/2. I can't drive yet, but my uncle--he'll be here in a few minutes--he said he'd take me to work and pick me up. And if I ever work at night, May Hicks is my neighbor, and she said I could ride with her."

"We're set for our night crew, but I really need someone early in the morning." The girl extended her hand. "Hi, I'm Candice. I'm the Shoppe Manager." Candice stepped back. "Let me get you an application. I'll be right back." She walked through a door that said "Corporate Office."

A wave of cold air gusted through the large doors behind Chloe. She turned around, expecting to see Gary.

Instead, an older black couple, all bundled up, walked in.

Chloe stared at the woman, trying to be discrete in her reaction. *A new outline!* A black outline? Next to the woman's jet black skin, the outline was hard to see, because it blended in. But, around the rest of her body, the thin black layer vividly contrasted the woman's silver hair, white pants, and red jacket, which made her resemble a gala apple. The outline was only on her, not him. They both had bright white *déjà vu* hearts, as bright as she remembered Mom's to be. Sunbeams protruded from their chests, illuminating the Shoppe lobby.

"Mornin', Child," the woman said to Chloe. "Sure is cold out." She set her purse on a nearby table.

"Good morning." Chloe stood close to the glass case, pretending to review an Anjou catalog. *What could a black outline mean?* She nonchalantly looked back and forth between the couple and the catalog.

At first glance, they whispered to each other. Second glance looked like they were praying--eyes closed and holding hands. And third glance? The elderly gentleman put his hand on her shoulders, and they kissed! Like three seconds long! Like something from a geriatric soap opera! Although tastefully done, it was clearly a passionate display of public affection.

Chloe felt a rush of adrenaline mixed with embarrassment. She stared. This was fascinating. Had she ever seen "old" people kiss?

It was just the two of them in their own little love world. Their bright white *déjà vu* hearts melded into one, creating a brilliant spotlight clearly focused on the reunion of their longing lips.

Before their kiss had ended, the large Shoppe doors flung open and in walked Gary and a formal-looking, wiry gentleman whose eyes landed on the couple. Candice simultaneously opened the office door and was back with a sheet of paper.

"Marg! We have customers," the wiry gentleman said.

Mr. Elderly Black Kisser turned and smiled. "Have a good day, Namby." He turned to his wife and said, "You too, Sweets." Then he quickly darted out the door.

Gary hovered in the background, smirking.

"Hey, Sweets. I need that batch of pralines by 9:00 a.m.," said Namby, as he headed for the office.

"Sure thing, Boss." Marg laughed and retreated to the back, like a polar bear returning to its cave after eating the last fish.

"Here you are, Chloe," said Candice, laughing. "Are you sure you want to work here with all these crazy people?"

"Are they hiring?" said Gary, walking toward Chloe.

Candice stiffened like a lollipop on a stick. She looked at Gary. "Hi . . . you're Gary, right?"

A mix of surprise with a drop of glee came over Chloe. "Do you guys know each other?" she asked.

Gary's face blushed. "Yes. She helped me with the chocolates for the funeral favors."

"Funeral favors?" Candice asked. "I thought those were wedding---"

"Oh, those were for my mom's funeral. It was like a wedding," Chloe interrupted. "Long story. Anyway, this is my uncle."

Candice turned to Chloe, looking compassionate. "I'm sorry you lost your mom. So, you live with your uncle and his wife now?"

Gary's face went one shade pinker.

"Yes," said Chloe. "Well, he's not married." Chloe registered Candice's response and smiled. She looked at Gary, examining his face. Did he even catch that Candice was sweet on him? "Gary, Candice says that they need somebody in the morning and that I have a good chance . . . ."

"Hold on there," said Candice. "Mr. Namby, the owner, has the final say on new hires, and he's not too fond of workers under the age of 16, because of all the child labor law stuff." She turned to Gary, "But, you'd be willing to drive her and pick her up from work?"

"Not a problem," said Gary.

Candice handed Chloe the application. "Here, fill this out and bring it back sometime. It's really short and straight-forward."

"Oh, I'll just fill it out right now," said Chloe. "Is that okay, Gary?"

"Sure. Can I have a large coffee while I wait for her?" said Gary.

"It's on the house," Candice said, smiling and heading for the kitchen.

A rush of excitement went through Chloe. Candice and Gary sitting in a tree, K-I-SS-ING! This new development could only help her chances of getting hired. She walked to the back corner of the Shoppe, sat at a table and pulled a pen out of her purse. She looked over the application, and then looked up toward the register.

Gary and Candice seemed to be hitting it off.

After some basic application questions and a few customer-service essays, Chloe felt confident her answers showcased that she was the perfect match for the job. She walked back to the register and handed it to Candice.

"Finished?" said Candice, looking it over. "Looks good. I'll talk to Mr. Namby and give you a call. Is this your home number?" She looked at the phone number, smiling.

"Couldn't you ask him now?" said Chloe, pushing slightly.

"Sure." Candice seemed to admire her determination. "Be right back." She walked through the office door. "Oh, there you are. Do you have a minute?" she said to someone in the office, as the door shut behind her.

Chloe stretched her ear toward the door, trying to hear their muffled conversation.

"Is she related to Marg?" said Mr. Namby.

"No. She just moved here from California. She'd be excellent, and I need someone for the mornings, Henry. Besides, how many 15-year-olds memorize the whole catalog before they even apply?"

"She's fifteen?" said Namby. "No way. Case closed."

Candice opened the door, returning to the Shoppe, smiling. Nonchalantly, she said, "Mr. Namby is going to review your application. I'll be in touch."

* * *

Chloe closed her Bible and put a checkmark on her mental TO DO list. *There. I just read two chapters,* she prayed.

I DON'T WANT TO BE A TASK ON YOUR CHORE LIST, CHLOE. I WANT A RELATIONSHIP WITH YOU . . . I LOVE YOU.

* * *

Apparently Anjou didn't want to hire the Memorizer-of-the-Year or a brown girl who sees *déjà vu* hearts. For the past month, Chloe jumped like a jack-in-the-box every time Gary's phone rang, but it was always a salesperson or some guy wanting a helpless creature mounted. Or Jefferson High School calling to stunt her academic growth by making her a sophomore instead of a junior next fall. Bummer.

Outside Chloe's window, a robin sat perched amidst hundreds of tiny white dogwood blossoms, inviting her to ditch homeschool for the day. Not an option. Her biology lesson was due by 3 p.m. online, and she and May had plans to go running at 10:30 a.m., since May was on spring break this week.

A sick feeling came over her as she clicked open her biology lesson: The Female Reproductive System. She leafed through the pages, hoping to see a topic like "Onset" or "Timing" or "When puberty happens." Nothing. Just diagrams and the basics of how a typical female's cycle works. *I wish I were typical.*

A wave of concern went through her. She clicked on the blank search engine box and typed in TYPICAL AGE FOR GETTING PERIOD. Quickly, she scanned the screen and read, "A girl's period will happen approximately two years after her breasts start to develop." So not comforting. *I've seen bigger breasts on boys at the pool.*

She continued reading.

"In the United States, the average age is 12."

Twelve? I'll be 16 in a few months.

She glanced at Mom's photo on the desk. *I need you, Mom. What should I do?*

The next line told her.

"If a girl has not had her first period by age 15, she should see a doctor."

Doesn't that sound like fun? Chloe thought. She wasn't sure what she was dreading more: going to the appointment or asking Gary how she should pay for it.

Chloe's cell phone chimed with a text from May. "I'M UP. MEET U AT THE TREE. GOOD NEWS 4 U!"

Thankful for the reprieve, she did some quick stretches, put on her tennis shoes from the porch, and trotted to meet May.

About halfway between the farms, a huge oak tree towered above the gravel road. It had been spared generations ago when a Hudson ancestor was clearing the field to make it tillable.

Today, the tree was covered with green buds and surrounded by the dark spring earth. In the distance, Gary's planter-gizmo hummed, combing the field, dropping its seeds, and covering them in a fluid, rhythmic motion.

"It's a future fellow Anjou Diva!" yelled May. She started jogging in place, awaiting Chloe.

Curiosity propelled Chloe's legs a bit faster. "Anjou Diva?"

May joined Chloe, her legs jogging in sync. "A girl quit last night. I heard Candice and Namby arguing over you. She won! He said she could use you on days for awhile, and then he might move you to nights. We would have *such* a blast working together."

Excitement rushed through Chloe. Yay! She closed her eyes, felt the spring sun on her face, and breathed in deeply. And again. "Yuck. *What* is that smell?" Chloe said.

May laughed, out of breath. "Mr. Corbin says it's the smell of money."

"What?"

"Pigs, City Girl," said May. "Swine--you know--snouts and curly tails?" May reached up and plugged her nose. "They don't smell like Piglet from the Hundred Acre Wood in real life," she said, in a nasally voice.

Chloe scrunched her face. *Note to self. Do not air out the farmhouse-of-an-ashtray when this aroma is in the air.*

"We used to raise them, too, before Dad switched to cows. I had the 4-H Grand Champion one year," said May with a mixture of pride and embarrassment. "Corbin lets them out in the spring."

Both girls plugged their nostrils and increased their pace as they ran past a large pen, bordered with an electric fence, with about fifty pigs rooting around in the mud.

"You're so lucky. You'll get to work with Jason on days," said May. "We've been together for 47 days." May looked at her watch and smiled. "And six hours."

"What's he like?" asked Chloe, knowing May wanted to gush.

"Oh, he's really funny. And nice. And super cute," said May. "I can't wait for my birthday. He said he's planning something special." May's face glowed with excitement.

"What color does he . . . ." Chloe stopped herself abruptly.

"Oh, he drives the coolest red Jeep," said May.

* * *

At 6:30 a.m., Chloe sat at one of the small round tables in the Anjou break room, studying her catalog and munching a crushed pear from the small plate of duds. She took off her coat and smoothed her black pants. Today was showtime. Candice would be in at 7:00 to train her on all the finer points of chocolate selling.

Anjou's employee break room was way-cool, resembling a large coffee shop dotted with small round tables. On one end, two sofas and two chairs formed a cozy sitting area, with a stainless steel coffee table in the middle, accented with a centerpiece of peach-colored roses. On the other side of the room was a kitchenette with a coffee bar. Contemporary artwork tastefully adorned the walls, highlighted by track lighting. One of the walls was entirely made of windows, showcasing Anjou's production kitchen, where all of Anjou's fine chocolate came into existence.

Chloe's heart beat nervously. *Why did I get here so early?* She stared into the kitchen, watching workers in white overcoats stir, brush, package, or operate a machine. In the corner of her eye, she saw one of the workers walk out of the kitchen room and into the hallway.

"Mornin' Child," said a voice, barreling through the double-swing doors into the break room. "I'm Marg."

It's the geriatric kisser with the black outline and bright white déjà *vu heart!* Chloe jumped in her seat, startled.

Marg's voice was deep and kind and weirdly familiar, bringing a sense of peace to Chloe's heart. Marg's facial expression was a cross between joy and mischief. Today, her silver hair was tucked neatly under a hairnet, which made Marg look like she had a Brillo pad on her head. Her bright white heart shone like a full moon on a dark night, which was a bit blinding for this time of the morning. And Marg's chest behind her heart?

Chloe was fairly certain she had never seen breasts that large before. *Those have to be size HH or N or some letter close to the end of the alphabet!*

"Good Morning. I'm Chloe. Today is my first day."

"Oh, I know all about ya, Child," Marg said. "I'm sorry to hear about your mama. You just come on over to Marg if you need anything." Marg smiled and her teeth matched the bright white of her heart. "I had a few kids in my day. But they've all grown up and left Elmer and me." Marg whipped out a small photo wallet from her pocket and told Chloe about each of her kids and grandkids--where they lived and what they did.

Curiosity egged Chloe on to ask why all of Marg's kids were white, and obviously adopted, but she restrained. "What a great family," she said. "Have you been with Anjou for a long time?'

"Since the doors opened thirty some years ago," said Marg, resting her hands on her giant mound of a stomach. "I'm the Kitchen Manager. I come up with the recipes for Namby. Always have." Marg glanced at the wall clock. "I need to get the ladies cookin' some butter creams. My office is back there, Child. You stop by any time, all right?"

"Thanks," said Chloe. She stood and watched Marg slumber out the door across the hallway into the kitchen.

Several hair-netted women smiled and greeted Marg before she went into a separate glassed office to the right of the manufacturing floor.

"Ready, Chloe?" Candice said, sticking her head through the office door. "So, I see your uncle got you here on time for your first day," she said, smiling. "I punched you in already. We'll go over that once we get you a locker, and a uniform, and your employee picture."

Chloe followed Candice down the hallway, past an area marked "Mail Order," to a set of gray lockers.

"A10 will be yours," said Candice. She opened the locker door and a pink plastic bag, marked with H & H in gold letters, fell out. "Oh, shoot. It was supposed to be empty by now. The girl whose spot you took will be in today for her paycheck. I'll make sure she cleans it out then." Candice gently slammed the metal door shut. "You can put your coat in mine today."

After a short tour, Candice fitted Chloe with an Anjou signature pear apron and a black beret. "You look great. You're ready for the floor!" She led Chloe to the Shoppe and said, "Pick your favorite chocolate from the case, and hold it up so I can take your picture for the employee wall."

When was the last time I had my picture taken? Wasn't it the photo shoot? Chloe gingerly opened the case and reached for . . .

"Oh, I forgot to tell you . . . you have to put a white glove on before you touch the chocolates." She pointed to a small circular container full of gloves. "There are three sizes. Let me see your hands."

Let me guess. I need a large.

Candice pulled a glove out with yellow stitches around the opening. "I'm not sure this will fit with your ring, but let's try it."

The glove fit snugly. Chloe's ring finger looked like it had a huge growth on it underneath.

She reached into the case and pulled out a rose caramel, holding it up for Candice's camera.

"Say, Cheese."

A pang of grief went through her as she thought of Mom. *Chloe, say Jesus Loves Me.*

Chloe waited for the flash of Candice's camera. Which *déjà vu* color would she see a glimpse of? She feigned a smile, and waited for dust, veranda, or peekadilly to briefly appear. *Would* they appear? Or were they too busy being outlines and covering hearts?

Candice's camera clicked. She checked the image.

Nothing? No more *déjà vu* colors when a camera flashes? Get out! After fifteen years? Too entirely weird.

"Looks great. You're really photogenic," said Candice, stuffing the camera under the register and greeting a customer who just walked in. Candice listened to the customer's order, nodding, and punching a few of the hundred buttons on the register. "We'll be right back with your order, Sir," she said, handing the gentleman some change and closing the register. Walking through an open door, she motioned for Chloe to follow.

"This is our prep kitchen, where we make all of our desserts and coffee drinks." She grabbed a grande to-go cup and set it next to the cappuccino machine that looked like a robot.

Candice did everything like a DVD being fast-forwarded. "For cappuccinos, use this pitcher. For expresso, use a cold pitcher from the fridge. An 8-ounce gets one shot of espresso, so use the attachment with one spout and put one scoop of coffee beans in the grinder. For . . . ."

Chloe's head was spinning.

"And then top it off with whipped cream and a chocolate-covered coffee bean," said Candice, walking the drink out to the register. "Here you are, Sir. Have a great day."

Chloe's nerves felt caffeinated. She looked around the prep kitchen for a towel to wipe the counter.

Candice wistfully walked back to the kitchen. "Any questions?" She pointed at a large laminated poster above a large dish sink that had a picture and instructions for each item. "You can always check the Instruction Guide, if you need to."

Chloe felt like a baby barista. *All those years of going to CoffeeCups with Mom. Why didn't I pay attention?* "Oh, I'm sure I'll get the hang of it."

The Shoppe had gotten busy, so Candice said, "Best way to learn," as she pointed at the register and then to Chloe. "I'll take the other register," she said, walking to the other end of the counter.

Chloe looked down at the intimidating register. *Please order chocolates. Please don't order a coffee drink*, she internally pleaded with the customer in front of her.

Chloe looked beyond the woman's dust outline to see her sighing heavily and tapping her long nails on the counter.

Nervously, Chloe choked out the words, "May I help you?" *Please order chocolates. Order chocolates. Please, order chocolates.*

"I'll have a two-scoop sundae with caramel and peanut butter and pecans. And that's all." She pulled a twenty out of her wallet.

Chloe took her money. So far, so good. She hurried to the prep kitchen and stared at the sundae on the instruction poster. Where are the chocolate cups? She fiddled around until she found them, and plunked one on a square plate. Okay, now scoop. Where's the ice cream scoop? She opened the cooler and found one stuck in a huge barrel of ice cream. She plunged it into the vanilla and formed a mound the size of a baseball. So far, so good. Next, she squeezed hot caramel out of a clear bottle to look like a starburst and pressed four large blobs of peanut butter from a pastry bag. A sprinkle of pecans. *Voila!*

Candice was back in the kitchen, making another coffee drink. She looked at Chloe's sundae and scrunched her nose. "Here, let's try that again."

Chloe's face blushed. She looked down at her caramel creation. It looked like someone with an allergy to pecans had thrown up.

"Here, I got it. Stick this in the walk-in cooler. You can eat it when you're off work," said Candice. Candice finished her coffee drink and Chloe's sundae order in the twenty seconds that Chloe was gone.

After ten coffee drink attempts and two gift card redemption disasters, Chloe was relieved when Candice said to punch out.

"And don't forget your sundae in the walk-in," Candice said, smiling.

A sundae is a good way to drown your sorrows at 10 in the morning. Chloe pulled up a chair in the break room, facing the kitchen where the hairnets were busy cooking chocolate creations. She slurped a spoonful of melted ice cream and started to choke on a pecan that had purposely disguised itself as a glob of caramel. She coughed profusely, reaching for a napkin and catching the pecan before it went projectile.

Then . . . in Marg's office, she saw . . . Miss Sparkly Gold. Of course. *My day wouldn't be complete unless I saw her.* Chloe wiped her mouth and cleared her throat . . . and stared.

Sparkly gold is so beautiful! I wonder if sparkly gold outlines always have a peekadilly heart for a pal? And what could Marg's *black* outline mean?

Miss Sparkly Gold buttoned her coat as she talked to Marg. Her eyes looked red and puffy. She and Marg hugged for several minutes; Marg's bright white *déjà vu* heart kissing the girl's peekadilly heart. The girl blew her nose and stuffed the tissue in her pocket. She picked up a pair of black shoes and dangled a small purse and pink plastic bag on her elbow. As she exited Marg's office, she caught a glimpse of Chloe as she walked past the break room and stared back at her, like she was trying to place her.

Chloe sunk down in her chair.

℞

Chapter 8

God doesn't create redeemed caterpillars, He makes butterflies (author unknown)

If you don't *have* a mother, and you're worried you can't ever *be* a mother, Mother's Day is really hard. Yet, from the time she arrived in Indiana, Chloe planned on celebrating Mother's Day with Mom. The last time she'd visited the Hudson Family Cemetery was when she was a kid and Mom took her out to "meet her grandparents." Chloe remembered carrying a bouquet of flowers and holding Mom's hand. Mom told her which stone to place the flowers by, and then Mom prayed.

Back then, the whole thing seemed weird and boring. Now it seemed surreal.

Chloe slowed to a jog as she approached the freshly planted field. She walked along the perimeter of a small irrigation ditch, looking for the small wooden-stick cross marking a dirt path that disappeared through thick woods.

She breathed in the fresh cool air and exhaled a prolonged breath to completely empty her lungs. Was she ready for this?

Huge trees, sprouting with green, lay on both sides of the path, forming a tunnel, and green shoots poked through dead leaves on the floor of the landscape. A few birds chirped and darted through the bare branches above, as if they were playing tag.

Chloe's running shoes squished in the soft mud of the path, as she walked slowly toward the light of the clearing ahead. The spring sun streamed in diagonal lines over the cemetery as golden threads leading to heaven. Hundreds of tiny crocuses bloomed in yellows and purples along the base of a small black iron fence that looked new. The cemetery looked perfectly manicured, as if Gary had just tended it.

A warm sensation went through Chloe. *Gary knew I was coming today. He's been really good to me.*

Chloe looked over what she guessed to be five or six generations of Hudsons. Many of the stones were flat and most of them looked really old, except one. In one of the back corners, a large pink granite gravestone glistened in the sun.

A feeling bubbled inside of her that she couldn't identify. Grief? Sadness? No. Mom's having the time of her life! Chloe walked slowly toward the stone and stared.

An intricate pattern of tiny butterflies, swirls, and hearts outlined the words on the front and spilled over the sides and back of the stone. The front read:

Lisa Marie Hudson
Created . . . Saved . . . Loved . . . Forgiven
Joyfully Wed to Christ

Loving mother to Chloe Rahab

2 Corinthians 5:17 "Therefore, if anyone is in Christ, he is a new creation; the old has gone, the new has come!"

Emotion went through every thread of her body. Joy? So not there yet. Bubbling from deep within, her tears started to swell, stinging her wounded heart as they rose to the surface. *I miss you, Mom.* Chloe's tears exploded like a fiercely burning phoenix flame. Her long, guttural cry, cleansed her grief and brought a release that surprised her. When the tears couldn't come anymore, she knelt and began to trace each letter on the gravestone.

Her diamond ring caught rays of sunshine as she traced.

Chloe sat on a dry patch of grass and talked to her Mom for hours. First, she told her about how beautiful the wedding was, and about the move, and Indiana, and her new friend, May. And about her romantic new job at Anjou and how she hoped to improve at making coffee drinks.

Then she gave Mom a *déjà vu* update. "I don't think dust means what you thought it did, because I've seen it on several men. I mean, I know men probably suffer from the emotional pain of abortion, too, because what if he wants to keep the baby and his girlfriend or wife says, 'I don't care what you think, it's *my* body.' That would be so emotionally painful! Or, if memories haunted him about driving his girlfriend to the clinic, or paying for it, *that* would be painful, too. I don't know yet what dust means for sure, but I just kind of think it means something else." *If only Mom could tell me from heaven!*

"And Mom, I've seen some new outlines too." And Chloe told her all about sparkly gold and black. "Sparkly gold is so beautiful! Is that what the streets up there look like? Have you met my brother or sister? Are you having fun with your One and Only?"

CHLOE, I WANT TO BE YOUR ONE AND ONLY, TOO. I LOVE YOU.

And just then a bright red cardinal landed on Mom's gravestone, looking like a red apostrophe on a contraction.

Thank you, God. I love you, too.

When the sun began to set, Chloe's stomach grumbled. She kissed her mom's grave, stood and walked toward the gate of the iron fence.

A new sense of strength welled up inside her as she glanced back before trotting out of the clearing. Once she came to the end of the woods, where the bare cornfield was in sight, she broke into a full run.

Oh, Lord, you have searched me and you know me. You know when I sit and when I rise . . . went through her head as she remembered running on the beach with Mom. *If I rise on the wings of the dawn . . .* Chloe felt a gentle breeze behind her, pushing her wings as she flew home.

* * *

Chloe stood by the Anjou time clock, waiting for 7:01 a.m. exactly, so she could punch in. Mr. Namby had given her a small laminated sheet with the heading "child-labor-law-specifications for a 15-year-old," which outlined what time she could punch in or out, and how many hours she could work on a given day. She was to keep it in her Anjou apron at all times and follow it precisely. She plucked a smushed raspberry cream from the dud box and popped it in her mouth as she studied her notecard on how to make coffee drinks. Today, she would leave the ranks of the cappuccino-challenged and press on, running the race for a gold medal in the Espresso Olympics!

Nervousness brewed inside of her.

Candice stuck her head in the desk area, just as Chloe punched her time card. "Oh, good. I didn't see you come in. Ready?" She led Chloe out to the counter behind the case, showing her a huge case of tiny gold boxes. "You'll be working on these today. We need 1000 four-piece boxes." Candice held out a laminated diagram showing the arrangement of each of the chocolates. "I need them finished by the time you leave at ten."

Packing chocolates? Easy compared to coffee drinks. Chloe looked at the diagram. *Same as Mom's wedding.* She fanned several hundred boxes out on the packing island and removed the gold lids, throwing them temporarily back into the empty case. She pulled out a case of dark Anjou pears and started plunking one in the corner of each box, working in mindless motion, allowing her mind to drift.

The large Shoppe doors flung open and a woman, noticeably pregnant, outlined in sparkly gold came in with a pre-schooler in tow.

Sparkly gold means the woman is pregnant? Chloe studied the woman's small frame dotted with a perfect basketball-sized stomach. *No* déjà *vu heart, just the beautiful gift of sparkly gold!*

Chloe thought about the girl who used to work here, the one whose locker was now hers. *Does she know she's pregnant? Is that why she quit?*

The woman's preschool daughter pressed her face against the glass case, fascinated by the rows of tiny chocolate masterpieces. "Look, Mommy. They're pretty." She skipped down to the opposite end of the case, her ponytails bouncing behind her. The mom perused the case, asking Candice a few questions about prices and bestsellers.

Minutes later, as the mom and daughter walked out of the Shoppe, a stout guy who looked to be in his early twenties came in, followed by a spurt of customers.

"Hi, Jason," said Candice. "We need you right away. Chloe's on project today."

May's Jason?

Jason placed his stuff on the countertop and manned the open register. "Can I help who's next?" he said.

Jason looked like an Italian wrestler. His jet black hair matched his bushy unibrow and his hairy arms. His body was thick around the waist, perhaps evidence of frequent visits to the dud box. Across his chest, was a large, bright peekadilly heart.

Jason was nothing like Chloe had envisioned him, based on May's descriptions. Super Cute? Not. Maybe he had a sparkling personality? Didn't she say he was super funny and sweet?

Chloe nonchalantly continued to pack the boxes in front of her as she watched Jason interact with customers.

One customer, a girl who also had a peekadilly heart, seemed to be magnetized to Jason's register.

Chloe couldn't help eavesdropping.

"You're looking good," Jason said to the girl. His eyes scanned her body and landed where her butterfly tattoos played peek-a-boo from her bust area. "Haven't seen you since graduation. Where you working?"

"Right over there," she said flirtatiously, gesturing out the window across the street. Her lip ring moved with her smile.

"I'm a supervisor here now," Jason said proudly.

"Are you going out with anyone?" said Tattoo, fluttering her mascara-caked eyelashes.

"Not really," said Jason.

What about May? Chloe accidentally dropped the gold box that she was closing with an elastic bow.

"We should get together sometime," said Tattoo, turning her head behind her as she neared the exit. "I'm over at Speedy Mart, if you need some gas."

Jason's eyes followed her undersized jeans out the door and smiled. He turned to Chloe and said, "You must be the new girl."

"Yes. I'm Chloe. I'm a friend of May Hicks."

Jason coughed and then paused, extending his hand. "Good to meet you, Chloe. I've heard a lot about you."

"Chloe, hurry up and punch out," yelled Candice from the other side of the Shoppe.

Chloe swallowed hard as she looked at about a hundred boxes still needing to be filled.

"I'll finish those for you, Chloe," said Jason sweetly.

Chloe whipped through the door, rifled through the time cards, and punched the clock. She looked up at the bulletin board and noticed a Nambygram addressed to her. Opening it, she read, "Chloe, To accommodate a last-minute scheduling change, your Shoppe hours this coming Thursday will be 3:59 - 6:59 p.m. You'll be shadowing May Hicks. Anjouly Yours, Henry Namby."

Cool.

* * *

On Thursday at 3:30, Chloe and May primped in front of the mirror, fixing their berets.

"Whoo hoo!" said May. "Last day of school! Sweetness."

Fifty-five degrees at the end of May? Chloe was just about out of patience with the weird Indiana climate.

May tied her apron tightly around her waist, forming a fat bulge above it. She squeezed it, like she was measuring it, then loosened the apron. She looked at Chloe, "Ready, student?" she laughed. "Where's the apple for your teacher?"

Chloe smiled, holding out her hand flat, extending it to May. "Make a wish," she whispered, "and take a bite."

"You kind of look like the witch in Snow White," May said, teasing her.

May and Chloe punched their time cards, and headed for the Shoppe, where Candice was finishing an order.

Candice looked at Chloe. "Oh, Hi, Chloe. Did your uncle drop you off? I didn't see him," she said. "Do you need a ride home later? I can take you. I'll just run some errands and stop back."

"She gets off the same time as me," said May, with a touch of sarcasm, like she'd been slighted. "Hi, Candice. Remember me? The one you haven't seen for a while who doesn't have an uncle that you're hot for?"

Candice's face turned red. "Hi, May. Nice to see you, too," she said, heading for the time clock desk. "Have fun training Chloe. Bye, girls."

Have fun training Chloe? Did she mean something by that?

The Shoppe was empty for the moment.

May started organizing the catalogs and chocolate cigars by the cash register. "Hey, once some customers come in, I'll take the order, and you go and make it? K?"

"Yes, Ma'am," said Chloe, saluting May and laughing.

Chloe grabbed a bottle of glass cleaner and a towel from a shelf under the register. She walked out to the front of the case and started squirting.

A gust of cold air ushered in a group of teens.

Chloe quickly wiped the glass case clean and hurried to May's side by the register.

A group of teen girls stood in front of them, looking at the paper menu. One of the girls had a dust outline and both had peekadilly hearts.

May's elbow brought Chloe back from déjà-vu-la-la land. "Are you going to get that?"

"Sure," Chloe said, heading for the prep kitchen.

"No nuts," yelled May. "I accidentally rang it with nuts, but she doesn't want any."

Chloe went back to the kitchen, and pulled the order ticket from a small black machine. A sundae on her first order! Good sign. Sundaes were becoming her forte. She even got a compliment on one yesterday, with the sweet old gentleman leaving her a $2 tip. Scooping a hunk of vanilla ice cream into the cup, she swiftly drizzled caramel and dark chocolate over the entire plate, creating a beautiful lace-like presentation. She quickly sprinkled a handful of almonds on top and delivered it promptly to the girl at table 21.

"Ew." The girl scrunched her nose and pulled her head back. "I ordered it without nuts. I'm allergic." The other girls sighed their discontent.

"Oh, I'm sorry. I'll get you a different one. Be right back," said Chloe, scooping up the plate and heading back to the kitchen.

The foyer door opened again, ushering in two more teens, each with a bright white *déjà vu* heart. The girl was pretty with long blonde hair. The guy was tall, about 6'3", the height Chloe had determined was perfect for Mr. Right. He wore a deep purple letter jacket that looked like it might be hiding a solid build. His smile filled his face, showing off his Crest-white teeth. The girl with him was laughing at something he said.

Chloe's heart fluttered. She wanted to put her reject sundae down and get a better look at his bright white heart. It had a clear white, brilliant center bursting with sunbeams that protruded beyond his body's frame.

At the register, May gave Chloe a hurry-up-already look.

Chloe brushed by her. "I'll be right back." She put the first sundae in the slop sink and quickly created another ice cream masterpiece, minus allergens. She hustled the new sundae to table 21, feeling like Letter Jacket Boy's eyes were following the delivery. She plunked the sundae in front of the girl. "Here you are. Sorry about that."

"Could I have a refill on my water?" asked the almond hater.

"Sure," Chloe said, sighing.

As she passed the register on her way back to the kitchen, Letter Jacket Boy flashed a smile her way.

May followed her into the prep kitchen. "Chloe! What's taking you so long?" she said, in a breathy tone. She tore a white order ticket from the machine and handed it to Chloe, exchanging it for the water pitcher in Chloe's hand. "Here. Make this. Where's the water go?"

"Table 21," said Chloe, glancing at the ticket. *Please let this be a sundae.* She read the ticket. No such luck. "One petite café latte and one grande café mocha to go," she read under her breath. Crap. Chloe rifled through her pear apron, looking for her coffee cheat sheet. She landed on the ESPRESSO card and stayed. How many espresso shots in a grande mocha? And what kind of chocolate again? She fumbled through the steps for a few minutes, finally pouring a mixture into a styrofoam cup and topping it with whipped cream. When she applied the to-go lid, the hot liquid overflowed, splattering down the side.

May drew it quickly from Chloe's hands, wiping it with a wet towel. "Here's the latte. Take it out a sec. It goes to the cute guy in the purple and his girlfriend."

Chloe cringed at the thought that Letter Jacket Boy might drink the grande disaster she just prepared. She appeared in front of the register and applied a smile. "Here you are. Sorry for the wait." Looking at the girl, she handed her the large cup of goo.

"Oh, that one's mine," he said, extending his hand to Chloe. "Thanks." He reached for the other cup, too, handing it to the girl. "Here you go," he said sweetly.

All of her cuteness smiled back at him. She took a sip, and smiled at Chloe, then turned and walked toward the Shoppe door.

May stuck her head out of the kitchen and yelled, "Chloe, are you okay?"

Letter Jacket Boy cupped both of his hands around his drink and looked at Chloe. “Thank you, Chloe,” he said, with a smile, then turned and left.

On the back of his letter jacket the word “Smith” was embroidered.

Too bad he has a girlfriend.

* * *

Evan Smith

“Lord, I can’t stop thinking about her.”

Evan Smith didn’t believe in love-at-first-sight. Not that he’d thought about it--until yesterday. Throughout his high school years, he’d asked a few girls out, but nobody twice. He’d invite them to family functions or to stuff at church, and he went to prom as a junior. He tried not to be critical, but each girl had the same problem: They said exactly what he wanted to hear, which is *not* what he wanted to hear. Or, they talked about things that measured “zero” on his interesting scale.

Aren’t there any girls who talk about their walk with Christ, or a book with substance, or politics, or . . . anything besides what was on the latest edition of “Hollywood Half Hour?” *I wonder what she would talk about.*

“You know her, God. Did I see You shining through her?” he prayed, as he walked back to the house, craving a mocha.

℞

Chapter 9

Feminine Care OB/GYN was in a medical building adjoining the new Dodge Regional Hospital. Chloe's appointment was at 9 a.m. At 8:45, Gary steered his pick-up around the circular drive and parked in an open spot.

A mixture of anger, nerves and nausea swirled inside of Chloe. *God, why did you have to take my mom? I need my mom today.* Chloe looked down at the diamond ring on her finger, and cupped it with her left hand. *I love you, Mom.*

I LOVE YOU, CHLOE. I'VE ADOPTED YOU. YOU ARE MY CHILD.

Gary seemed nervous, too. He'd smoked two cigarettes on the way and talked nonstop.

"Do you really *have* to come in with me?"said Chloe.

"Yes. They need my insurance stuff," said Gary. "I'll just hang out in the waiting room."

Chloe followed Gary through a revolving door, missing her cue to exit into the lobby. *Walking in a perpetual circle . . .* She continued around once more, and jumped off the rotation, like she was getting off of a spinning merry-go-round.

Inside the lobby, several office suites formed a border in the shape of a square. In the center of the lobby was a koi pond that was close to an elevator. Feminine Care was the first suite on the right.

Chloe tried to calm herself. Was every girl nervous before her first female exam?

A door on the opposite side flung open, and out walked---

"Hello, Hudson. What brings you here?" said a voice in a Dutch accent.

Crap. Like I really want to see someone I know right now.

"De Veen. Good morning," said Gary. "How's the latest addition look in your trophy room?"

"Superb." Dr. D turned to Chloe. "Good morning, Miss Hudson."

Chloe's heart palpitated. Dr. D's voice struck fear within her. Was it his height? No. She liked to see people who were taller than her. She stared at his designer glasses. No. Was it his Dutch accent? *No, I like accents. It's just him.*

"Great to see you again," said Dr. Creepy D. "Haf you met Ty yet?"

Chloe looked like she'd swallowed a bottle of anxiety. Her pale face stared at him. After a long pause, she quietly said, "No, not yet."

"She's got an appointment at your place this morning," said Gary, nervously. "She's got some female issues."

Oh, Gary, Shut up! And wait. Feminine Care OB/GYN is Dr. D's place? *No way. I am not, I repeat, NOT, seeing Dr. D!*

Gary continued to babble. "Her appointment is with Dr. Secus."

"Oh, she's superb," said Dr. D. He touched Chloe's shoulder. "You'll really like her."

Chloe's shoulder felt like it had been taser-gunned with a shot of panic of-the-creepy-kind. Instinctively, she jerked away and paused. She turned to Gary. "I'll meet you in there."

Gary stayed to chat a few minutes.

Feminine Care's waiting room was full and colorful.

Chloe checked in with the receptionist. "My uncle will be right in with the insurance stuff," she said.

"Oh, it's no hurry, Honey. Dr. Secus is doing a delivery, so she's running about an hour behind. Just have a seat," said the receptionist.

Chloe turned around, ingesting a big-picture view of the waiting room, mesmerized. *I wish I'd brought my déjà vu journal.*

The waiting room looked like a Monet painting done in muted colors of dust and peekadilly, with accents of bright white, sparkly gold, and black.

She'd hit the sleuth's mother-load of *déjà vu* clues! Chloe looked for a pen and something to write on in her purse. She pulled out a tissue and flattened it on her thigh, gazing around her and jotting notes.

A middle-aged woman without a *déjà vu* heart watched her and gave her a weird look.

Oops. Some nonchalance might be good. Chloe picked up a magazine off the end table by her chair and stuck her tissue in it. She leafed through it, pretending to read it, then stared at the cover.

A naked baby lying on his tummy smiled back at her. *What if I can't have kids?* Not that having a period sounded like much fun, especially the way May talked about it.

Gary talked to the receptionist and sat next to Chloe. "How's it going?" he said.

Fine, except for my over-talkative-at-the-moment uncle. "Just fine. But, I want to read my magazine, okay?" she said, trying to mask her perturb-sion.

"Sure," Gary said, looking sorry.

Now, back to déjà vu sleuthing.

Chloe stared at a couple who looked to be in their late twenties and married, based on their wedding rings that sparkled while they held hands. Neither had a *déjà vu* heart--neither peekadilly or bright white. The woman looked stylish, and pregnant. *Very* pregnant and very much outlined with sparkly gold. But just her, not her husband. *Aha! So if a guy whose wife is pregnant doesn't have a sparkly gold outline, then a guy suffering from the emotional effects of an abortion, probably wouldn't have a dust outline! So dust must mean something else.*

The man showed his wife something from the magazine he was reading, and they laughed softly.

Chloe's heart felt warm. *They look like they're in love. That's what I want with Mr. Right someday.* Her mind flashed to Letter Jacket Boy from Anjou, but she stopped herself. *He has a girlfriend.*

As Chloe admired the couple, a mother-type and a sparkly gold teen girl with a peekadilly heart sat next to them. The teen girl seemed pleasant and asked the couple when they were due.

Wait. Chloe felt a miniature *déjà vu* epiphany coming on. *Married lady with sparkly gold has no déjà vu heart. Teen with sparkly gold has a peekadilly heart.* She quickly jotted a note on her tissue.

The intercom throughout the waiting room beeped and the receptionist's voice came on. "Patients of Dr. Secus. She is back in the building and will be starting her appointments shortly."

No, not yet! I'm still sleuthing. Chloe scanned the waiting room some more.

A teen girl with pink hair and a saturated dust outline sat alone. Not surprisingly, her dust outline had a peekadilly heart pal. She leafed through a women's magazine and checked her watch. She scanned the waiting room, seeming to notice that the seat next to her was the only one still empty.

A highly professional and attractive woman, who appeared to be in her early forties, turned from the receptionist station and eyed the seat. She wore a navy power suit with a starched white blouse, accented with a silk scarf. Her black hair was neatly pulled back and up into a professional braid. Her expensive purse matched her leather high heels. Her only jewelry was a pair of diamond stud earrings and a diamond tennis bracelet that subtly enhanced her French manicure. She gracefully walked to the empty seat and smiled at the girl with pink hair. "Hi," she whispered, as she sat down.

Chloe was impressed. This woman kind of reminded her of Mom when she'd interacted with customers and her highly-professional demeanor came out.

She caught Chloe staring at her and smiled. Then, her eyes appeared to glue on a mom with a toddler and a newborn in a stroller.

With one hand, the mom held open a picture book in front of the toddler, reading to her. With her other hand, she gently pushed the stroller back and forth.

The professional woman stared at the three intently. She looked as if she was straining to hear the picture book's cliff hanger ending. With each minute of staring, her demeanor hiccuped between sadness and longing.

Chloe watched as the woman's face turned blush, and she quietly bubbled.

She reached into her purse and pulled out a tissue. She dabbed the tissue to one of her eyes, and then blew her nose. As the girl next to her stood up and left, the woman put her purse in the chair and grabbed a magazine, not looking up again.

About twenty minutes later, a voice bellowed out of the intercom. "Chloe Hudson, Room 6."

"You need me to come with you?" asked Gary, looking compassionate.

Puhleese. Like I really want my uncle holding my hand while I'm in the stirrups! Chloe almost snapped back, then stopped herself. Gary was trying. Today probably wasn't easy for him either. "No, thanks," she said.

Chloe picked up her purse and walked down a hallway, painted pink on one side, and light blue on the other. She passed a large bulletin board covered with pictures of naked babies and families with kids of all ages. She continued walking past the nurses' station.

Room 3, Room 4, Room . . . .

As Chloe approached, the girl with pink hair burst out of Room 5 and stood, momentarily paralyzed, as if she was still registering news. Her dust outline clung to her body, like chalk on a victim at a crime scene. Her peekadilly heart now swirled with the color of dust, too.

The girl's face was red and puffy, and tears were streaming down her face. Wiping her nose with her bare arm, she muttered a profanity under her breath. She gave Chloe a dirty look, like she was mad at the world.

Chloe turned around to catch one more look, feeling the girl's eyes sear through her back. She opened the door marked Room 6 and entered.

The room looked hygienic and institutional, much like the pediatrician's office that she went to for check-ups as a kid. A patient's table sat on the diagonal, pointing toward the center of the room. On the wall next to the schedule was a picture poster about birth control pills. Two chairs lined the wall.

If only my mom could be sitting in one of those chairs. Chloe stepped up onto the examining table, hearing the paper crinkle under her jeans. She glanced above her at a poster of a cat hanging by its claws that said, "Hang in there."

The door flung open, making Chloe jump.

"Good Morning, Miss Hudson. I'm Dr. Secus. Sorry for the delay this morning." She sat down in one of the chairs and glanced at Chloe's chart.

Dr. Secus had short black hair with bangs that matched her horn-rimmed glasses. Her white overcoat contrasted with her peekadilly heart.

Chloe looked at Dr. Secus' hand. No ring. "Are you married?" she blurted out.

Dr. Secus pressed her eyebrows together and looked annoyed. "I don't see where that's your concern, but no." She tapped her pencil a few times on her clipboard, then put it behind her ear. "I see you're here for a consultation. What can I help you with?"

"Well, I haven't had my period," said Chloe. "I'm getting a little worried."

"You're turning 16 in July?" said Dr. Secus. "Are you active?"

Running. Working. Painting. "Yes, I'm very active."

"Do you use protection?"

Protection? *Mom always told me to carry pepper spray when I went running on the beach or in the neighborhood, but I've completely forgotten lately!* But that was California. This is Indiana.Was pepper spray really necessary in Gary's neighborhood? Does a rural route even qualify as a neighborhood?

"Ahem," said Dr. Secus. "Do you use protection?"

Chloe, you have to do more than just treasure your purity. You have to fight to protect it. Mom's words ran through Chloe's mind as she looked at the diamond ring on her finger, and suddenly craved a chocolate soldier. *The fighting Psalms Mom gave me! Where did I even put them?*

"Miss Hudson?" said Dr. Secus. "I need you to tell me the truth, so I can give you accurate medical information."

"No, I don't really use protection," Chloe stammered.

Dr. Secus shot Chloe a look from behind her glasses. She crossed her arms. "Young lady, practicing safer sex is extremely important," she said, emphasizing the word *safer*. "Even this morning, I diagnosed another patient about your age with an STD."

"The girl with pink hair who was crying?" asked Chloe.

"Yes, I mean, uh, I'm not allowed to discuss other patients with you," said Dr. Secus.

Dust means STD?!? Whoa.

"If only she had used protection," continued Dr. Secus, "she could have cut her chances of infection quite substantially."

"Safer sex is protection?" Chloe stammered.

"Yes, in some cases, you can reduce your risk by 50%. Think about how significant that is, Chloe," said Dr. Secus, looking at her intently.

I'm no gambler, but those odds don't seem that good! "What is safer sex," she paused, "safer than?"

"Than not using protection," said Dr. Secus, with a touch of sarcasm. "Do you want to end up with cancer?"

Cancer? Chloe's demeanor rapidly divided and mutated. A shot of grief went through her veins. The C word was one that she couldn't even bring herself to say yet. Would she ever? When something steals the life of the most precious person in the world to you, it's *more* than a disease. It's a Killer. A Thief. A Destroyer. *Did an STD cause Mom's cancer?*

"Some STD's cause cancer," said Dr. Secus.

"That people can *die* from?" Chloe stammered.

"Yes. It can happen to a woman later in life."

"Like when they're in their early thirties?"

"Could be."

Chloe's mind raced with bits and pieces of Mom's letter. *Sex with lots of boys . . . An abortion at 15 . . .*

"Does having an abortion ever cause cancer?"[3] asked Chloe.

Dr. Secus stood, held her clipboard under one arm, and put her hand on her hip. She shot Chloe a dirty look and paused. "I've *never* seen *any* studies whatsoever that link abortion to breast cancer. Let's not change the subject, Chloe," she said. "Some STD's can render a girl sterile."

Sterile? Chloe's eyes went to the counter where a jar was labeled "sterile bandages." *Isn't sterile good?* Chloe fidgeted. "St--Sterile?" she stuttered.

"Yes. Some STD's can take away a girl's ability to conceive or carry a child," said Dr. Secus.

Was Mom sterile? Maybe she couldn't have any more kids after me, even if she wanted to.

A sudden panic overcame Chloe. "Are STD's hereditary?" she asked.

"No. But it is possible for a baby to get the mother's STD during delivery. We usually do a C-section in those cases." Dr. Secus stood and pulled open a drawer under the counter. She took out some little square packets and held them in the air to show Chloe.

" . . . and so, Miss Hudson, we'll need to do a pregnancy test on you today, and test you for STD's. Then, we can look at some birth control options, and I can give you some free samples to protect yourself and the men you are putting at risk." She put the packets next to Chloe's purse on the chair. "Here," she said, handing Chloe a white cape. "Put this on. It opens to the front."

Chloe's face went bright red with embarrassment, realizing the levity of her DUH moment. *How can I be so clueless?* "Dr. Secus, I'm really sorry, but I think I just now caught what you meant by *active*. Did you mean *sexually* active?"

"Of course I did," said Dr. Secus, looking empathetic. "Chloe, it's okay. You shouldn't deny yourself. Sex is an *appetite* that should be discovered and explored from womb to tomb. You're entitled. You just need to be safe, well *safer*, about it."

Chloe was weirded out by Dr. Secus' emphasis of the word *appetite*. "No, really, I misunderstood.

I'm not sexually active. I've never done anything." Chloe held out her hand, so Dr. Secus could see her diamond. "It's a purity ring. I promised my mom."

Dr. Secus looked first at Chloe's fingers, and then at the ring. "Those don't work," she said sarcastically. "But, that certainly is a rock." She looked at Chloe's hand again. "Your hands look a little swollen. Chloe, are you *sure* there's no chance you're pregnant?"

Chloe sighed. "Yes. I haven't had my period yet. That's why I'm here."

"So you've *never* had a menstrual cycle? Menstrual cycle is the medical term for your period, Chloe," said Dr. Secus, as if she were talking to a kindergartner.

"No. The reason I came today was to see if there's something wrong with my body."

"Well, most girls do start younger, but that doesn't necessarily mean there's a problem. Are you eating healthy and not purging?" Dr. Secus perused Chloe's chart. "You do know what purging means, right? That means making yourself throw up."

"No--I mean, yes," said Chloe, trying to clarify. "I mean, I eat really healthy, and I don't *try* to throw up, but I guess I have puked a few times lately, when I'm really wigged out."

"Have you had any unusual stress lately?"

Like losing my mom? Like seeing weird outlines and hearts on people? Like becoming an orphan? "Yes. My mom died of cancer last year. That's why I moved here--to live with my uncle."

Dr. Secus paused, looking like she was in deep thought. "Unusual stress can cause a girl to be late. I think we should just watch you." She put some checkmarks on a thin yellow piece of paper and handed it to Chloe. "Let's see you back in six months." She opened the door and motioned down the hallway. "Scheduling will do your appointment."

Chloe walked out of the room toward the receptionist. She handed her the yellow paper, then glanced at the wall behind her, noticing an extensive selection of brochures. She pulled one out of each compartment in rapid-fire succession and stuffed them in her purse.

"Is Gary Hudson your father?" asked the receptionist. "I need to collect a co-pay for today's visit."

"Oh, that's my uncle," said Chloe. *Did Gary know about Mom's STD?* she thought, as she motioned to Gary in the waiting room.

℞

Chapter 10

Chloe punched the Anjou time clock and opened the Nambygram addressed to her. "Chloe, You are assigned to Prep Kitchen duty for the coming weeks. Please do a review of the coffee guide poster and ask for help, if needed. Anjouly Yours, Henry Namby."

Apparently four customers complained anonymously about their coffee drinks, and all fingers pointed toward Chloe. What about the artistic sundaes she made? Didn't they count for anything?

Chloe opened the door of the industrial dishwasher. Hot steam hit her face. She waited a few seconds until the hot plates were warm to the touch, then pulled them out and stacked them in a tower on the wire shelf. She wiped the dessert area with a towel and filled the pecan container to the brim.

The menu machine clicked and whirred, spitting out a small white ticket.

She leaned in, looking at the ticket: 2 cappuccinos w/ shot vanilla.

In the Shoppe out front, she heard Candice say, “Thank you. Those will be right out.” And then, “Hi. May I help you?”

Within twenty seconds, the order machine whirred again, spitting out an order for fudge cake.

A shot of nerves made Chloe’s heart race. *God, please help these drinks not to taste like crap*, she prayed. She double-checked the poster, completed the five-steps and topped the two cups with plastic lids. She rounded the corner and abruptly stopped for just a second.

Standing to the side of the register was Letter Jacket Boy, craning his neck in her direction. His bright white *déjà vu* heart shone brilliantly, highlighting the smile that filled his face. An attractive girl, about his same age, stood close to him, sending a text.

Smith! Why couldn’t he order a sundae, for heaven’s sakes?

Chloe’s eyes met his, and she felt her face instantly blush. She walked toward him, feeling his eyes glued to hers. “Here you are,” she said, steadying the cups and handing them both to him.

“Thanks,” he said, handing one to his date as she flipped her phone shut.

The girl took a quick sip and scrunched her face. Then she took another sip. “This is---”

Smith gently grabbed her arm. “Just fine,” he interrupted. Still smiling at Chloe, he nudged the girl toward the door. He turned to Chloe. “Thanks. Have a great day.”

Chloe stood in Smith-La-La Land, watching him leave. *What kind of car does he drive?* She peered through the front window.

Outside, Smith approached a mid-sized car that Chloe couldn’t label. He opened the passenger door for his date and shut it behind her. On his way to the driver's side, he took a sip of his coffee drink.

Is he going to make a face? Dump it out? *I hope he doesn't have tastebuds!*

"C-h-l-o-e, can you get the cake order?" said Candice from the register.

Chloe snapped to and bolted back to the prep kitchen.

Candice came back, pulled a ticket from the machine and picked a mug from the shelf, smiling. "Do you know him?" she asked. "He seems to come in a lot lately.

"Who's this?" bellowed Marg cheerfully, as she sauntered in. She plucked an empty mug from the shelf and plopped in a tea bag. "Somebody coming in for eye candy?" Marg teased.

"Are you on break, Marg?" said Candice, glancing at the clock.

"Sure am."

Candice took the plate of fudge cake from Chloe's hands. "Chloe, hurry! Go punch out right now, or Namby will have a fit about the child-labor stuff," Candice said, topping the cake with a dollop of whipped cream.

"Okay, sure," Chloe said, leaving quickly. She punched her time card and placed it back into the gray slot. She opened the dud box and pulled out a semi-crushed truffle, nibbling it.

Marg was sitting alone in the break room, stirring her tea. "Hello, Child," she said to Chloe, pulling a chair out, inviting her. "How'd it go out there today?"

Child. I love it when she calls me that.

Marg reminded Chloe of Mom, which was kind of weird, since Mom was thin and white, and Marg was large and black. "Okay, I guess," said Chloe, wanting to change the subject. "How are you?" she said, taking another nibble.

"Oh, Child--the Lord really blessed the Hope and Help Center yesterday." Marg's face was lit up with excitement. "The ladies and I have been prayin' for an ultrasound machine for each of our locations. Then, yesterday, out of the clear blue sky, we got a notice that somebody's estate left a big donation of $100,000--the *exact* amount we need to buy three machines. That's no coincidence." Marg took a hatless nutcracker from the dud plate and popped it into her mouth.

Ultrasound machines . . . babies. "What does the center do?" said Chloe.

"We help girls who get in trouble," said Marg.

Just like my mom used to do on Tuesday nights. "Like Miss Sparkly Gold?"

Marg used her finger to pick a nut out of her tooth and gave Chloe a weird look. "Who is Miss Sparkly Gold?"

I can't believe I just said that! "Um, nobody. Sorry," Chloe stammered. "So how do you help them?"

"We tell them how to fall in love," said Marg, closing her eyes for a moment.

I think they figured that out already.

"We give them hope . . . and help," said Marg. "And show them how to make a redemptive choice."

"What's that?"

"It's when you give your mess to Jesus and let Him redeem it."

Chloe looked confused.

"It's like a coupon. You surrender your situation to God by stopping *exactly* where you're at, and acknowledging you messed up and that you want a do-over. Then you let Him show you the next good choice to make and you trust Him. And then He starts fixin' and healin' and workin' things out for you."

The word *redeem* went through Chloe's head, as she looked at Marg's black outline. *Did God redeem Marg from something?*

"I just wish we could reach the girls before they get to us." She took off her hairnet and fluffed her tight silver curls. "They have the rest of their lives to be doin' it with their husbands." Marg elbowed Chloe. "Like Elmer and me." She smiled.

TMI! TMI!

"Child, you're not doin' that stuff, are you?"

Chloe's eyes popped. Do people come right out and ask you that sort of thing? Apparently mincing words was not Marg's specialty. Chloe hesitated, then put her hand on the table, showing Marg her ring. "No, I promised God."

"A-a-a-men, Child. I'm proud of you," said Marg. "That ring's a beautiful reminder." Marg looked at the clock, stood up and drank the rest of her tea in one gulp. "I need to get back to work."

10:45 a .m. Gary's probably waiting for me out front. Chloe hurried out of the break room, through the offices and to the Shoppe. She looked around. No Gary. She sat down at a small table next to the window and waited. *This is when Gary's lack of a cell phone is really annoying.*

* * *

Was a dead animal messing up my ride again? Gary was late one other time due to a taxidermy emergency. A suburbanite from Chicago, who had gotten lost on a rural route, hit a beaver masquerading as a jaywalking pedestrian. He called Gary and then waited while his roadkill got turned into a porch ornament. Poor Bucky.

Candice walked through the quiet Shoppe and stuck her head in the office door. "Henry, Jason's here now, so I'm going to Office Junction for more register tape." She headed for the door, noticing Chloe. "Do you need a ride? I could take you home," said Candice.

"Oh, my uncle's place is the opposite direction," said Chloe.

"It's really no problem," said Candice, yearning.

Chloe shrugged her shoulders. "Well, okay, thanks." She followed Candice out the door to her hot pink Jeep convertible parked on the side of the building.

"Hop in," said Candice, putting on a pair of large white sunglasses. Candice pulled a small tub of lip gloss from the dash and applied some pink shimmer, pursing her lips in the rearview mirror. She took off her black beret and fluffed her fiery red hair. With the top down, she sailed out of Anjou parking lot as though she knew exactly where we she was going.

The sunny June day was perfect for cruising the country in a convertible. Several wind-blown miles later, Candice turned into Gary's lane and drove up, passing a pick-up truck on its way out.

Gary's expression told the fact that he'd forgotten Chloe.

Candice parked the Jeep as Gary approached it. She smiled at him. "Special delivery."

Gary turned to both of them. "I'm sorry." He took off his baseball cap and wiped the sweat from his brow. "I got wrapped up in a project and lost track of time." He smiled at Candice. "Nice Jeep."

"Thanks," she said. "I took a Pink Jeep Excursion in Sedona, Arizona last summer and fell in love with pink Jeeps."

"Did you go to the Grand Canyon, too?" said Gary.

"Yes," Candice said, pushing her sunglasses to the top of her head and tucking a red lock of hair behind her ear. "It was awesome. Some friends and I hiked to the bottom of the canyon and spent the night. And we did whitewater rafting through the canyon." Candice shimmied out of the Jeep and brushed her black pants. "It was really beautiful."

Chloe watched the scenario with delight. Words like "hiked" and "whitewater rafting" were having a visible effect on Gary. Candice was reeling him in like a pro.

"Have you ever been to Yellowstone?" said Gary.

"Yes. I actually used to live near there," she said. "My brother and I would go on hunting trips to Canada sometimes. He bagged an elk once," she quickly added.

"Did he have it mounted?" Gary asked, visibly interested. "Chloe probably told you that I'm a taxidermist." He glanced in Chloe's direction.

Candice looked surprised. "No, I didn't know that." She smiled at Chloe. "But I guess that sort of thing doesn't come up in chocolate conversations."

"Would you like to see my taxidermy shed?" Gary asked.

Oh, Gary! Puhleese. What woman wouldn't find the suggestion a total turnoff?

Candice flipped open her cell phone and dialed Namby. "Henry, I've been delayed. I'll be back later this afternoon." She turned to Gary, smiling from ear to ear. "I'd love to."

* * *

CHLOE, HAVE YOU READ MY LOVE LETTER TO YOU LATELY?

When the air conditioner kicks on at 7 a.m., you know it's going to be hot in Hoosierland. On Saturday morning, Chloe sipped her iced green tea then nibbled a bite of her lemon-soy scone as she waited for her computer to boot up. She checked her cell phone, noticing a missed text from May. "HEY, LTRJKT IN 2NT. THINK HE WAS LOOKING 4 U, BUT DIFF. GIRL W/ HIM AGAIN. BTW, DID YOU GET THE BOOK I LEFT 4 U IN MAILBOX?"

Chloe texted her back. "GOT THE BOOK. DID HE PAY W/ CASH OR CRDT?" Why does the guy always pays with cash? *How am I supposed to conduct research with only a last name, and one that half of Americans have?*

Chloe signed into her Facebook account. "Jason Barillo wants to be your friend."

The words "slime" and "pig" came to her mind. *He wants to be friends with anyone with a uterus!* How can May be so blind? *Should I warn her that Jason has a bright peekadilly heart? Should I tell her about the gas-station-tattoo-girl who eats a lot of chocolate?*

She clicked "Ignore."

Where did I put that book? She leafed through her "To Do" tray and pulled it, looking at the front cover. Pure black with the title, *The Bed Beckons*, in red block letters. No author listed. She flipped the book over to read, "What people are saying about it," but nobody had said a word.

Last week, Jason gave May the book as a "just because" gift, which May thought was so sweet.

"Chloe, you *have* to read this book," she said. "It's about a photographer wallflower who gets swept off her feet by a world video game champion. It's *so* romantic."

Chloe set the book back down and clasped her computer mouse. She focused the cursor on the white search box and typed in Smith. Maybe today she'd be luckier than the other times she'd tried to find Letter Jacket Boy.

Nope. Futility again. There were at least a bajillion Smiths. And you can't google "Letter Jacket Boy!" *Or can you?* Chloe did a 60-mile radius search of northeastern Indiana high schools, then narrowed her search for those with the school colors of purple and yellow. Aha! Cedarville High School. She looked both ways and quietly entered the high school's website, unannounced.

What sport did he play? Were those wings on his jacket? A soccer ball? Do they give letter jackets for academics? Maybe he's a bright white braniac! She clicked on football. Nothing.

Baseball? Nada.

Basketball? . . . Bingo!

A warm feeling came over her as she stared at the screen.

Smith stood in the center of Cedarville's basketball team.

He gets better-looking every time I see him. What a great smile. And kind eyes with a sparkle. Chloe wished his picture showed his bright white *déjà vu* heart.

Her heart raced. Where's his first name? She quickly scanned the black lettering under the picture, looking for the name Smith. Yes!

Team Captain: Smith (top row, middle, center). That's it? She scrolled through several action photos, each of them void of captions. What kind of a hack did this website? Who wants to look at a picture of someone, without even knowing his name? Like he's an object and not a person?

Chloe zeroed in on one of Smith being heavily guarded by a tall guy in a Jefferson High School jersey, with the words De Veen printed across the shoulders.

De Veen?

Curiosity teased Chloe. *This must be the Ty De Veen I've heard so much about. I wonder if he's on Facebook?* There can't be that many Ty De Veen's! She maximized her Facebook account and typed in his name. Double Bingo! . . . Whoa.

Two parts hormones and one part adrenaline formed a gooey mocha in Chloe's heart. A tingling sensation flew through her, like hundreds of butterflies tickling the insides of her body from top to bottom. She stared at Ty De Veen's picture, with her eyes wider-than-wide, before making a declaration in her mind.

Never before, in all of my almost-16-year-existence, have I seen a more gorgeous member of the male race!

Ty De Veen looked more like a Pacific coast surfer than a Midwestern basketball-type. And he must be super friendly or famous, because who has more than 4,000 Facebook friends?

A pang of embarrassment hit Chloe as she thought of her feeble 50 friends.

Fortunately, Ty's FB page had open access to anyone who was interested, providing the perfect avenue for hours of research and development. Twenty-seven photo albums? Sweet. This would be delicious.

Chloe quickly clicked through each photo, watching a picture show of Ty's entire life, from babyhood to hottytude.

Then she did a rewind back to chapter one of Ty De Veen's life, zeroing in on a family picture of Dr. D, his wife, and "Tyler" standing in front of a windmill. Hmm. Must be an only child. Got his height from his dad.

Mrs. De Veen looked short next to Dr. D. Maybe 5'3" or so? Her tight, wrinkle-free face made her look a lot younger than him. She had thick, bleach-blonde hair, shoulder-length. And she wore lots of make-up, including bright pink lipstick on her plump and pouty lips.

Back to the Dutch hottie . . . Played basketball since he was a toddler. Lived in the Netherlands until moving to Dodge two years ago. Was he a model at one time? (In some of these pictures, he looks like he just walked off a Fitch runway!) Likes to party. Idol is Davion Griffin? *Where have I heard that name?* What does "in an open relationship" mean?

Chloe blushed inside. Is this how stalkers start out? She looked around her, slightly paranoid. *I'm fine. Nobody can see me. Should I "friend" him?* I could send him a message and say something like, "Hey, next time your dad brings a dead carcass to my uncle, stop by and say Hi. Or, "Hey, what a coincidence, I'm tall too!" Or, "Do you like chocolate pears, because I work at Anjou!" Chloe reached for the "Send a friend request" button and stopped. She looked down at her large brown fingers, took off her purity ring and put it on the little eagle ring holder next to Mom's picture. *Mom, I'm fine. I'm just looking. Stop overreacting.*

Chloe clicked on Ty's home page and read some of his posts. What does "The count-1, 2, 3" mean? Must have something to do with basketball. After a re-look of each photo album, Chloe glanced down and saw May's book, *The Bed Beckons,* next to her computer. She picked it up, deciding she needed a break.

Outside, the hot July humidity had changed to a steamy downpour.

Would Gary be home anytime soon? She plopped on her bed and read for the next couple of hours. Then, she went back and reread, and pondered, and imagined . . . , and reread, and pondered, and imagined some more. She, the photographer wallflower, and Ty, the video game champion, doing the things on page 23, and 117, and 153, and 205 . . . , and then once again in the epilogue of her mind.

* * *

May's 17th birthday was coming up, and Chloe wanted to make it special. May was the best thing that had happened to Chloe in Indiana. *What would I do without May?*

Gary inched the truck to a stop in front of the entrance of Ray's Foods so Chloe wouldn't have to walk in the rain. "I'll park the truck and be right in," he said. "Why don't you see if they have pot roast on sale this week?"

Chloe stepped out into a puddle, splashing her sweats. Her flip flops squished as she approached the sliding doors that swung open automatically. She tugged a grocery cart loose and headed for the produce section, stopping to look through the ad. No pot roast on sale. Poor Gary. How could he not like her California pastas, wraps, and sushi? Wonder if Candice knows about Gary's enchantment with mashed potatoes and gravy?

Fragrant scents perked Chloe's nostrils, detouring her to the Floral Department. *Maybe I should get May a bouquet to go with her birthday present.* She pushed her cart to a case of fresh flowers and pulled out a bouquet of bright-colored daisies. She lifted them to her nose and sniffed. Setting them back into the water container, her hands brushed a bouquet of pink tulips.

Tulips. *I wonder where the De Veen's shop for groceries?* Do they have gardens of tulips? A windmill? Does Ty ever wear wooden shoes? Chloe laughed to herself.

Gary came behind and tapped her on the shoulder. "Am I buying flowers for May's birthday, too?"

"Maybe you should buy some for Candice?" Chloe teased.

Gary looked like he was pondering the thought. "I wonder if she'd like a nice pot roast instead?" he said, laughing.

"Do you like tulips?" Chloe held the bouquet in front of Gary.

"I guess."

"They're Dutch flowers, right?"

Gary shrugged his shoulders.

"Just like your friend, Dr. D, right? He's Dutch, isn't he?"

"De Veen? Yep."

"Why did they come over here?"

"I guess he worked on some research project until the new hospital recruited him," said Gary, putting the tulips in the cart. "Alice, his wife, is originally from North Bend. They met when Harding was in med school at the university there. Alice wanted to move back to the States and be close to her family again." Gary picked up a bouquet of white roses and looked at the price tag. “Plus Ty wants to play in the NBA someday.”

“What’s the NBA?”

“National Basketball Association,” Gary said, heading toward the produce department.

Chloe followed him with the cart, plunking in an avocado, an artichoke, and several small packages of herbs on her way to the strawberries. *I wonder if Ty likes strawberries?* she thought, as she inspected them. She selected two packages and caught up to Gary. “Are you going to be there for May’s birthday lunch tomorrow?”

“No. I’m leaving in the morning for Lafayette, but I’ll be home around suppertime. Purdue has a seminar about a new soybean hybrid that I want to check out.” Gary grabbed a ten-pound bag of potatoes and added them to the cart. “I’m gonna get a few other things. I’ll be right back.”

In the bakery Chloe peered through the glass case, eyeing an individual heart cake with white frosting, topped with crystal cake glitter. She stepped back, contemplating if “Happy Birthday, May” written in cursive letters would fit on top.

A reflection of peekadilly bounced off the glass.

“Do you like our tiny heart-tart cake? It has raspberry filling, and we can personalize it for you,” said the bakery lady from behind the case.

Chloe looked up, expecting to see a *déjà vu* heart on the worker. No heart. She turned behind her, and scanned the area for a customer with a peekadilly heart, but no one else was around. Weird.

“Well?” said the worker.

Chloe paused. “Yes. Could you write “Happy 17th, May,” on it in petal pink icing?”

Gary was back, his arms filled with a case of frozen burgers, four cans of Pringles and two family-size Doritos. He dropped them into the cart, taking care not to crush the tulips. "I'll meet you at the register."

Chloe placed the small bakery box in the open space next to her purse and headed for the check-out lanes.

Gary raised a gallon of chocolate milk halfway in the air from a long line in Lane 8. Chloe veered through a glut of carts and joined him.

Oh, I wonder if Ty drinks milk. Chloe smiled, envisioning him with a white mustache as the star of a milk commercial.

Gary picked up a copy of *Field and Stream* and started to read.

Chloe scanned the grocery scenery and dug through her purse, hoping she'd stuck her journal in it.

Shoot. Forgot it again. And too bad, because grocery stores were good sleuthing spots. She looked around at the *déjà vu* mix. *A lot* of peekadilly hearts, which seemed to be the case, no matter where she went.

Peekadilly was definitely the most popular of her colors, and the least discriminating in terms of age, race, or gender. A peekadilly heart didn't always have a dust outline, but a dust outline always seemed to have a peekadilly heart. Unless the person had a bright white heart, or a weird two-tone heart like Gary's.

Chloe's peripheral vision caught some dust entering the line behind her. She fidgeted, wanting to turn around and look. Nonchalantly, she turned her head behind her, pretending to look at the cookie display. A young couple, both outlined in dust, stared right into her eyes, like they were surprised to see a brown girl in Dodge. *I wonder if they know they have an STD?* They *would* know, wouldn't they?

A slow shot of anger steeped inside of Chloe as she faced ahead, trying to rid her mind of dust. Ever since her appointment with Dr. Secus, she hated dust. *Dust stole my mom.*

Chloe glanced over to Lane 7, where she saw a father-son *déjà vu* duo.

Dad looked normal, even clean cut. No wedding ring. Was he a single dad? Junior couldn't have been more than 10 or 11 years old. He held a cell phone in his hand and appeared to be playing a game. Both of their chests looked like someone had spray-painted a bright peekadilly heart tattoo on them.

Chloe looked at Gary's two-tone heart, peekadilly, with a white center. What could her uncle have in common with Peekadilly Pop and Son? Did Gary's heart used to be entirely peekadilly before he became a believer? Or was it entirely bright white and then attacked and surrounded by peekadilly?

The boy put his phone in the pocket of his shorts, picked up a king-size Snickers bar and waved it front of his dad, begging. The dad nodded to the cashier to add it to their order. Junior opened the package, took a huge bite and headed for the movie machine. H*ave I ever seen peekadilly on a kid?* What could a tween kid have in common with Old man Tipton from Seaside?

"Can I have a carton of Marlboro Lights?" Gary asked the cashier.

Chloe winced at Gary's request. She helped Gary empty the cart, so she could get back to her *déjà vu* examination.

The next person in line, a female with no outline, plopped a huge bag of diapers and a large can of something on the conveyor belt.

Chloe waited for Gary to pay the cashier, then followed him toward the exit, pushing the cart. She glanced over at the girl in Lane 7 who was handing a fifty to the cashier. "Thanks," she said.

Miss Sparkly Gold! Chloe stared at the girl's face for several seconds, confirming it was her. No more sparkly gold? And now her peekadilly heart was two-toned like Gary's, punctuated with a large, bright white center. The girl looked tired, but peaceful.

* * *

On Sunday morning Chloe's eyes flew open and her heart beat furiously. She sat up in bed and gasped for breath, breaking into a cold sweat. *Breathe deep! In and out, in and out.*

Her panic attack continued.

Help me, God! Why aren't You helping me? She fell back again on her bed, trying to calm her tense body. *What if these colors are making me clinical? What if dust, veranda, and peekadilly begin invading my sleep psyche on a regular basis? Isn't having them in my days bad enough?* Especially since learning the icky meaning of dust. *I don't want these colors any more. Did you hear me, God? I don't want this anymore.*

Chloe pulled her diamond ring from her finger and held it up in the air, feeling disdain. *This thing started it.* Chloe turned it back and forth in different directions.

Flashes of bright white danced in the air, with each turn, like a miniature flash of lightning.

And one of the tiny flashes struck Chloe in the chest. She lay there, still and quiet, feeling an eerie peekadilly presence.

The ring in her hand was repelling her *déjà vu* heart.

She got up and ran to her full-length mirror.

A large, bright peekadilly *déjà vu* heart stared back at her, with a bright white eyeball. With her fingers, she traced the curves of the heart down to the point where they met.

Sheepishly, she looked down. A sense of guilt and shame oozed over her body, and she wanted to run and hide.

It's a lot easier to see a peekadilly heart on someone else than on yourself.

She glanced outside and saw a bright red cardinal, perched in the weeping willow tree near her window. He stared at Chloe, and seemed to chirp something to her.

"Be quiet," she said.

℞

Chapter 11

They say misery loves company. Maybe that's why May's new peekadilly heart seemed to befriend Chloe's two-toned heart. Were hearts everywhere being painted with peekadilly graffiti by *The Bed Beckons?*

Chloe fanned a linen table cloth under the shade of the large oak tree and looked at her watch. May should arrive any minute. She opened the picnic basket and carefully removed the bouquet of pink tulips, then centered it on the cloth. She set May's custom table setting, which consisted of a pink ceramic plate that she'd found at the Goodwill, a linen napkin, and a sterling silver fork that she'd pulled from a storage box in Gary's barn and polished. She pulled May's cake from a bakery box and placed a white candle in the center of the small "a" in May's name, and then filled a wine glass with icy cold Diet Dr. Pepper.

"Chloe, you are so nice," said May, approaching. She sat down on the corner of the cloth and smiled big.

"Happy Birthday, one-day-late." Chloe struck a match and lit the candle to flicker in front of May. "Make a wish," she said.

May smiled, closed her eyes and blew it out. "O goody gumdrops, my wish will come true." She ran her finger through the icing and licked it. "Thanks, Chloe. You are a really good friend."

A tingling feeling went through Chloe. *May is my good friend.* She cleared her throat and began to sing. "Happy birthday to you . . . Happy birthday, dear May, happy birthday to you."

"Jinkies," May said softly.

"I know," said Chloe. "I'm not a great singer."

They both laughed.

"So how do you like working at Anjou by now?" asked May.

"I love it. Everyone is super nice."

"Have you met Large Marg?"

A warm feeling went through Chloe. "I love her. She reminds me of my mom."

"Because she's black?"

"No. Besides, my mom was white," said Chloe. "Like the majority of the population in Dodge," she said, with a hint of frustration. Chloe got a serene look on her face. "Marg seems pure."

"Pure?" May said, raising her eyebrows skeptically. "I saw her make out with her husband once at Anjou."

Chloe smirked. "I know. Me, too. But that's her husband. She and Elmer have been married for 49 years. She told me they both saved themselves for each other, and that their sex has become more passionate as their love for each other has grown through the years."

May's face cringed. "Ew." She closed her eyes. "Don't do a visual," she said, laughing. "It's a good thing they never had kids, because Marg's boobs would scare a nursing baby half to death."

Chloe laughed. "But they do have kids. They have four."

"But they're adopted, right?"

"Well, yes . . . but they are still their kids." Chloe looked to the sky and thought of her mom. "So, do you think there's something to that?" Chloe asked, changing the subject.

"To what?"

"You know," Chloe stammered. "Staying pure for your husband?"

May was silent for a moment, as if her left and right brain were in an argument. "Oh, that is so old-fashioned," she said finally. "My sexuality is supposed to be part of how I express myself as a woman. If two people love each other. . . ."

A sick feeling came over Chloe. Should she tell May about Jason? *But I don't want to ruin her birthday.* Avoiding the risk, Chloe reached in her purse and pulled out a small square box, wrapped in silver foil paper, and tied with iridescent pink ribbon. "Here," she said handing it to May.

May looked surprised. And thrilled.

And emotional?

May unwrapped the paper neatly to find a white velvet box. She flipped open the lid, and her eyes lit up.

Inside, tucked inside a small horizontal canyon, was a sterling silver band with a beautiful pearl centered between two tiny diamonds. Swirls of the faintest pastel colors gleamed in the small white globe.

"It's so pretty," said May, placing it on her finger and looking surprised that it fit perfectly. "How did you know my size?"

"I asked your mom," said Chloe, smiling. "It looks great on you!" She lifted May's hand, coveting her slim fingers. "It could be your purity ring, if you want," she said, looking up at May.

May shunned a tiny hint of disgust, then looked like she was getting choked up.

I've never seen this side of May. "So, tell me all about your birthday, yesterday! Did you and Jason have a blast?"

May gave her a blank stare and then her eyes started getting puffy and red.

"What's wrong?"

A tear rolled out of each of May's eyes and dropped into her lap.

What did that peekadilly jerk do to my friend? A pang went through Chloe as the word peekadilly cut through the synapses of her mind. *I have peekadilly, too.*

"He didn't even mention my birthday the whole day," said May, now blubbering softly. "I kept thinking he had some big surprise planned, or even a little surprise . . . but nothing."

"Did you go anywhere?"

"We went to a movie and then back to his apartment." May hesitated. "But then some of his buddies stopped by, and they just played video games." May sniffled a big snork. "I would have had more fun working at Anjou."

"What a jerk," said Chloe, disgusted.

"What?" May gave Chloe a surprised look through her tears. "He's not a jerk. He just forgot. Anybody could accidentally forget."

"But wouldn't he remember if he really cared?"

May was quiet. "You don't like him, do you? You never have," she said, defensively.

Why is she sticking up for that slime ball? "It's just . . . ." Let's see, how do you say a guy is a loser and a pig in a nice way? "May, he doesn't deserve you. You're pretty and smart and kind and he's . . . ." Chloe stopped herself and looked for a detour out of the conversation. "Do you want some cake?"

"No. I just ate a whole box of donuts." May wiped her nose on her bare arm. "But he's the only guy who's ever liked me. He's all I ever think about."

"You should be thinking about your photography and your scholarship stuff," said Chloe, glancing at the bouquet of tulips and hoping May had left her hypocrite-detector at home. "You're the women's libber. Aren't you always saying that a guy shouldn't define you? Like your poster in your room that says 'A woman needs a man, like a fish needs a bicycle?'"

"I know you're right, but . . . ." May paused, weighing her next words. "Well, you're probably going to think this is ridiculous, but ever since I was a little girl, I've dreamed of one thing."

But you already have a dad. And he calls you Princess.

"Until this year, I didn't think it could ever happen, because I was so---"

"So . . . what?"

May snorked again and choked out the word, "Fat."

Could a life dream really be thwarted by some extra weight? Chloe tried to look patient. “What is it, May?”

“You have to swear not to tell anyone,” May said.

“I promise. May, you’re my best friend in the whole world.”

“I just want to go to prom next year, and Jason is my only shot.”

* * *

Chloe stared at herself in the mirror of the Anjou employee bathroom.

This two-toned déjà vu heart is sucking the life out of me. A pair of puffy eyes with bags under them stared back at her. Her shoulders slouched from the heaviness of peekadilly pulling her down. Was that why she could barely drag her butt out of bed this morning? The fact that Gary had to drop her off at work an hour early to attend some pesticide seminar at Purdue hadn’t helped. *I can’t wait to get my driver’s license.*

The sound of a flushing toilet in one of the stalls startled her.

The door flung open and out sauntered Marg. She saw Chloe and flashed a bright smile that matched her large bright white heart. “Mornin’, Child,” she said. Marg pushed on the soap dispenser and swirled her hands together, looking at Chloe’s face. “You look terrible. You okay?” Marg washed her hands and wiped them dry, then put her hand on Chloe’s back, “What’s wrong?”

A shot of warmth pulsated from Marg’s moist hand. Chloe’s lip started to quiver. “I don’t even know,” said Chloe. *I can’t tell Marg about stupid peekadilly! If only I had my mom.*

Marg opened her large arms and engulfed Chloe in a big bear hug.

Will my peekadilly heart stain her bright white heart?

Chloe melted in Marg's embrace. Her legs felt like wet noodles. How long had it been since she'd been hugged like this?

"God loves you and so do I," said Marg, not letting go.

God? I forgot about Him, just like He forgot about me. Chloe broke the hug before it got awkward.

Marg looked into Chloe's eyes. "Do you know Him, Child?"

I showed Marg my purity ring. Doesn't she remember that?

"I don't mean knowing *about* Him," said Marg. "I mean *knowing* Him. Child, have you ever accepted Christ as your Savior? You know, asked Him to forgive your sins?"

Chloe bit her lower lip and took a step back. "Yes. I did that right before my mom died . . . but He let her die anyway. He let me become an orphan."

Marg's face filled with compassion. Her hand stroked the side of Chloe's head lightly. "Child, we're all orphans until He adopts us into His family. He's our daddy, our Abba Father, and He takes us from our mama's wombs."

And then he took my mom from me. "What about your kids?"

"God gave Elmer and me four beautiful kids. We're their parents on earth, but He's their Daddy for eternity."

"So all your kids were adopted?"

"Yes. Praise God, they've all asked Jesus into their hearts," said Marg.

"I mean, did you give birth to them?" Chloe asked, remembering that Marg's kids were all white.

Marg's black outline surrounded a hint of disappointment, like a conversation bubble. "No, Child. None of my babies are from Elmer's seed."

"Seed?"

"His sperm, Child."

Gross. TMI!

"Donovan and Grace and Levi and Mary were from courageous young ladies who chose to let God take them from their wombs, so He could adopt them . . . and bless Elmer and me with them."

"But do they *feel* like orphans? Why do I feel like an orphan? I mean, if I've accepted Christ, why don't I *feel* like His child?"

Marg looked puzzled. "Feel?" she said, pondering the word. "My kids know I'm their mama whether they *feel* like they came from my belly or not. If you've accepted Christ as your Savior, you are His child whether you *feel* it or not!" Marg cupped Chloe's face with both of her hands. "The question is whether or not you're depending on Him as your daddy. If you want to *feel* like His child, you have to treat Him like your daddy."

"But I've never had a dad."

"Well, He's been there all along. You just never chose to have a relationship with Him," said Marg. "Child, you can't have a relationship with a stranger. Depending on God means you talk to Him . . . and listen to Him . . . and run to Him when you need help . . . and go through your day with Him. And if you mess somethin' up, He won't disown you. He'll just wait for you to confess your sin, so the two of you can get close again. That's how you depend on Him as your daddy."

A tingling sensation went through Chloe. *Marg sounds a lot like Mom.*

Marg glanced at the clock on the bathroom wall and tucked her gray curls under her hairnet. "Namby needs a batch of caramels by lunch time. I'd better get them going. Why don't we go out for breakfast or lunch sometime?" she said, heading out the door.

"Thanks, Marg," Chloe responded. She turned back to the mirror and fitted her black beret on her head. The diamond of her ring beamed a ray of bright white on the eye of her peekadilly heart.

CONFESS YOUR SEXUAL SIN, CHLOE. CONFESS AND REPENT, AND I WILL FORGIVE. I LOVE YOU, CHLOE.

Sexual sin? But God, I didn't actually do anything.

WHATEVER YOU DO IN YOUR HEART OR MIND, YOU'VE DONE.

Chloe went into a stall, locked the door, and closed her eyes. *Abba Father, please forgive me. Help me stay pure in my heart, and mind, and body. Thank you for adopting me. I promise I won't ignore You anymore.*

I FORGIVE YOU, CHLOE. YOU ARE MY CHILD, AND I LOVE YOU. I WILL NEVER LEAVE YOU.

Urrnt. The intercom buzzed and Candice's voice spilled out. "Chloe to the Shoppe, please. Chloe to the Shoppe."

A sense of peace flowed through her, filling the pores of her soul. She unlatched the door and glanced in the mirror as she headed for the door, then stopped. Her *déjà vu* heart was now mostly solid bright white, except for the tiniest thin peekadilly outline! *Whoa.* No sunbeams, and not as bright as Marg's, or Mom's, but still white.

She hurried toward the time clock, her bright white heart leading the way. She punched her time card and untacked a Nambygram addressed to her, sticking it in the pocket of her apron. She burst through the wooden door to the Shoppe.

"Chloe, can you take the register for me?" asked Candice, smiling.

Chloe looked over and saw Smith, laughing and talking with the cute girl who was with him.

His bright white *déjà vu* heart, exploding with sunbeams, was magnetized to hers.

Th-thump. Th-thump, she heard her heart inside of her. "May I help you?" she said, choking slightly.

The girl turned to him. "I'll be right back."

"Okay," he said. A pleasant look came over Smith's face as he turned to Chloe. "Sure. I need a one-pound package of truffles," he said, smiling.

A drop of adrenaline formed on Chloe's forehead. She froze. *What should I say?* Finally, she blurted out, "Would you like anything to drink with that?"

Smith contemplated for a moment. "Sure, I'll have a mocha with an extra shot of espresso," he said, looking into Chloe's eyes.

Of all times to remember Namby's suggestive sell! What was I thinking?

She took Smith's money, placed a box of truffles in a carryout bag, and then prepared his coffee drink, blowing a kiss and a prayer on it. She handed it to him, and said in a robot-like tone, "Have a great day."

Smith smiled big. "Thanks, I will. You have a great day, too, Chloe."

Chloe? He called me Chloe again!

Then he and his date left.

Hey, Daddy, did you hear Smith call me Chloe? Just want to let you know I'm not opposed to an arranged marriage! Especially with letter-jacket-wearing boys or tall Dutch hotties.

For the rest of the day Chloe felt like she was floating. She replayed the scene in her mind and thought of all the funny and cute and coy things she could have said to Smith. *Next time*, she thought.

As she rode home with Gary, she sent May a text: LTR JCKT BOY CAME IN TODAY! NAMBYS SWITCHING ME TO NIGHTS BEG. NEXT WEEK. CAN I RIDE W/ U? GOT MY SCHOOL SCHEDULE YESTERDAY IN MAIL. I HAVE B LUNCH. YOU? DO U KNOW LILY HUNT? MY WELCOME TOUR IS W/ HER NEXT FRI. SEE YA. Chloe tapped the send button.

May replied right back. DRIVING TO ANJOU RIGHT NOW. YAY ABOUT NIGHTS! POOP--I HAVE C-LUNCH. LILY HUNT=JINKIES. LUV U, MAY.

℞

Chapter 12

On Chloe's 16th birthday, she awoke early to the smell of breakfast cooking. She put on her white fluffy robe and headed downstairs. Gary had prepared her favorites--a spinach and artichoke omelette, fresh strawberries and cut mango, and a giant cinnamon roll. In the middle of the kitchen table sat a large bouquet, a dozen white roses addressed to her with a tag simply signed, "Happy Birthday, Love, Gary."

A bittersweet feeling flowed through her. Everyone was trying so hard to make her birthday special, yet she couldn't help thinking about her life a year ago--how it was so different, so wonderful, and so with Mom.

May had given her a handmade card. The card's front was sepia photo of a bare tree with a bright red cardinal photoshopped in. Inside, May wrote, "Chloe, you are the best friend a girl could ever have. Your BFF, May." She also gave her a gift bag with a Starbuck's gift card, a home-made coupon good for free transportation to Jefferson High School, and a book entitled, *How to Talk to Boys Without Peeing Your Pants.*

Candice and Marg gave her a one-pound special-made collection of Anjou Chocolate strawberries, not available to the public. Henry Namby gave her the day off, with pay, as was his custom with every employee.

Chloe smiled at Gary as she munched her omelette. "Thanks, Gary. This is great." She looked at Gary's *déjà vu* heart. *Is his bright white growing and his peekadilly getting smaller?* "No cigarettes this morning?" she asked.

"Nope," he said, smiling. "Day seven. Not bad for me."

After Chloe finished her breakfast and made it through Gary's rocky rendition of *Happy Birthday,* he said, "Okay. Come with me. You have some more gifts."

"Should I go get dressed first?"

"Naw."

Chloe followed Gary, sliding on a pair of flip-flops from the porch and letting the screen door slam behind her. *I hope my present isn't in his taxidermy shed!*

Gary led her to the large white barn and then stopped. "Okay, you have to close your eyes now."

Chloe could hear him undo the latch and slide the huge door half open. *I think I know what it is . . .* Chloe held out her hand and she felt Gary pull it toward the center of the barn.

"Keep your eyes closed."

Chloe felt air rustle against her face and heard what sounded like a huge sheet being shaken.

"All right. Open up," said Gary.

Mom's convertible! "Can I drive it?"

"Not until you're legal. We'll get you signed up for driver's ed," said Gary. He looked across the barn at his John Deere tractor. "You can drive *that*, if you want," he said with a smirk.

Chloe laughed. She looked at the tractor, remembering. "Did I ride on that once, when I was a baby? And I was sitting on your lap and wearing an orange jacket and sunglasses and a baseball hat?"

Gary's eyes widened. "Did you see a picture of that? I remember that," he said. "That was right before you and Lisa--I mean, your Mom--moved to California. You had to be less than a year old."

"And you were singing me that song, *Don't Worry, Be Happy,* right?"

"Could have been," said Gary, shaking his head. "You want me to sing it for you now, for your birthday?" he added, teasing. "I better not, or I might scare the mice out of the hay loft."

Chloe started humming the song in her head and smiled.

"Your mom gave me explicit instructions about your present today," said Gary. "It's been washed, waxed, cleaned out, and topped with a daisy."

Chloe looked inside and saw a large, dainty white daisy with a yellow-button center basking in the small, clear flower holder. On the driver's seat was a present wrapped in white iridescent paper tied with light pink curly ribbon. Tucked under the ribbon was a letter-size, light pink envelope with several tiny white pearlescent butterflies randomly fluttering on it. *Mom's grave resembles her stationary.*

Chloe thought back to the last time she'd opened one of Mom's pink envelopes--when Mom thought dust might mean the pain associated with abortion. Would this one have new revelations too?

Maybe Mom wrote about her STD? *Did Mom even know she had an STD?*

A sense of thrill, mixed with a pang of grief, went through her. Chloe reached in the car, carefully removed the letter from the package and held it in her hand. *Mom touched this. She wrote this for me.*

"I'll leave you alone for awhile," said Gary. "We're still going for Mexican tonight, right? I'm going in to town for an appointment. I'll be back later."

He seems to have a lot of appointments lately. "K. Thanks, Gary."

Gary ran from the barn to the house, dodging raindrops that were now falling.

Chloe opened the door, sat in the driver's seat, and turned the key to lower the roof. She breathed in the scent of sweet hay and listened to the rain beat softly on the roof. She held the letter to her heart. "Mom, I have a bright white heart too now, just like yours," she whispered.

A sparrow flew through the rafters of the barn, then playfully into the rain.

Chloe carefully unwrapped the package, neatly folding the paper to save it. Inside, was a copy of the book entitled, *Fall in Love & Learn to Fight*. Inside the front cover Mom wrote: "Happy 16th Birthday, My Sweet Mocha--I know God has a great purpose for your life, Chloe. You'll discover His plans, and take your promised land, as you fall in love with Him. Love you, Mom."

Thank you, Mom. Funny you gave me this, because I'm starting to think I'm not supposed to be an artist. Maybe God gave me my colors for a different reason?

Chloe leafed through the book, set it down and carefully opened the envelope. Two pages of stationary, crisp and tightly creased lay inside, inviting her to unfold them. Mom's ornate script, written in thin black marker, was perfectly centered in the middle of each page. The first page was a short note; the second was filled with writing.

A sense of love swelled in Chloe's heart as she focused on the words, imagining they were being read to her in her mother's voice.

My Dear Chloe,

I've prayed, in faith, for years that you would accept, believe, and know Christ. If you don't already, I have faith that God will continue pursuing you, as He did me. He is what you long for--your Knight in Shining Armor, riding on a white horse, coming to your rescue, protecting you, and fighting for you.

The enclosed verses caused me to fall in love with Him. They formed the prayer of my life and enabled me to realize I am accepted, secure, and significant. May you also make this the prayer of your life as you fall in love. Love, Mom.

Chloe flipped to the next paper and read the familiar words.

"Our Father and Creator, We thank you for being our Savior and Great Physician, our Closest Companion, Provider and Protector, and the Lover of Our Souls. We love you and long for you."

He is our Father and Creator . . .

Matthew 6:9 Our Father in heaven (Chloe, the word "our" is extremely intimate. In prayer, the Holy Spirit living in me, joins with Jesus the Son, as we unite with our Heavenly Father).

Genesis 1:27 So God created man in his own image, in the image of God he created him; male and female he created them. (God created you *Imago Dei*, which is Latin for "in His image." This means you are like Him in *some* ways. But, realize that *He* is God; you are *not*! God made you to crave love, fellowship and relationship with Him and others, *and* He made you with the ability to *choose* if you want these relationships. True love is always "free," never coerced or out-of-duty.)

Psalm 139:16 . . . your eyes saw my unformed body. All the days ordained for me were written in your book before one of them came to be. (Chloe, He *chose* you . . . created you . . . and planned the day in history that you would be born and the day you will die. Your time on earth is to be a beautiful serenade with Him, preparing you for eternity.)

Psalm 139:13-14 For you created my inmost being; you knit me together in my mother's womb. I praise you because I am fearfully and wonderfully made; your works are wonderful, I know that full well. (Chloe, You are an amazing work of art that He made exactly the way you are. I know you don't like how your hands look, but God does! He formed every detail of your body, and He doesn't make mistakes.)

Ephesians 1:4-6 For he chose us in him before the creation of the world to be holy and blameless in his sight. In love he predestined us to be adopted as his sons through Jesus Christ . . . (Every single one of us in Christ is adopted.)

We thank you for being our Savior . . .

I John 3:16 This is how we know what love is: Jesus Christ laid down his life for us. (How much did Christ love you? Spread your arms out as far as you can. When Jesus' arms were spread wide on the cross and nails driven through them, He was thinking about you. That's love!)

Isaiah 1:18 "Come now, let us reason together," says the LORD. 'Though your sins are like scarlet, they shall be as white as snow; though they are red as crimson, they shall be like wool. (When we admit, confess, and repent of our sin, Christ covers our stained hearts with purity and righteousness.)

II Corinthians 5:17 Therefore, if anyone is in Christ, he is a new creation, the old has gone, the new has come! (Chloe, this is my favorite verse. Christ saved me, healed me, and gave me the Holy Spirit to live in me. After this happened, I wasn't the same person! The new me had hope and a future. He redeemed my past.)

John 14:25-26 All this I have spoken while still with you. But the Counselor, the Holy Spirit, whom the Father will send in my name, will teach you all things and will remind you of everything I have said to you. (Chloe, God will never leave you or forsake you. The Holy Spirit will constantly remind you of all of God's promises.)

He is the Great Physician

Psalm 147:3 He heals the brokenhearted and binds up their wounds.

John 8:10-11 Jesus straightened up and asked her, "Woman, where are they? Has no one condemned you?" "No one, sir," she said. "Then neither do I condemn you," Jesus declared. "Go now and leave your life of sin." (Chloe, Jesus heals without condemnation. Regardless of what we've done, even if our own sin has brought us painful consequences, Jesus gives us mercy. And then He prescribes prevention by telling us to stop sinning.)

Matthew 4:23 Jesus went throughout Galilee, teaching in their synagogues, preaching the good news of the kingdom, and healing every disease and sickness among the people. (Chloe, Christ became my Great Physician when I heard "the good news of the kingdom." As I write this today, I know He has the power to heal me physically, but even if He chooses not to heal my body, don't ever forget that He healed my heart and soul!)

He is our Closest Companion.

Hebrews 4:15 For we do not have a high priest who is unable to sympathize with our weaknesses, but we have one who has been tempted in every way, just as we are--yet was without sin. (Chloe, Jesus understands everything you're going through! He will strengthen you, and show you a way out of every tempting situation.)

He is our Provider and Protector.

Hebrews 13:5 Keep your lives free from the love of money and be content with what you have, because God has said, "Never will I leave you; never will I forsake you." (Chloe, don't love money! God will provide what you need. True wealth is a blessing from God that doesn't bring trouble with it. When money becomes your idol--or anything other than God--it will destroy you.)

Psalm 18:1-2 I love you, O LORD, my strength. The LORD is my rock, my fortress and my deliverer; my God is my rock, in whom I take refuge.

Psalm 119: 9-11 How can a young man keep his way pure? By living according to your word. I seek you with all my heart; do not let me stray from your commands. I have hidden your word in my heart that I might not sin against you. (The Bible is no ordinary book. It's the "Word" of God--living, breathing, and powerful. Chloe, you can't truly fall in love with someone you don't know! The Bible is how you get to know God--what He's like, what's important to Him, how He works, and how much He cares for you. It's His love letter to you, written by the Holy Spirit through men of God. Memorize it! Take it with you, each day. Pray it back to Christ. Meditate on it. If you can worry, you can meditate. Just switch what you're thinking about! If you study God's Word, it will also help you learn to fight! It will protect you, warn you of *T*he *E*nemy's methods, and empower you against spiritual attacks.)

John 17:11b Holy Father, protect them by the power of your name--the name you gave me--so that they may be one as we are one. (Jesus Himself prayed for you, Chloe. That's intimate.)

He is the Lover of Our Souls.

Deuteronomy 3:22 Do not be afraid of them; the LORD your God himself will fight for you. (Chloe, Moses said this to Joshua about the enemies that were living in the Promised Land. God promised them this land of blessing, but they had to conquer it in order to receive it. You also have a "Promised Land"--a future full of spiritual blessings that God has for you! Allow God to fight your spiritual battles--in you and through you--so you can fulfill your destiny.)

Jeremiah 29:11-13 " . . . For I know the plans I have for you," declares the LORD, "plans to prosper you and not to harm you, plans to give you a hope and a future." (A lover wants his beloved to discover her plan and purpose. He completes her by bringing out the best in her. Chloe, God loves you and has a great future for you!)

Revelation 2:17 . . . To him who overcomes, I will give some of the hidden manna. I will also give him a white stone with a new name written on it, known only to him who receives it. (This is the most romantic verse in the Bible to me. Just think, you will get a new, secret name, known only to you and Jesus. I will have mine soon!)

We love you and long for you.

(Chloe, I'll soon be reunited with the Lover of My Soul. He and I will be waiting for you.)

A sense of warmth went through Chloe, and she felt completely loved. *Thank you, Mom.* She reread the letter another time and closed her eyes. *I wonder what her secret name is?* She crossed her arms in front of her, squeezing the terry cloth of her robe into her arms, pretending Mom was hugging her.

God, I think I finally get how much Mom loved you and how much she wanted me to make you the Lover of my Soul.

Chloe kept her eyes shut, basking in the moment, then prayed. *My Father and Creator, Thank you for being my Savior and Great Physician, my Closest Companion, Provider and Protector, and the Lover of my soul. I can't wait to learn my secret name someday! God, thank you for always being with me. Help me to discover how You want me to use my déjà vu colors for your kingdom. I love you and long for you.*

Quietness fell outside as the rain stopped.

Chloe opened her eyes. Faintly, she heard a vehicle coming up the driveway. Was Gary back? *How long have I been out here?* She watched a black pick-up truck drive past and park.

Dr. D's truck!

Chloe looked down at her bathrobe and was embarrassed.

She heard one truck door shut, then another. “Ty, why don’t you knock on the door? I’ll check the shed,” said Dr. D.

Oh, crap! Bathrobe. No make-up. I don’t want to meet Ty De Veen looking like this! Chloe tried to slide out of view in the front of the bug, but that’s not easy when you’re 6-foot tall! Her heart pounded fast. She shimmied over the top of the door, avoiding the noise of a door slam. She tiptoed behind the sliding door of the barn. *Okay, God, time to admire your Dutch Hottie creation in person!*

“Gary,” said Ty loudly. “Are you home?”

What a beautiful Dutch accent!

She peered out and saw Ty’s muscular, cut, athletic back-side, and . . . .

And dust . . . Bright dust. Dust to the exponential! Layers and layers of dust, far beyond the typical outline of the body. Ty De Veen’s dust was like a thick, heavy covering that clung to his every movement like a dark cloud.

Ew.

Ty let the screen door slam behind him as he turned and walked toward his dad.

Peekdailly. Bright and Bigger. Ty’s *déjà vu* heart shone brightly from his chest.

“Sometimes Hudson parks his truck in the barn,” said Dr. D. “I’ll see if it’s in there.”

Chloe’s heart raced. He was coming! Where should she hide? She looked around, deciding to take cover behind the combine. She looked down to make sure her feet were out of view, and held her breath.

“Hey, Ty. Check dis out,” Dr. D called.

“He doesn’t drive *that*, does he?” said Ty.

"No, it must belong to his niece, Chloe," said Dr. D. "She'll be going to Jefferson High School zis fall. I haf a feeling you're going to like her."

A cold shiver went up Chloe's spine. *Why? Why is he going to like me?*

* * *

Chloe aced her online driving course, but why did Indiana have to change the driving age from 16 to 16 1/2? That wouldn't be until next February!

At least I can ride to school with May this year.

Chloe gripped the steering wheel like she was bracing herself for the big hill on a roller coaster. Surely the third time out would be a charm, right? Her first time behind the wheel, she accidentally ran over a squirrel. Gary teased her by making up an original song entitled, *Little Dead Squirre*l to the tune of *Jesus, Take the Wheel.* Her second driving venture resulted in a cop pulling her over for rolling through a stop sign at the intersection of two country dirt roads. When she saw the red flashing lights in the rear-view mirror, she nearly pee-ed her pants. Fortunately, Gary had once done a taxidermy job for the cop, which equated to the Dodge version of a get-out-of-jail-free card.

"Turn in here," said Gary, pointing to a shopping plaza up ahead. "I want to look at something at the jewelry store."

Hmm. Chloe carefully made the turn on a green arrow and drove grandma-slow through the parking lot. She pulled into a space in front of Glisten's Jewelers.

A doorbell rang as they entered the quiet store, void of customers. Soft music piped through the air. The Windex-clean glass cases sparkled.

S*omeday Mr. Right will take me to a jewelry store just like this, and he'll buy me a pearl ring* *surrounded by tiny diamonds. He'll gently take my hand and practice saying the words, "Chloe, with this ring, I thee wed." Then he'll take me into a passionate embrace and kiss me right then and there, in front of the watching little old man wearing a jeweler's eye piece on his head.*

"May I help you folks with something?" said a gentleman in a suit, making his way to the front case where Gary was peering at several rows of diamonds.

"Oh, no, I'm just looking," Gary stammered. "How much is the one in the top row that's shaped like a football?"

Chloe raised her eyes from the pearl case. *Gary's looking at diamonds? He and Candice have been spending a lot of time together, but isn't it a little fast?* Chloe rushed to Gary's side. A smile filled her face.

The jeweler laid a small piece of black velvet on top of the case. He opened the glass door and removed the gem with a pair of gold tweezers, carefully placing it on the black background.

The diamond shone all the more brilliantly against the black background.

"This particular gem is a one-carat oval that runs $3000," said the jeweler.

Gary appeared to be doing calculations in his head. "Do you like this one, Chloe?"

Chloe reached her hand toward the gem, her purity ring catching the light and the attention of the jeweler.

The jeweler stared at the gem for several seconds, and then looked at Chloe, then at Gary, and back at her. "You're buying her another one?" he said to Gary.

Oh, gross. He thinks I'm with Gary.

Gary interrupted her thought. "No, this is my niece."

The jeweler stared at Chloe's hand, mesmerized. "If you don't mind my asking, where did you get that diamond, young lady?"

"It was my mom's. I think she bought it in Europe somewhere."

"Can I take a look at it?" Anticipation dripped from the jeweler's lips. He looked like a desert-wanderer just seeing a waterfall-mirage.

Maybe this guy could see weird colors in the diamond too? *Part of me wishes my déjà vu colors had stayed hidden in that diamond, just making random appearances when a camera flashed. But another part of me realizes that God must have a reason for putting my life in the center of this Dodge déjà vu paint-by-number.*

Chloe slipped the ring off her finger and handed it to him.

He pulled the eyepiece perched on his head, over his eye, magnifying his black eyeball through the hole. He turned the diamond in several directions while examining it. Finally, he handed it back to Chloe. "I don't believe I've ever seen a diamond with internally flawless clarity like that."

"Yes, I remember my mom saying something about that."

"What's a diamond like that worth?" asked Gary.

The jeweler began to say something, then stopped himself. "Oh, I'm not sure what the market is right now," he said, turning to Chloe. "Listen, Young Lady, if you ever want to sell that rock, you come to me, okay? I'll give you more than a fair price."

Chapter 13

Mayble Hicks

May Hicks lay in a fetal position on her bed, staring blankly at her bedroom wall. She rolled over on her back and zeroed in on the poster hanging above her bed. It was an antique that she'd found last year at a flea market while shopping with her mom. At the time she thought it to be retro, and kind of cool, but not now. The poster's lioness stared back at her, exclaiming, "I am woman, hear me roar!"

Stupid poster.

A pit continued its formation in her stomach. *I thought it would be different.* She closed her eyes. *What if . . . ? No, I'm not even going there yet. It's too early to worry.*

Does everybody feel like this? *But I did everything the February issue of Cosmo Chic said to do! And it worked. Jason said he didn't want to wait for me to lose my last ten pounds. He said we were ready. "We're really good friends, May."*

As soon as it was over, he was like, "Okay, you should probably get going."

"Don't you want to snuggle and just talk for a while?" I said.

"Not really," he said matter-of-factly. "I have to be at work tomorrow at 10, and my gas tank is on empty."

I thought the second time would be better . . . but it was like he was playing a video game, and I was a level to be conquered. And then I got really worried and said, "What if it breaks?" Jason's idea of consolation was to say, "Don't worry. I totally know how to use these things." (And did he have to mention that he bought it with a $1.00 coupon out of the Sunday paper?) Then I asked him if we could plan a date or something, and he said, "I thought we agreed on being friends-with-benefits?"

Did I miss something? Because now he only seems interested in the benefits and not the friendship.

The last time I felt like this, like someone shot a bullet through my heart, was in 7th grade, when Billy McCoy called me a fat pig in gym class.

I keep trying to put the whole thing into a compartment and forget about it. But, I just can't! It's like when I try not to think about donuts, ALL I can think of is donuts. Why is that?

Jinkies. How am I going to concentrate at school next week? What if I don't get good grades or a scholarship this year? I'll be stuck in Dodge forever. Chloe will go to college in Chicago or New York or California, and I'll be left here, working at Anjou until I'm Large Marg's age. Then I'll probably marry some jerk, gain eighty pounds and live in a trailer park. I don't even care about prom anymore! Screw prom. I just want to feel back to normal.

* * *

At 3:30 p.m. on a Thursday, Chloe sat on the back porch waiting for May. *Working nights is going to be fun!* She took the cappuccino-cheat-sheet notecard from her apron and fanned herself. The black of her uniform drew the August heat to her skin, making her sweat. *I hope I don't get pit stains.*

The Hicks's silver mini-van pulled up the driveway.

Weird. Is May's green pickle in the shop? Maybe it's been bumped one too many times? May's car reminded Chloe of a square pickle chip. For the most part, it was kelly green, except for the extensive silver duct tape on the bumper and rearview mirror, the result of a little mishap with the Hicks's mailbox. Mr. Hicks had encased it in a solid brick shrine last spring, after some teens were busted for mailbox bashing.

Chloe opened the screen door and yelled to Gary, "May's here. We're off at 7."

The door on the side of the van opened slowly and automatically. Baby Louie's car seat filled one of the middle seats; Timmy and Tommy were in the back and May was in the front. "Hello, Dear," said Mrs. Hicks, pleasantly. "I haven't seen you in awhile. How have you been?"

Chloe crawled in the seat behind May on the passenger's side. "Hi. I'm good." She tapped May on the shoulder. "Hi, May. Is the green pickle sick?"

May grunted.

Awkward silence.

Chloe could feel four little eyes peering at her from the back seat. She turned to Timmy and Tommy. "How are you guys?"

"Good." They giggled. "May got grounded," said Tommy with a twinkle in his eye. "And lost her phone."

"And she can't drive," said Timmy with a smirk. "Cuz of her test. Mommy said she can die from it."

Test?

"Shut up!" barked May from the front seat. "The word is text, you moron." She turned to her mom. "You set me up."

"No. You made your own choice. And I'm giving you a consequence because I love you, and I don't want you to get killed, or kill someone else," said Mrs. Hicks. "May, it's not just the texting while you were driving. It was also missing curfew twice and then not having an explanation."

"A whole week isn't fair," said May. She craned her neck around the top of the seat and looked at Chloe. "Sorry that my mom is making you ride the stupid bus on your very first day of public high school."

Mrs. Hicks pursed her lips. "I *am* sorry about that, Chloe," she said.

Chloe looked at Mrs. Hicks's dust outline, like she was seeing it for the first time. *No way. Mrs. Hicks has an STD?*

Mrs. Hicks pulled into the Anjou circular drive, close to the entrance. "Have a good night at work, girls. I'll pick you up at 7:10."

May got out and slammed the door. She waited for Chloe to get out of the van. "I don't want to talk," she said.

May's peekadilly heart shone brighter than before.

"Okay," said Chloe. "But if you change your mind, I'm here."

Chloe opened the large door for May and followed behind her.

Jason was behind the counter, filling the truffle case. Now, his hulk-like frame was entirely encased with a dust outline!

"Um, hey," said May quietly, looking at him expectantly.

Jason continued stocking the truffles, not looking up. "Hey," he mumbled.

Noticeable awkwardness.

May burst through the back door and grabbed the dud box. She shoved in a mouthful of caramels and chewed them with rounded cheeks, like she was swishing around goo mouthwash. Her face was turning redder with every chew. She put her hand over her mouth, like she was contemplating saying something and stopped herself.

Her pearl ring shimmered on her finger.

Chloe took the dud box from May and looked inside.

Several chocolate soldiers looked like they'd been hit with hand grenades. She took one out and nibbled it, as she stood silently, remembering Mom's words. *Chloe, love is a battlefield. You have to fight to protect your purity.* She glanced at May's ring, and an instant pit formed in her stomach. Did May throw her pearl of purity to the pig of Jason?

"Chloe, you were right. He's such a jerk," May whispered, turning toward the Shoppe.

Chloe thought of his new dust coating. "And he's changed," Chloe said.

"Wait," May said, confused. "You're not defending him, are you?"

"No, no, no, no, no," said Chloe. *Oh, thank goodness she doesn't have Jason's dust outline. Thank you, God.* She closed the dud box and tucked it in the shelf under the time clock area. "May, let's go running this weekend," she said.

May nodded, swallowing hard. "I don't think the warden will let me."

"The warden?"

"Mommie Dearest . . . AKA Beverly Hicks."

* * *

"You have to be kidding me," said Chloe, looking up from a map of Jefferson High School.

"It's just until Monday afternoon," said Gary. "Candice is going to stay here with you. She rearranged her work schedule for tomorrow so she can drive you to Jefferson in the morning and pick you up on her lunch hour. And May's driving you to school Monday, right?"

Chloe didn't say anything.

"Look, I'm really sorry, but this kind of opportunity doesn't come up very often," said Gary. "I have to be there tomorrow. They've got her in cold storage right now. My flight's at 5 a.m." He flung a small travel case open on the sofa and threw in a Bible, a flashlight, and a toiletry bag.

Chloe grimaced."What exactly are you doing to it?"

"Bertha. She's a rhino that's been living in a nature preserve in Texas for several years. The owner contacted me awhile back and said he'd heard I was a really good taxidermist," Gary said, obviously flattered. "He asked if I could come out when Bertha passed. He's going to donate her to a museum."

Anger seared a few butterflies in Chloe's stomach. *So she had to croak the weekend before I go to public high school?* "But May's grounded from driving for a week," Chloe said, with a huff.

Gary thought for a moment. "Indiana has these great inventions called school buses," he said, teasing her.

* * *

Chloe's heart beat furiously on the way to Jefferson High School.

Candice flipped the turn signal on her pink Jeep and turned into the lot by the front office. "Want me to come in with you?" she asked.

"No, it's okay. I know you have to get to work. Thanks for the ride, Candice."

"Good luck today."

Jefferson High School was in its day-before-school-starts-mode. Teachers were making copies and carrying boxes to their classrooms. Two janitors were doing paint touch-ups in the front foyer, and another was slowly pushing a huge floor-cleaning machine across the wide hallway off the gym.

Breathe in, breathe out. Am I ready for this? How will I survive Monday if I'm a wreck today, when there aren't even any students?

Chloe opened the office door and walked toward a secretary finishing up a phone call.

"How can I help you?"

"Hi. I'm new this year," Chloe said nervously. "I'm supposed to meet someone for a tour."

"I'm Miss Marilyn. I run this office." She rummaged through a few files and looked at Chloe. "Are you Chloe Hudson or Fran Fingers?"

Chloe folded her hands and tugged on her purity ring. "Chloe." *Fran Fingers? Thank God my last name is not fingers!*

"Okay, then. You're with Lily Hunt. She should be here any minute." Miss Marilyn's face brightened. "Oh, you will just love her! She's our head cheerleader. I'm the coach for our girls," she said proudly. "Lily's the president of this year's Junior Class, *and* President of the Sunshine Society. She's also the prettiest and nicest girl I know!" Miss Marilyn took a deep breath before adding her post script. "And she gets straight A's! She's Mr. & Mrs. Hunt's daughter."

Chloe wondered if Miss Marilyn was president of Lily Hunt's fan club. "Are the Hunts teachers here?"

"No," said Miss Marilyn, surprised. "George Hunt is the CEO of the new Dodge Regional Hospital and the Chairman of the School Board--a leader in our community," she said, almost patriotically. "Oh, here's Lily now!" She turned. "Hello, Dear," she said, her tone dripping with a sugary-sweet coating.

Chloe turned to see a beautiful petite girl, dressed preppier-than-thou, with long blonde hair and a striking resemblance to . . . *Mom. Lily even has a thin layer of dust around her body the way Mom did.*

Chloe glanced at the *déjà vu* heart on Lily's chest . . .

A peekadilly center, surrounded by a *thick* layer of . . . *black*? Chloe stared intensely--for a split second, that is. *If there's one thing I've learned about sleuthing* déjà *vu hearts, it's that most girls get creeped out when another girl is staring at her chest.*

Had she ever seen a black *déjà vu heart?* The only black Chloe had seen was Marg's black outline, which was still a mystery to her. What could a *black heart* mean? *I have to write this in my journal!*

"Hi, Chloe, I'm Lily. It's great to meet you! I know you're going to love Jefferson High School." Lily extended her toned, tan arm to Chloe. Her fingernails were perfectly manicured in Jefferson royal blue.

Chloe reached her hand to return the greeting. Her ring caught a ray of the office's fluorescent light and sparkled.

"Wow. What a beautiful ring," said Lily. She held Chloe's hand. That's the prettiest cubic zirconium I've ever seen."

"Oh, actually, it's real," said Chloe. "It was my mom's. She gave it to me to be my purity ring."

"Oh, that is *so* cool," said Lily, genuinely. "I'd love to meet your mom. Is she picking you up later this morning?"

One of those pangs of sadness went through Chloe. It was weird. She never knew when to expect them, but she'd gotten good at masking any outward appearance of them. "No, I live with my uncle."

"Oh, are your parents divorced?" said Lily, compassionately.

Chloe smiled a half smile and shook her head slightly. "No, my mom passed away, and I don't really have a dad, so I'm with my uncle."

"Oh, I'm so sorry."

Chloe looked at the sincerity in Lily's eyes. *What a nice person. I can see becoming friends with Lily.* "You actually kind of remind me of her. She had blonde hair and blue eyes, just like you."

"You mean she wasn't black?"

"No." Chloe paused. "My mom was white. She actually went to school here a long time ago."

"Well, I'm sure she was beautiful," said Lily. Lily took a file folder marked "Chloe Hudson" from Miss Marilyn and politely smiled. "Ready to see Jefferson High?" She headed for the door, opened it, and waited for Chloe. "Thanks, Miss Marilyn," she said, over her shoulder.

"Oh, it's my pleasure, Dear."

Chloe and Lily walked out of the office and down the hallway. "Isn't she *so* annoying?" said Lily.

"Who?"

"Miss Marilyn. She's so over-the-top." Lily stopped briefly and looked into the file. "I'll show you where your locker is first, and then we'll walk your schedule." Lily pulled out two class schedules and gave one to Chloe. "Oh, cool, we're locker neighbors. Hunt. Hudson. I guess that makes sense." Lily smiled and walked toward a large hallway that formed a T with the foyer. "Right this way."

With every step, Chloe's nerves took a small jump. She followed Lily like a mouse in a maze on a cheese hunt. Would she remember how to get to her locker on Monday? Jefferson High School was even bigger than she had envisioned.

"Here we are," Lily said. She pointed to a tall, slim locker. "This one is yours. Your combination is on your schedule. You might want to try your lock a few times." Lily twirled the lock on her own locker and clicked it open.

Inside, she had a lighted mirror with a makeup brush and lip gloss, and lots of pictures of . . . Ty De Veen.

Chloe's heart beat faster as she looked at Ty's picture. He *was* good-looking. But that extra-thick dust coating that he donned in real life had quenched any attraction that Chloe had for him. And thankfully so, because apparently he was with Lily. "Is that your boyfriend?" Chloe asked nonchalantly.

"Yes. That's Ty De Veen. Today's our anniversary. We've been together six months."

I wonder if he's the one who shared his dust with you? "Congratulations," said Chloe. "Do you have anything planned?"

"Yes. Both of our families belong to the Twin Eagles Country Club, so we're all going out for dinner tonight," said Lily. "Our families are good friends. My dad recruited Dr. D from the Netherlands to run the Women's Health Services Department for the hospital when it opened."

"My uncle knows him," said Chloe.

"Is your uncle a member at Twin Eagles?"

"No," Chloe said with a laugh. Changing the subject, she squatted to eye level of the lock, trying to crack the combination. After more tries than she'd hoped, she successfully clicked it open to find textbooks already on the shelf for each of her classes."

"Miss Marilyn gave me your combination. We got all your books together for you," said Lily. "Just to make you feel more at home."

A big smiley face doodled itself on Chloe's heart."Thanks, Lily."

"No problem. On with the tour," said Lily with a smile.

Chloe followed, wishing she'd brought her map of the school to take notes. After more hallways than her mind could hold, they wound back to the large foyer, just past the gym.

Lily stopped in front of a huge trophy case and smiled big.

Next to the case was a 6-foot-7 life-size cutout of Ty De Veen holding a basketball.

"Isn't this great? The cheerleaders had it made," said Lily excitedly. "He's going to love it."

And she thinks Miss Marilyn is over-the-top?

“We have a great chance at winning state this year. Did you know that Indiana University has already signed Ty?”

“Signed?”

“You know. Full-ride scholarship? Davion Griffin signed him the first day he could last year.”

“Wow, he must be pretty good. Who is Davion Griffin?” Chloe asked.

Lily looked slightly shocked. “He’s the head basketball coach for Indiana.” She walked to the end of the trophy case and pointed to a black and white picture next to a huge trophy. “He used to go here. After Jeff, he went to I.U. and then to the NBA, until he got injured. Now he’s the head coach at Indiana. He’s kind of Ty’s idol.” Lily peered at the picture and then stepped back to give Chloe a look. “It’s weird, but you kind of look like him.”

Chloe peered inside the glass trophy case. Which one is he?

Lily playfully rolled her eyes. “He’s the tall one. In the middle.”

“The black guy?” Chloe asked.

Standing a foot taller than his teammates, Davion Griffin looked more like a man than a teen. His skin was blackish brown, at least one shade darker than Chloe’s.

Chloe continued to stare at the picture, scanning the two rows of players, her eyes landing on a familiar face. She smiled big. “That’s my uncle,” she said. “In the suit and tie.”

“Oh, funny,” said Lily. “Is he still friends with Davion Griffin?”

Chloe thought for a moment. “I don’t know. He’s never mentioned him.”

℞

Chapter 14

"Chloe, thank you for rescuing me!" said May, pulling the front door shut behind her. "I couldn't take another minute in that house," she whispered.

"I wasn't sure if she'd get mad at me for asking," said Chloe.

"Jinkies. My mom *loves* you. She'd do anything for you," said May.

"Well, glad I could help you with parole," said Chloe with a laugh. "Even if we only get an hour."

"Let's go to Gary's hunting blind," said May.

"You mean the treehouse?" said Chloe.

"Sure thing, City Girl."

May chit-chatted about the weather, the hang-nail on her pinkie, and an episode of "Scooby Doo" that she'd just watched with the twins.

Chloe feigned interest the whole walk, praying in her head. *What should I say to her? Should I tell her about You? And how You heal sick hearts?*

Chloe stared at her friend's condition, her heart pounding. May looked as if she was suffering from a peekadilly heart attack in progress. *Why wouldn't I tell her?* If your best friend has a disease, and you know the cure, wouldn't you tell her?

Gary's hunting blind was in a thick woods behind one of the soybean fields toward the back of the Hudson Farm. Gary built the blind a few years ago, when the area was designated as "set aside" land for some government program. The woods teemed with wildlife, nearly year-round. The stand resembled a lookout tower built atop posts, elevating it about twelve feet in the air. A sturdy wooden ladder was fastened to the floor of the blind through a square hole. Two of the sides had large square windows that opened to the woods.

Chloe climbed up the ladder first. She took the broom that leaned in the corner and swept the dust from the floor. "Okay," she yelled to May. "It's good."

May climbed up and slid carefully across the floor into pretzel position.

Chloe sat on the edge of the opening and dangled her legs.

The two sat in silence until May burst.

May looked pale. Then red. Then sad. Then completely unraveled. "Chloe, I did it," she blurted. "Jason and I did it."

It? So peekadilly means "it" too? "You did?" Chloe asked slowly.

"Do you think I'm a slut?"

"May, of course not," said Chloe. "But are you okay?"

May squished her upper and lower lip together and closed her eyes. "No. I'm a mess." May leaned her head against the wood. "I gave it away, and now I can't ever get it back again."

"You mean your virginity?"

"Yes." May crossed her hands and felt the pearl ring that Chloe gave her for her birthday. "You know when you said this could be my purity ring?"

Chloe nodded.

"Well, I thought you were such a square when you said that."

Thank you.

"But, I don't now. I feel so . . . ." May got quiet.

"What? How do you feel?"

"Used . . . and scared."

Anger swelled in Chloe. "Is Jason trying to hurt you?"

"No. He's just ignoring me." May's lip began to quiver. "But, I don't even care about that right now. Chloe, what if I'm pregnant? I'm supposed to start this weekend, and I haven't gotten my period. What if I have an STD?"

Chloe looked May's direction, like she was in a trance. No sparkly gold or dust outline. *Thank you, God. Should I tell her about my colors?* Chloe closed her eyes and continued thinking. *Telling another person about the biggest secret of your life is a big deal!* Chloe hesitated and prayed some more, then felt peaceful. And then something more than peace . . . something more like a prompting to tell May. Her face brightened.

May looked hurt. "Chloe, why are you smiling?"

"May. You are *not* pregnant, and you don't have an STD."

"O--kay," said May. "And you know this *how*?"

"Well," Chloe said, "I'm going to tell you something. May, it's pretty bizarre. I've only ever told one person in my whole life."

"You mean, you're not a virgin, either?"

"No. I mean, yes. I am a virgin. But I have this gift . . . ."

May's eyes bulged as she listened intently to the first several chapters of the *Story of Many Colors* by Chloe Rahab Hudson. A short while later, May's face brightened, and a sense of relief came over her entire body. "You mean you don't see a dust or sparkly gold outline around me?"

Chloe shook her head and smiled. "Only your peekadilly *déjà vu* heart."

May saddened and looked down at her chest. "I feel it, Chloe. I can't see it, but I feel it in my heart. I don't know if it's pain, or shame, or regret. I don't know if it's in my heart or in my soul, I just know it hurts."

Chloe smiled again.

May made a face. "There you go again. That's really creepy how you smile when I tell you something bad," she said.

"May, I'm smiling because I know a good heart doctor! I had a peekadilly heart a while back, too."

"But I thought you said you've never done it?"

"I did. I mean, I didn't do *it*. I did something else." Chloe looked frustrated. "What I mean is that I think a peekadilly heart can mean more than one thing." *I wonder what Gary's peekadilly means? Are he and Candice doin' stuff?*

"Well, what did you do?" said May.

Chloe blushed and hesitated.

"Come on. I spilled my guts," said May. "Chloe, I promise I won't tell a soul."

"You know that book you loaned me?"

"The trashy novel from Jason?"

"Yes. Well, one day, I did a bunch of that stuff over and over in my mind."

"With Letter Jacket Boy?" May asked.

"No, with somebody else," said Chloe.

"Who?"

Chloe sighed. "Okay. Ty De Veen."

"Jinkies . . . I don't know him, but, Chloe, I think he's bad news. I think you should stay away from him." May sounded proudly prudent.

"I know. I don't like him anymore . . . anyway, I got a peekadilly heart after that, well, it was actually two-toned."

"Wait, didn't you say you had some other color of heart?"

"Veranda? Yes, When I started seeing my colors on people after I got Mom's ring, I was the only one with a veranda heart. But then when I accepted Christ as my Savior, He covered my veranda heart with bright white. But then when I lusted over that book, my heart was stained with peekadilly, except for a white eyeball in the center. And then when I confessed my sin, my *déjà vu* heart became mostly bright white again, except for a tiny layer of peekadilly." Chloe stopped and caught her breath. "But, I still don't get why some people have sunbeams radiating from their bright white hearts . . . like my Mom, and Marg, and Letter Jacket Boy, and . . . *your parents."* Chloe cleared her throat. "Anyway, I don't have any sunbeams on mine."

May appeared to be in deep thought and then her face looked like it was having an "aha" moment. "I think I get it," she said.

"You do?"

"Sure. Beverly and Chet--the 'rents, you know--have been telling me about this my whole life, but I wasn't going to believe in something just because my parents did. But I think I get it."

"Really?" said Chloe.

"Yes. Christ can't cover your sin, until you see it for yourself and admit it, because if you don't see yourself as a sinner, you can't see your need for a Savior. So He gave you the gift of seeing your veranda heart."

So veranda was all my sin?

"And then, for some strange reason, He's given you the gift of seeing peekadilly, which must mean different types of sexual sin," said May.

Some strange reason? Didn't Mom pray for some special discernment for me about purity? And then my colors came out of her ring! Chloe looked down at the ring on her finger, then held it out and gazed at it. *Wow. How did May come up with that?* Chloe replayed her *déjà vu* discoveries in her head, then looked over at May.

May's eyes were closed. A look of peace was emanating from her . . . and her *déjà vu* heart was bright white, except for a tiny bit of peekadilly around the edges.

I see you met my Friend, and Physician, Chloe thought, smiling. She waited for May to open her eyes. And waited about 15 minutes more. Then closed her own eyes. *Thank you, God.*

"Chloe," May said. "I don't think you should tell anybody else about your colors. I won't tell anyone either."

* * *

Am I ready for Jefferson High School? When I am afraid, I will trust in you.

I AM WITH YOU, CHLOE.

The bus ride Monday morning wasn't that bad. May seemed like a new person, back to her bubbly self, but different, too, in a way Chloe couldn't quite describe.

Unfortunately, May's and her class schedules were like two ships that passed in the night. No classes together. No "B" lunch together. But at least their lockers were in the same general vicinity.

The bus turned into the circular drive of Jefferson High and screeched to a stop.

"Are you okay?" said May. "You look pale. You're not going to ralph, are you?"

Butterflies were fluttering in Chloe's stomach. *Breathe in, breathe out. When I am afraid, I will trust in you.* "No, I'm okay." Chloe forced a smile and swung her backpack over her shoulder, following May off the bus.

The main foyer of Jefferson High was crowded. May and Chloe joined a herd of *déjà vu* students headed for the hallways with lockers.

May introduced Chloe to a few students on the way. After each one, she stopped and whispered, "So, does she have dust? Do you see a color on him? Oh, this is going to be so much fun!"

Annoyance instantly formed inside of Chloe. "May," she said, searing a gaze. "Stop. You promised."

"I promised not to *tell* anyone, but not to *ask* about anyone."

"May, I'm not kidding. Seriously. You *have* to promise never to bring up my colors again. *Never* again," Chloe said. "I mean it." She stared into May's eyes and put her hand on her arm. "Please."

May looked remorseful. "You're right. I'm sorry."

"So, you promise?"

"Yes, I promise."

A bell rang throughout the hallway.

"Jinkies, I have to pee," said May. "You better get to your locker. If I don't see you today, look for me in the bus line, K? Good luck."

Chloe walked toward her locker, feeling a group of guys staring at her every move. Did she just hear the words "hot?" and "black?"

One of them laughed and elbowed the guy next to him. "Fresh meat," he mumbled.

The guy laughed back. "So go make your kill, or is she too tall for you?"

Chloe felt her face blush. *Yes, I'm way too tall for you!* She walked faster, ignoring them.

"Hey, Chloe!" called Lily. "How was your weekend?"

A group of pretty girls congregated by Lily's locker, waiting for her.

"Good. Did you have a nice dinner with your boyfriend?"

Lily smiled. "It was mint. He gave me this," she said, pointing to a plastic white rose that she'd wound through the coils of a notebook. "Wasn't that thoughtful of him?"

A fake rose? *I hope my Mr. Right never gives me a fake rose!* The terms *fake* and *rose* should *not* go together. *So* unromantic. *So* cheesier than Cheese Whiz. "Nice," Chloe said, nodding.

Lily looked like she'd stepped off the cover of a Today's Prepster catalog, except for her black and peekadilly *déjà vu* heart and her dust outline. She wore a cute, pink and green polo shirt with walking shorts and sequin boat shoes. Her make-up was tastefully applied, accenting her beautiful features, and she wore lots of gold jewelry.

I wonder if Mom looked like that when she was in high school here?

Lily introduced Chloe to her group of friends. "Check out this ring, guys." Lily lifted Chloe's hand to show them.

I hope they don't think my fingers are fat.

The girls seemed to like Chloe's ring more than they liked Chloe.

"So, do you know where you're going first?" said Lily, pleasantly.

Chloe looked at Lily. *She's so pretty, yet so nice. She has tons of friends, but she's still trying to make me feel welcome.* But Lily's eyes looked sad, in spite of the smile that was painted on her face.

"Yes. I'm headed to French class first, Room 352."

"Well, bonjour," said Lily.

* * *

Room 352 reeked of cheap perfume. The name Pamela Pip was written in large, purple cursive letters on the blackboard in the front of the room. A world map hung on one wall with the country of France outlined heavily in black. Strings of Mardi Gras beads lay in swirls on the counter that spanned one whole wall of the classroom.

The room buzzed with small talk. Students were shuffling in and finding seats. A few guys turned around and smiled at her.

Chloe's heart raced. *Why do I get so nervous around guys? It's just a smile. It's not like they're asking me to marry them!* Chloe chided herself, squirming nervously in her chair. Though it was only first period, she'd already bagged the idea of being Miss Outgoing and Miss Talkative today. That would come, right? Today was about survival. There were plenty more days ahead to learn how to talk to boys. *Heck, by the end of the year, I'll probably be speaking in full sentences with some of these guys!*

From the back row, far corner, Chloe hoped to be invisible. She quietly pulled out her *déjà vu* journal to make a quick note. "Lots of peekadilly hearts in French class--and *lots* of guys. Some have a dust outline, but no dust swirls in their hearts. *Does that mean they don't know they have an STD?*

Chloe's bright white heart felt like a minority, and so did she, in more ways than one. First, she was the only person in the class with skin color deeper than a light tan. And second, weren't there *any* other girls interested in learning French at Jefferson? She checked her schedule again. *French I with Pip, Room 352. Yep, that's here.*

The intercom chirped, and the sound of Miss Marilyn's voice piped into the room. "Welcome back to school, Jefferson students. I have a few general announcements for you. First, remember your cell phones must be turned off during all classes or they will be confiscated. Second, our Cheerleader Fundraiser is beginning today. If you'd like to buy a life-size cutout of our very own Ty De Veen, be sure to stop by the office or see Lily Hunt. And, finally, please help us in welcoming our two new students, Chloe Hudson and Fran Fingers."

Chloe cringed and slouched in her chair. Was the guy next to her staring at her hands? She looked over at him.

"Are you Fran?" he said.

No, my name is not Fran Fingers! "I'm Chloe."

A rhythmic tapping sound was coming down the hallway and getting louder. A silver high heel tapped through the doorway of the classroom.

A shot of shock jolted in Chloe and her eyes popped. *Oh my.* She stared as her mouth dropped open. *She's my French teacher?*

A hush fell over the room as Pamela Pip strolled carefully to the front of the room. Miss Pip wore fuchsia-colored jeans that looked painful and a tiny white jean jacket over a low cut black T-shirt with obscure white letters. Her long, mousy brown hair was as crispy as bacon, perhaps the result of over straightening. Her lips looked like they had kissed a bottle of Botox and her eyelashes were the kind only seen on mascara commercials, not on real people. It was hard to tell her age. Maybe mid-thirties? Miss Pip put some copies on the desk and turned to greet the class. "*Mon nom est Pamela Pip. Vous allez aimer m'avoir comme enseignant*," she said.

Miss Pip's welcome dripped with seduction. At the end of each phrase, she pursed her bright pink lips, zeroing in on one of her male students and twitching her penciled eyebrows up, teasing him.

Miss Pip's *déjà vu* heart was distinctly bright peekadilly.

Chloe heard the sound of steps coming from the hallway again. In walked the largest shoe she'd ever seen. That had to be size 16 or something! Attached to it was a beautiful masculine tan leg smothered, coated, and top-coated in dust. Ty De Veen!

The strong scent of Fitch cologne wafted behind him. He walked to the front row of the class and took an empty seat, front and center.

"Hello, Mr. De Veen," said Miss Pip in French.

Ty responded with something in Dutch, making Miss Pip smile.

"Okay, guys," she said, turning and walking toward her desk. "I have a syllabus for you." She took the pile of papers and tapped the stack's edges on the top of the desk. Then set them down again. She squared her shoulders and clasped the sides of her jacket, pulling it open and off of her arms, then hung it on the back of the chair and picked up the papers again.

Apparently, Victoria's Secret was out of the Size Large T-shirts. Consequently, Miss Pip had poured herself into what looked like an extra small--so small, that the letters spelling P-I-N-K were distorted. The black cotton material heaved two inches of cleavage, reminding Chloe of a baby's butt.

Chloe felt some puke forming in her stomach, but not from nerves. *Oh, Puhleese! Now I know why I'm a minority in here.* She looked around the classroom at her fellow classmates--twenty or so guys, hungry to learn French.

Chapter 15

Ty De Veen

Ty De Veen counted three things: Basketball points, Facebook Friends, and the number of girls he'd had sex with. Moving from the Netherlands to Dodge had paid off in every area. Last year as a junior he dominated the team, the boards, and local news media coverage. The Jefferson Bobcats made it to State last year, the first time since his idol had played here more than 15 years ago. *We would have won it if that j@*!x had passed me the ball.*

Indiana University had promptly signed him on his first day of eligibility, and Davion Griffin had even attended the signing. One more year at Jefferson High School and he'd shake the dust off this scummy little town and get to Bloomington--his next stepping stone to the NBA.

Ty entered the cafeteria and spotted his buddies at the front of the Ala Carte Line. One of them waved him over, offering him cuts.

He wiped a bead of sweat from his forehead and placed his cell phone back in his pocket. He walked across the cafeteria, feeling heads turn as he went.

"Yo," his friend grunted.

Ty looked around the cafeteria, his eyes landing on a new specimen. Who was she? He stared at her brown face, framed with long, shiny black hair and zeroed in on her eyes. Black. Piercing. Sexy. And familiar. He looked her up and down. How could she look like Davion Griffin? After all, Griffin never had kids--it would have ruined his basketball career.

Ty felt two arms loop around his waist from behind him. He clasped the hands and turned around. "Hey, Lily."

"What's for lunch today?" she asked flirtatiously.

Ty ignored her question. "Hey, do you know who that black girl is over there?" Ty motioned to the corner of the cafeteria where the girl sat by herself, eating Mexican. He stared on.

Lily scanned over to that direction and looked at the girl, then turned back to Ty. "Nope." She stood on her tiptoes, cupping his face downward toward hers, inviting a kiss.

Perturbed, he pulled away. "Hey, not here. Coach warned us that they're writing athletes up this year for PDAs."

Lily looked disappointed. She placed a salad and a bottled water on the tray, moving it to the side to make room for Ty's two foot-long sandwiches.

He pulled his wallet from his Fitch shorts and tossed a $20 bill on the tray. "I'll get us a table," he said, leaving Lily at the register. Then he walked past several empty tables, straight toward the back corner.

* * *

The *déjà vu* Dutchman was coming toward her.

Chloe could smell the scent of his Fitch cologne mix with her Nacho cheese sauce as he got closer. Was he going to sit here? A month ago she had dreamed about this moment, but not anymore. She crunched her tortilla chip, looking straight ahead.

"Is dis seat taken?" he said, towering over her.

She looked up. And looked up some more.

A very tall pillar of dust with a Big and Tall peekadilly heart stared back at her, hovering.

A jolt of fear went through her, surprising her. How could I go from drooling over this guy to being afraid of him? "Um . . no," she said nervously. "Go ahead."

"Hello, I'm Ty De Veen," he said. He extended his large arm toward her.

Chloe popped the tortilla chip she was holding in her mouth and reciprocated.

Ty clasped it, and put his other hand over the handshake, holding it for one second too long--just enough to make it uncomfortable. Ty let go, and looked at Chloe's hand. "You have a goot, firm handtshake," he said, smiling.

Chloe finished chewing the soggy chip in her mouth, swallowed hard, and quickly popped another chip in.

"So, what's your name?" said Ty.

"Chloe," she said, accidentally spraying a tiny triangle of chip in the air. She looked up, relieved to see Lily.

Lily gave Ty a disgusted look. She banged the tray down and began transferring the food to the table. She sat down and removed the lid from her salad and speared some lettuce like she was pitchforking hay.

Ty returned her disgusted look.

"Hi, Lily!" Chloe said. "How are your classes?"

Lily looked up from her tray, stared at Chloe, and cocked her head. "What's your name, again?" she said with a snippy tone.

A shiver went through Chloe, then hurt. Really? *I can't believe this! I thought we were going to be friends.* Chloe's spirit inside of her picked up a brick and quickly stacked it on two other ones, forming the beginning of an interior wall. She stared back at Lily, her look communicating, "You don't intimidate me."

The temperature of Chloe's blood went from 98.6 to 100 in a split second. *I'd like to tell you about your little STD, Missy. And who knows what that black heart on you means!*

CHLOE, I WANT YOU TO LOVE LILY, AS I LOVE YOU. I WANT YOU TO BUILD A BRIDGE, NOT A WALL.

Even when she's being a big poop? I mean, come on, she totally knows my name!

CHLOE, I LOVED YOU, EVEN WHEN YOU WEREN'T LOVABLE, AND EVEN WHEN YOU STILL AREN'T.

God, did you just call me unlovable?

NO, CHLOE. I CALL YOU MY CHILD, AND I LOVE YOU AND FORGIVE YOU, EVEN WHEN YOU DISAPPOINT ME.

Chloe's fight-or-flight instinct bit the awkward silence. She feigned a smile as she stood and gathered her lunch trash. OK. Maybe Lily is just having an off moment. "Hey, great to see you guys. I actually need to get going."

"Bye," said Lily, with distinct punctuation.

Chloe walked out of the cafeteria, feeling two Dutch eyes seared on her back side.

* * *

On Tuesday, May was on parole for driving again. She steered into the parking lot of Jefferson High School. "This car is so embarrassing," she said.

Chloe's heart beat nervously as she looked at the entrance of Jefferson High. *Let's hope day two is better than day one.* "It's better than riding the bus," she said.

"Which reminds me," said May, rolling her eyes. "I have to text the warden that I drove cautiously to school and that I'm sending this text when the car is parked." She pulled her phone from her purse. "Next year we're riding in your cute, blue bug, right?"

Next year? I just want to make it through today! "Right," said Chloe. *I just have to get used to it,* Chloe reassured herself. Hadn't she dreamed of going to public school most of her childhood?

A girl with sparkly gold leaned against one of the tall lampposts, looking like she was waiting for someone. The girl looked tired and like she didn't feel well.

Moments later, a black hummer flew into the parking lot. It screeched to a stop in a space down the way from her.

The girl walked to the driver's side and waited.

Ty De Veen emerged from the SUV, opened a notebook and handed her a small, square piece of white paper.

Chloe saw the girl mutter, "Thanks," and then walk into the building alone.

"Okay. C'mon," said May. "Day two, here we come."

"No, wait," said Chloe, crouching down in her seat. "Wait until Ty De Veen goes in."

"Chloe, you're crazy if you think you'll be able to avoid Ty De Veen."

A shadow went behind May's green pickle.

A tap on Chloe's window just about made her pee her pants. She turned slowly and looked out.

"Hi, Chloe," said an extremely large, dust coated, peekadilly Dutchman flashing a smile her way. "I'll valk you to French class."

"Speak of the devil," whispered May, teasing her.

* * *

Friday . . . finally. Chloe breathed a sense of relief. Hadn't this been the longest week of her life? She stood by her locker, compiling a mental checklist of weekend homework. She pulled her French and biology books from her locker and put them in her satchel.

Chloe felt . . . watched. Like a paramecium under a microscope. Was it Ty De Veen again or Queen Bee Lily and her worker bees?

For the past week Ty De Veen appeared to be *everywhere* Chloe was. Every time she came out of the girls' bathroom, he'd be leaning against the wall, as if he was waiting for her. In Pip's class, Chloe would intentionally come in late and sit in the back. Right away, Ty would move from his front row perch and sit next to her, even if it meant carrying a chair four feet in the air above everyone's head. On Thursday afternoon, Ty came up to Chloe and said, "I heard you were talking to Jake White in biology. And Kirk Brown in study hall. Big Mistake."

It was enough to creep a girl out.

And make another one furious.

By day two of school Lily had recruited forces to eradicate this new unwanted pest. She and her cheerleading friends formed a Share & Stare Club, with Chloe as the bullseye. Between classes they would high-tail it to the lockers, so they could be waiting. Queen Bee Lily would come up with the verbal-sucker-punches to Chloe's stomach, while her worker bees looked and cheered on.

"That ring is so fake," said Queen Bee.

And all her mindless colony would reply, "You're *so* right, Lily. It's *so* fake."

"What a loser," said Queen Bee. "She can't even get a boyfriend, so she's trying to steal mine."

And everyone in the hive said, "Anybody who doesn't have a boyfriend *is* a loser!"

"Did you see those hands?" Lily impersonated Porky Pig and said, "Th-th-that's all, folks." And then one of the cheerleader bees used her thumb to make a pig nose at Chloe.

But yesterday's sting was a new low.

"Stop staring at us, you . . . ." said one of the girls.

Chloe felt like she'd been hit with a stun-gun. A shot of angst mixed with hurt and humiliation pooled inside of her. No way. *Did she just call me the N word? I can't believe someone would use a word like that! Really?*

That was the other thing. A high school *this* size with no minorities?

Chloe had counted how many black kids she'd seen at Jefferson High School this week. The result? Zero. Zilch. Zip. Nada. She felt like an Oreo in a sea of milk, or perhaps in a *déjà vu* milkshake.

"She's such a freak," said Lily. "She stares at people's chests."

And I stare at their outlines. Oh, I'd like to tell her about that little dust problem of hers!

Slowly, she turned her head, zeroing in on one of the girls, and her mouth dropped open. Sparkly gold! She did not have sparkly gold yesterday. Did she get pregnant last night? Chloe held her glance for a few seconds, *Should I tell her?* It's not like you can really tap a girl on the shoulder and say, "Hey, by the way, I was just wondering, do you happen to know you're pregnant?" or, "Just curious, did you study more than your homework last night?"

"What are you looking at?" snapped Lily.

Chloe's insides began to bubble. She wasn't sure if it was tears or anger, but whichever was about to explode. She slammed the door of her locker and walked quickly past them.

God, how can you love people like that? Like Lily?

CHLOE, I CREATED LILY AND CHOSE HER. I LOVE HER, AND I HAVE A GREAT PLAN AND PURPOSE FOR HER.

But she's so mean.

I DON'T WAIT UNTIL PEOPLE ARE PERFECT TO LOVE THEM.

Chloe silenced the voice in her head, then ignored it. *Who's side is He on, anyway?*

"Party on, it's Friday!" said a skinny red-headed boy darting down the hallway past her. He scurried to pull his jeans off the ground, scooping them back over his boxers.

Chloe fell in step with a herd of students walking briskly for the door. The warm summer air hit her face, encouraging her. She scanned the parking lot looking for May. *Thank goodness I have May. And Anjou.*

"Hurry!" May called to Chloe from across the parking lot, waiving her Anjou beret in her hand.

She and Chloe piled into the car. May gunned on the gas, putting her at the front of the parade of cars streaming out of Jefferson High. "Now would be a good time for some tunes, but this hunk-of-you-know-what doesn't work," said May, tapping the CD/radio player. She tapped her fingers on the steering wheel, her pearly ring bobbing up and down, as though she was singing a song in her head. "Got my research assignment today for my Hoosier history class."

"Did you get Johnny Appleseed, like you wanted?

"No," said May, scrunching her nose. "We drew numbers and the first chiquita picked him. I got the last pick--a guy named Alfred Kinsey. Ever heard of him?"

"Nope."

℞

Chapter 16

Wonder if Smith will be in tonight? For the past four weeks, at exactly 4:30 p.m. on Friday, Smith--AKA Letter Jacket Boy--seemed to crave his favorite coffee drink. Whenever the order machine spit out a ticket for a double cappuccino mocha, Chloe's heart would jump. She'd crane her neck out into the Shoppe, and there he'd be, looking back at her with his beautiful white smile, bright white *déjà vu* heart with sunbeams and tousled hair. But always with another girl.

Chloe opened the Nambygram addressed to her, before punching the time clock. "Chloe, You have come a long way on mastering your coffee drinks. I think we shall now utilize your excellent customer service skills on the register in the Shoppe. Anjouly Yours, Henry Namby."

"May, I'm in the Shoppe with you tonight," said Chloe, smiling.

May punched her timecard. "I wish. I'm on fall cleaning duty again," she said, making a face.

Poor May had been given the task of scrubbing every baseboard in the break room, Large Kitchen, and Mail Order, thanks to a certain Jason-who-had-lost-his-benefits.

The Anjou Shoppe was deserted, probably because the weather outside was perfect--a sunny, cool, crisp fall day.

Chloe tidied the area around the register and wiped a glob of hardened chocolate off the counter. She swept the floor, stocked the cases, and completed every task on the "extra jobs" list.

Customers trickled into the Shoppe every once-in-a-great while, interrupting her mental evaluations and analyzations of things like *déjà vu*, romance, God, and what to be when she grew up.

Chloe glanced at the clock. Could time go any slower?

Only fifteen more minutes and Gary will be picking me up.

Gary had been spending more time with Candice lately, and Chloe loved her, but she missed Gary. Tonight, they were going out for Mexican, just the two of them.

Chloe grabbed a tall blue bottle of glass cleaner and then walked into the lobby. She sprayed clouds of white foam all over the case and began wiping them away.

A gust of cool air blew on her back as the door opened. The silhouettes of several customers reflected from the glass case, calling her into customer-service mode.

She finished wiping the glass case quickly and scurried behind the counter, tossing the towel under the register. She turned to the new audience of customers. "May I help someone?"

Three *déjà vu* hearts shone back at her.

A warm feeling bubbled in her as she glanced at Gary and his bright white heart. *His peekadilly heart is getting covered by more bright white every day, just like mine!* She smiled at him and then glanced straight ahead at the customer before her.

Gary acknowledged, then hovered toward the side of the lobby next to . . .

Smith!

Smith looked as if he had just showered, his hair still kind of wet. He wore dark jeans and a button-down navy oxford shirt, which made his *déjà vu* heart sparkle brilliantly. He flashed Chloe that model-like smile, politely waiting by Gary, so the other customer could go first. "Hi," he said to Gary, in a friendly tone.

Chloe stared at Gary and Smith standing side-by-side. Smith's bright white heart was intensely bright, a few shades whiter than Gary's *déjà vu* heart. It had no visible traces of peekadilly, and lots of sunbeams bursting from it.

I hope he talks to Gary! I hope I talk to him! This is my chance. Hey, I'm not even that nervous.

Chloe turned toward the customer who was standing closest to the register and paused in surprise.

Miss Pip! Pam-eh-ooh-la-la-pip, as most of her students called her. Pip's peekadilly heart looked like a stain on her too-small, red halter top. Black leather pants and brat-doll shoes completed her outfit, making her look like she was on her way to a street corner. She appeared to be in her own little tech world, oblivious to the fact that Gary and Smith were waiting for her.

Maybe.

"Hi, Miss Pip. Can I help you?" said Chloe.

Miss Pip looked up and acted as if Chloe had startled her, causing her to drop her phone somewhere in the middle of Gary and Smith.

Four feet away.

She looked at them both and took tiny steps in her four-inch heels toward them.

Smith started to move like he was going to pick it up for her, but before he could . . .

She bent over. Slowly. Deliberately. Like a giraffe bending over to eat grass, legs locked, and body thrust forward and down. She held the stance for several seconds, as her long red fingernails hindered her ability to pick up her phone that she had clenched moments earlier. What little her halter top had left to the imagination, was now front and center as an eyeful to Gary and Smith.

Chloe stared at the situation. Would Gary and Smith react the way the typical French student at Jefferson High School did whenever Miss Pip dropped a pencil on the floor?

Miss Pip seemed to have butter fingers. She'd drop pencils, one at a time, then look up at her target to see if there was a reaction. Most of the French peekadilly students would get a far-off crazed look in their eyes, holding their gaze on the deep crevice on Pip's chest.

"May I help you?" Chloe asked again, watching the scene with anticipation.

Miss Pip ignored her second plea to help her with her chocolate order.

Both Gary and Smith, almost in sync, turned their heads to the side, bouncing their eyes like they were bouncing a basketball against a wall. Gary walked over to the case, as though he was analyzing the newest flavor of truffles.

Curiosity seared through Chloe's bones like a kitten that has just seen a baby mouse. She followed Gary's *déjà vu* heart. Did the few sunbeams on his heart just flicker and grow? She looked at Smith. Did his sunbeams and bright white heart just get whiter? *This is fascinating.*

Smith moved toward the register, pulled a paper menu from the plastic rack and began perusing it. After a few seconds he looked up and smiled at Chloe and gave her a look like they'd just shared a secret.

Miss Pip retrieved her phone and carefully tiptoed to the register, cutting in front of Smith. Her huff declared her defeat. She looked at Chloe and said, "*Vous n'êtes pas dans mon cours de français?*"

Chloe felt her face turn beet red as Smith watched for her response. "Um . . . I'm sorry. I don't know what you said."

A flare of disgust flashed behind Miss Pip's long eyelashes. "I said," she snapped, "aren't you in my French class?"

"Oh . . . yes," said Chloe. *Ahem. I haven't learned any French yet,* because *how is a person supposed to concentrate in a crockpot of peekadilly?*

"You're Fran Fingers, right?" Miss Pip laid her phone down on the counter, face up, displaying an image that was less than family-friendly.

Not again! Chloe looked at Smith. *Is he looking at my fingers?* "No. I'm Chloe."

"Well, Chloe," said Miss Pip, tapping her long nails on the counter. "Do you sell any chocolate . . . that's kind of fun?" she asked, glancing at Smith flirtatiously.

Smith smirked, then scrunched his face.

Chloe thought for a moment. She put on a white glove and opened the case next to her. She pulled out a white chocolate army guy and held it in the air for Miss Pip to see. “These are kind of fun. Do you want to try a sample?”

Miss Pip rolled her eyes. “How are those fun?” she said, annoyed. “Just give me a one-pound box.”

Anticipation was growing inside of Chloe. Only a few more seconds and she’d get to wait on Smith! She filled Miss Pip’s order and punched it into the register. “Thank you,” she said to Miss Pip, making change and handing it to her. Now . . . for Letter Jacket Boy! She turned her gaze to Smith, who was . . . gone.

In his place stood Gary. Gary registered Chloe’s apparent look of disappointment. “Nice to see you, too,” he said, sarcastically.

Chloe scanned the Shoppe. No trace. Nowhere. Did he go to the bathroom? “Gary, did you see where that guy went? The one who was standing here.”

“I saw him get a text on his cell phone, and he darted out,” said Gary. “You still off at 7?”

Disappointment trickled in the wellspring of Chloe’s heart. To think that she was actually talking like a coherent human being on the day Smith came in alone. What were the chances? Shoot.

* * *

Chloe was more interested in Gary’s *déjà vu* heart than she was in her fajitas at El Torpedo’s. She studied it throughout dinner, so much so, that he kept asking if he’d spilled something on his shirt.

Gary’s heart definitely got at least a couple of new sunbeams tonight during the little episode with Miss Pip, and Chloe wanted to know why.

“You’ve changed,” she said. “What’s going on?”

"Haven't had a smoke for 22 days now," he said, proudly.

Chloe stared at him, like she was waiting for the next part. "What else? I know there is something else."

Gary blushed and looked around like he was an undercover agent. "Okay," Gary began. "There is something else, but I don't want to talk about it here." He took a big sip of Coke and swished it around in his mouth. "When we get home."

Chloe brimmed with anticipation on the way home. What could Gary's revelation be?

Once home, Chloe made hot chocolate while Gary started a fire in the fireplace. She handed him a tall Anjou Fine Chocolates mug with two large marshmallows floating on top. "Gary, I want to ask you something. It's kind of embarrassing."

"About your female thing?" he said. "Have you had it yet?"

Ouch. "No, it's not about that," said Chloe.

"I wanted to ask you about tonight at Anjou."

"What about it?"

"Well, you know that lady who was there?"

"The one with the big boobs?"

Chloe did a slight double-take. Boobs? Do uncles say that sort of thing? "Um. Yes. That's the one. She's a teacher at my school. Her name is Miss Pip."

"What about her?"

"Well, do you think she's attractive?"

"I didn't really give myself a chance to notice."

"Precisely!" Chloe sounded like Inspector Clueso. "I saw you look away really quick." *And I'm wondering how your bright white heart got brighter, with more sunbeams, as a result of looking away from big boobs!*

Gary sat silent.

"Well?"

"Well, what?" Gary said with a smirk.

"Tell me." Chloe's stare pleaded for scoop. "Look, I know you're with Candice. But I want to know what went through your mind when you saw Miss Pip."

"Why do you want to know?" Gary teased.

"Because that other guy in the Shoppe did the same thing," Chloe hesitated, then softly finished her sentence. "And I kind of like him."

Gary smiled and took a sip of his hot chocolate. He paused, then said, "Okay. You're a big girl, so I'll tell you. I have changed, and I'm gonna tell you why. But I don't want your judgment. I'm telling you my junk, Chloe. It's between us, okay?"

This sounds bigger than I'm even imagining. Juicy! Chloe felt like a junkyard eagerly anticipating a new load of junk.

"When I saw your teacher, I bounced my eyes and said a Bible verse in my head. Then I prayed for help to resist the temptation to think lustful thoughts, and for strength to love her as one of God's children," he said, matter-of-factly.

Chloe sat in silence, processing. She rolled Gary's words around her head over and over, trying to absorb them. *The Word and prayer equals more bright white and less peekadilly?* Makes sense. Prayer and the Word would make someone more pure, right? Like Mom . . . and Marg, and . . . Smith! Smith must bounce his eyes too!

Little cupids started dancing in Chloe's heart as she thought of Smith. Any guy can lust. Any guy can give it away. But, it takes a *real* man to be pure. She smiled to herself. *Okay, God. I'm officially interested in Smith. Let the matchmaking begin!*

CHLOE, FALL IN LOVE WITH ME.

Then Chloe spaced off, reveling in her new déjà vu discovery.

Gary was in the midst of chapter two of his story. "Well, haven't you?" he asked Chloe.

"Haven't I what?"

"Ever wondered why I don't have a computer or cell phone anymore?"

Yes. I think that's weird. And annoying. "Kind of. Why did you get rid of your cell phone?"

Gary was silent. "And haven't you wondered what all the recent appointments are for?"

I thought they were farming stuff.

"Chloe, I've been seeing a counselor to help me."

"Help you, what?"

"Help me recover."

Recover?

"A few years ago, I got really lonely and bored."

Understandable.

"Well, Chloe, men are visual. That's how God made us . . . and, I got addicted."

"To drugs?"

"No. To porn," said Gary.

Ick.

"To sin, really," said Gary. "To lust. I've been seeing a counselor since last year, and he's helped me learn how to fight sexual temptation. He gave me some verses to memorize, but I think my real change has come from being in the Word every day and praying. I've been letting Christ fight my battle."

"Did my mom know about your problem?"

"Yes. She was praying for me. And she wasn't going to let you live with me, until she talked to my counselor."

"Wait. I thought Mom said you became a Christian a long time ago."

"I did . . . when she was pregnant with you. After she found Christ, she was a totally different person. I wanted what she had."

"Then how did you become . . . ?"

"I didn't stay connected to Christ. I stopped going to church when you and your mom moved. I didn't read the Word or pray. And pretty soon I didn't hear God speaking to me anymore. I just heard temptation whispering to me . . . and I started to answer it, but now I ask God for help."

"What happens to a guy who doesn't ask God for help?"

"Well, porn can lead to really bad things because its progressive. That means as time goes on, it takes more deviant acts to quench an addict's sexual desires."

G-ross.

"And my counselor says it can cause a lot of problems in relationships," said Gary, "and marriage."

Well, I would guess so! What girl dreams of her Prince Charming having a porn problem? Chloe looked at Gary's expression of worry. "Does Candice know?" she asked.

"No. I'm hoping it won't be a big deal to her."

A compassion welled within Chloe for Gary. "I hope so, too."

℞

Chapter 17

"Put on the full armor of God so that you can take your stand against the devil's schemes." Ephesians 6:11

"Good Morning, Ladies," said the hostess at Berry's Pancake House. She ushered Marg and Chloe to the last open booth. Marg scooted in her side, pushing the table out for more room. "Child, I've been looking forward to this all week." Marg flipped over her coffee mug.

The aroma of fresh coffee and cinnamon rolls wafted through the restaurant.

Warm sunshine streamed through the window, warming Chloe. Or was it coming from Marg's bright white heart from across the table? Chloe closed her eyes, basking in it for a moment. This past week had shivered her soul. She felt as though she was on the edge of a cliff, tipped forward and circling her arms to keep from falling into a canyon of colliding concerns.

Lily and her friends hate me. Ty De Veen is scary. I'm the only brown girl in my whole high school. I don't like seeing dust and peekadilly. I miss Mom. Maybe I haven't gotten my period because I'm sick. Miss Pip. French class. All of Smith's girlfriends. Gary was addicted to porn? What if I don't know what I should be when I grow up? Or go to the wrong college? Or marry the wrong Mr. Right?

"So how was your first week at Jefferson High School?" asked Marg.

Chloe pressed her lips together and looked at a coffee pot gurgling in the waitress station. She paused, then her lower lip quivered. Each of her fears had put on a pair of punching gloves and were in the ring together, inside her head.

Marg reached her arm across the table and touched Chloe's forearm. "You okay, Child?"

A thread in Chloe's heart began to unravel from Marg's tug. She felt raw. Lonely. Scared. *I don't want to cry.* But bubbles started to form in the corner of her eyes.

"Let's go," said Marg, shuffling her large body out of the booth. She took a five dollar bill and laid it under her coffee cup. Marg held out her hand for Chloe to grasp and headed for the exit. She opened the passenger door of her car for Chloe. "Come on," she said, motioning Chloe in.

Chloe sat on the seat and broke down. How embarrassing!

Marg started to drive. "You just let it all out, now. Everybody needs a good cry now and then. It's healthy."

Minutes later Marg pulled her car into the driveway of a small, brick ranch house. "We'll go to my house for a bit. I bought some of that green tea you like, and I was hopin' I'd get to share it with you sometime."

The thought gave Chloe's heart reprieve. She followed Marg, waiting behind her as she unlocked the door.

"Elmer! It's just us," said Marg. "I've got Chloe with me."

Chloe heard a door open down the hallway, then footsteps.

Elmer had a warm smile and a bright white heart that matched Marg's. But no black outline around his body like Marg's. "Chloe, I've heard a lot about you," said Elmer, extending his hand. "Welcome to our home."

The Workman's home was small and welcoming. The front door led into the living room, painted light cream with a pink-and-blue flowered sofa and two La-Z-Boy chairs. A small round table sat in the corner. It was topped with a doily and lots of pictures in frames. Above the sofa was a family picture of a much younger Marg and Elmer and four teens, all of them white.

Elmer noticed Chloe looking at the picture. "That's a nice family, wouldn't you say?"

I've always dreamed of a family, with a mom and dad and kids. "It really is," said Chloe, smiling.

"Marg and I will be married for half a century this year." He touched Marg's arm and rubbed it. Then he kissed her lightly on the lips.

"Yep." Marg smiled. "One of the families from our church is gonna have a big ol' party for us this summer. We'll put you and your uncle on the invite list, if you want, Child."

Elmer paused. "I was just practicing my sermon for tomorrow," he said. "You mind?" He turned and headed for the hall. "I know Marg has invited you before, but I want you to know you're always welcome at our church."

"Thank you," said Chloe.

"You sure are, Child." Marg smiled at Elmer. "Chloe and I are going to have some green tea."

"Green, heh?"

"It's new Elmer. That's what they drink in California." She turned to Chloe. "Come on in the kitchen, Child."

Chloe jotted a mental note of admiration. Marg and Elmer were cute. They seemed to really love each other, even after fifty years. Isn't *that* what girls dream of? Whose happily-ever-after includes getting divorced?

Marg quickly brewed some tea and set out a plate of home-made oatmeal raisin cookies. "Have a seat, and tell Marg what's been going on."

Chloe tried to be stoic, but that only lasted five seconds. Upon Marg's second gentle nudge, Chloe spilled her guts. She told Marg about everything--well, not her colors, or Gary, since she had promised--but all the other stuff going on.

Marg listened intently and nodded with compassion, occasionally asking a question or two for clarification.

After Chloe shared for at least an hour, and Marg had eaten the plate of cookies, Marg said, "You need to learn how to fight."

A small bead of confidence started to form inside of Chloe. *I would like to fight. These fingers of mine would make a mighty nice knuckle sandwich for a certain Lily's lunch!* "I think you're right. Have you ever hit somebody?"

"No, Child. You've got to understand the battle, so you know how to fight. You aren't fighting against a *person*--this Lily, or Ty, or anybody else at your school. They aren't the enemy. They're your neighbors."

"Well, then, who is my enemy?" asked Chloe.

"The Bible says our battle isn't against flesh and blood, but against the spiritual forces of evil in the heavenly realms. That means it's happening around us--in the sin of our hearts, in the deceptive and hollow philosophies of the world, and in Satan and his demons."

The sin of my heart? My veranda? My peekadilly?

"I collectively call them The Enemy because they all work together to kill and steal and destroy people's lives and futures, and keep them from doin' what they were created for."

"You mean their purpose in life? Like why they were born?" said Chloe.

"That's right," said Marg. "The Enemy knows if you've got people out there doing what God made them for--bringing glory to Him and advancing His kingdom--it makes Satan's time to go in the fire come quicker," said Marg.

H-E Double Toothpicks.

"And he wants as much company as he can get. So, he tries to get people to destroy themselves with their own sin. And he uses whatever he thinks will work on that particular person."

"Like what?"

"Well, the sin that brings a lot of people to the Hope and Help Center is sexual sin. It isn't the only sin, but it seems to get a lot of people."

Peekadilly.

"God meant for sex to be a beautiful blessing for married people--to bond them, like He did Elmer and me, and to bless them with children--but The Enemy tempts people into doing it outside of God's plan, before they're married, or in their minds, like with porn, or in ways that the Bible says is wrong. And then if the person falls for the temptation, The Enemy laughs and throws it in his or her face, and then smiles at the person's consequences. Because for a lot of folks, if the sin doesn't take 'em down, the consequence will, and there's always a consequence to sin."

Sin always has a consequence. Mom said that, too.

"And then the world works in it, too, because it tells people lies . . . like you evolved from a pile of goo or an ape, so sex is just your animal response. Or, anything and everything you want to do is *your choice*, and you are *entitled* to your choice, and if anyone tells you otherwise, then they are just a judgmental fanatic. Or, you don't have a creation of God inside of you but rather a medical condition that needs treatment . . . or, everybody is doing 'XYZ,' so it must be normal."

I don't think I want to know what XYZ is.

"And, Child, there is a devil, and he is real and roaming around the earth for the time being. He was created as an angel and named Lucifer. When he sinned against God, he and his followers--other angels--were thrown from heaven. Now they are called Satan and his demons, and they spend their time fighting against God and using people and institutions and governments as pawns."

"Why does God let them do that?"

"Well, Child, it won't be forever. The Word tells us how His-story will eventually end. But for our lives here and now, He wants us to love Him and love others, by fighting spiritual battles with faith and love. And He knows we can't do it on our own, so He fights *for* us, through the Holy Spirit shining *through* us."

Shining through us with bright white hearts and glistening Sonbeams! The Holy Spirit--speaking and praying to God and Jesus on my behalf--helping me understand God's Word and hear His voice. And fighting spiritual battles for me! "So, has sexual purity been your biggest battle?"

"No, Child. My biggest spiritual battle was forgiveness," said Marg. "Without Christ, I could have never forgiven some of the stuff that happened to me."

Chloe zeroed in on Marg's black outline. *Could it be linked to forgiveness?* She pondered the thought, but decided it couldn't be, since she'd seen only one other person with a black outline. Surely more people must know how to forgive than that?

Elmer walked through the kitchen, carrying his coffee mug. "Excuse me, girls." He put the mug in the sink and filled a glass with water, then left, brushing Marg's shoulder with his hand.

"If Elmer and I both didn't learn how to forgive, we never would have stayed married," said Marg. "Fifty years takes a commitment and a lot of forgiveness."

"Why, did one of you cheat?"

"No, Child. We made a promise to God before we were married, and *every day* after we were married. Love isn't easy, because we all are sinful and selfish, and if we don't kill the sin in our hearts each day, then anything can happen."

I bet it wouldn't be hard to love bright white Letter Jacket Boy!

"See, that's what a lot of people don't understand about marriage. The gooey love feelings come and go, and when you don't feel them, you have to love God by loving your husband."

"And having sex, right?" Chloe blurted, then realized she'd probably invited TMI.

"Yes, Child. God bonds me and Elmer together in that way, and it's beautiful and wonderful," said Marg. "But it wasn't that way until I had done some forgiving for things in my past."

Marg and Elmer certainly looked like they'd been bonded with a large glue bottle of oxytocin. "But I thought you said you saved yourself?"

"I did, Child. But I got a bad consequence from somebody else's sin. I know it doesn't seem fair, but it's not up to us. God will make it right in the end, and until then, He wants me to love and forgive."

"What happened to you?" Chloe asked, trying to reciprocate Marg's compassion. "What did you have to forgive?" Chloe nonchalantly looked beyond the kitchen to the Workman family picture hanging above the sofa. *Is there a reason that Marg and Elmer adopted their kids?*

"I can tell, Miss Chloe," said Marg, "that you're just itchin' to know why Elmer and I adopted our kids."

Oops. I guess I wasn't very nonchalant.

"I don't mind tellin' you, because now I see how God can take a mess-of-a-situation, even from somebody else's sin, and turn it into something beautiful," said Marg. "I grew up in the Deep South. My daddy left Mama to raise us three kids on her own. When I was twelve, Mama pulled me out of school and said my uncle was hirin' me to clean his house every day," Marg said, squeezing her eyebrows together. She took another tissue from her pocket and wiped her nose. "Chloe, his house wasn't dirty." Marg stopped and looked at Chloe to see if she was catching her drift.

"It wasn't?" said Chloe, missing her drift.

"Child, my uncle raped me, day after day. And my Mama knew." Marg's eyes welled up with memories. "After a couple of months, my belly started to get big. Mama took me to the nice new clinic[4]that had just opened in our neighborhood--said I was sick, and they'd make me better."

Chloe felt like someone had pricked her heart with a knife. Poor Marg. How could an uncle do such a thing? How could a mom? *My mom always protected me.* "Oh, Marg. I'm so sorry that happened to you."

"Child, they aborted the little life inside of me, and after that, my body could never have kids again." Marg's face was getting puffy. "I'm sorry, I've told this story a hundred times, and that part of it still gets to me." Marg grabbed the last cookie from the plate and took a big bite. "Anyhow, I ran away a few years later to Selma and met this nice fella who ran a hardware store. We were set to be married, until he found out I couldn't ever have kids--then he called off the wedding."

Chloe's heart brewed a potion of two parts sorrow, one part anger, and one part panic. *That was so unfair of him. What happened to Marg wasn't her fault! But, what if . . . ?*

"What's wrong, Child?" said Marg. "You look like you just saw a ghost."

What if that happens to me? What if I meet Mr. Right, and I can't have kids with him? "Nothing," said Chloe.

"But, then I met my Savior."

"Elmer?"

"No, Child. I met my Father in heaven." Marg's demeanor brightened again, and she smiled. "But if I hadn't met my Savior, I wouldn't have met Elmer. We met at a Southern Gospel tent revival when I was 22 and got married a year later. And Elmer said from early on that God always gave him a heart to adopt kids--black, white, brown--whatever color the good Lord gave him would be a blessing."

Sparkly gold.

"But sometimes that womb isn't your own. For Elmer and me, God used four courageous women to bless us with Donovan and Grace and Levi and Mary."

"Really?" Chloe said, hopeful.

"Yes, Child. I praise God, even for my crummy past, because if that stuff didn't happen, I may not have recognized my need for the Lord and found the purpose for my life."

Chloe contemplated Marg's statement. "Well, how *do* you know your purpose?"

"You ask God. He created you and gave you life."

That's what Mom said, too. "Okay, but, like, how am I supposed to know if I should go to art school or be a model, or stay in public school or go back to home schooling?"

"Child, when you have an intimate relationship with Him, you talk to Him every day. You tell Him everything you're feeling and ask Him questions. You do *life* with Him. You read His Love Letter to you, and ask Him how to love Him more, and how to love the people He brings into your life. And if you do that, you'll always be in His will, and you'll end up making good choices."

"But how did you love the people who were in your life, like your uncle and mom, after what they did to you?" *How could I ever love Lily?*

"Well, Child, that's where I had to *learn* how to forgive. God forgave me for all my sins, so He wants me to forgive others. Forgiveness is one of those spiritual battles. God will fight it for me, if I trust Him to, but I can't rely on my own feelings. Love is an action, not a feeling. I have to make a decision in my mind to choose love and forgiveness and let God judge the sin."

"So, did you go back to your uncle?"

"No, I had to get away from my uncle, so I could start healing and start the process of forgiveness. And Child, even though it was the worst, and most painful, season of my life, I can actually praise God for it now."

Praise Him for it? *That seems a little overboard,* thought Chloe.

"Child, God didn't take away the physical consequence of not being able to bear children, but He mended and restored my broken heart, and He brought good from the bad. I've had a great life."

Chloe's eyes popped and she took a quick breath. "Wait," she said. She stared at the black outline around Marg's large body, while her mind filled with *déjà vu* epiphany.

Black is a *physical* consequence of an abortion? *But Mom had an abortion, and she didn't have a black outline!* Chloe patiently waited to hear a knock on her epiphany door.

And then realized . . . *déjà vu* outlines are *physical* consequences, and *déjà vu* hearts show *emotional* pain, unless they get healed by the Great Physician.

So, Mom's bright white must have covered her black heart, and she must have been able to have more kids! Chloe thought for a moment more. *Well, duh, she had me! Her dust outline, an STD, didn't prevent her from having more kids, but did it cause her cancer?*

Chloe stared at Marg's bright white *déjà vu* heart as her words brought meaning. "He covered my sinful heart . . . *with bright white!* So, with Christ, the pure and lovely Light of the World, sin can be covered and broken hearts with emotional pain can be healed." *And the Word of God makes a pure heart even brighter white. But without Christ, there's no way to heal a déjà vu heart.*

"Child, let's get back to you. These kids at your school--maybe God wants to use your gifts and your personality and your past--everything that you've gone through with losin' your mama to help them.

My gifts? *My gift! God, do you want me to use my gift to help others? Others with sparkly gold or black déjà vu hearts? Or dust outlines?*

Epiphany squared! Wait, if a black heart means the emotional consequences and pain from an abortion . . . *then Lily has had an abortion.* Chloe envisioned Lily in her mind, with a dust outline, and a black and peekadilly *déjà vu* heart, and compassion began to trickle in her veins. *Lily needs bright white . . . she needs Christ to heal her heart.*

"Child . . . Child!" Marg said. "Sometimes you go all spacey on me." Marg looked slightly irritated. "Listen, Girl, as I was saying, you need to learn how to fight."

"But, I thought you just said I'm supposed to love people."

"Yep. Love is a powerful weapon when you're fightin' a spiritual battle. And that's what you've got on your hands."

On my hands? Chloe looked at her purity ring. *Purity fights sexual sin.*

"Chloe, you have everything you need to fight! God will fight *for* you and *through* you. You keep askin' Him what He wants you to do."

"Marg, do you have any brochures for the H & H Center here?"

"Sure do, Child." Marg went over to a small desk and opened the drawer. She pulled out some papers and sauntered back to the table. "Here you go," she said, handing a stack of pink H & H pamphlets to Chloe, as if she were giving marching orders to a soldier going to battle. Then she handed Chloe a paper that said *Fighting Psalms*, and a sticker that said, *Don't Fight Naked, Put on the Armor of God!* She touched Chloe's shoulder, commissioning her.

"Thanks, Marg." Chloe glanced at the *Fighting Psalms* and read the first one. Psalm 144: 1-2 "Praise be to the LORD my Rock, who trains my hands for war, my fingers for battle. He is my loving God and my fortress, my stronghold and my deliverer, my shield, in whom I take refuge, who subdues peoples under me." *I've seen these before! These are the fighting Psalms that Mom gave me.*

I LOVE YOU, CHLOE. I WILL FIGHT FOR YOU. BE STRONG AND COURAGEOUS. DO NOT BE TERRIFIED, DO NOT BE DISCOURAGED, FOR I WILL BE WITH YOU. DON'T FORGET MY BOOK OF THE LAW, MEDITATE ON IT DAY AND NIGHT.

Marg opened the tupperware container of cookies and motioned to Chloe. "One more left. You want it?"

"No, thanks. I think I've eaten about a dozen today. I need to go," Chloe said, feeling a sudden craving for chocolate soldiers.

* * *

Chloe climbed the ladder of Gary's hunting blind, slipped her backpack from her shoulder and hoisted it onto the floor. She unzipped the top pocket and pulled out a throw blanket, then fanned it over the wooden planks. She climbed two more steps and shuffled herself on top of the throw, feeling its softness and brushing it smooth. She reached inside her backpack again and pulled out her Bible, her journal and pen, and the Fighting Psalms. *Hey, God, it's me. I'm reporting for basic training. Please teach me how to fight a spiritual battle and strengthen me.*

* * *

Ty De Veen

"I'll leave it under the mat of our front door," said Ty. "The address is 600 Scarsdale Drive," he said, cutting off the caller.

Ty grabbed a tall bottle of beer from the fridge and walked down the hall to a large wooden door. He flipped on the switch in the De Veen trophy room, bringing two stories of synthetic nature to life. The dusk of the day and the woods outside shone through two stories of windows.

The room looked like a camping and boat store, or a nature room in a museum. The quiet sound of birds and running water filled the air. Strategic lighting streamed upon the ten-point buck, his doe and their two fawns. Oversized goldfish swam in safety under the watchful eye of a lifelike grizzly bear hunkered over them. Sensing Ty's motion, a flood light burst on, giving spotlight to a fully maned lion with green eyes and teeth bared. Two breeds of squirrels, a python, and one exotic bird watched from their perches.

Ty hunkered his solid body into an oversized chair fashioned completely from alligator skin. He scanned the lighted shelves on the panoramic wall in front of him. How many basketball trophies did he have by now?

He breathed in the delicious thought of solitude for the next few hours.

Harding and Alice were attending some sort of black-tie, philanthropic dinner. Alice had gotten touch-up surgery last week, tanned, and had spent the afternoon at the spa getting a mani and pedi for tonight's event.

A rush of adrenaline pulsed through his angry veins as he booted his laptop. He glanced into the trophy case again, zooming in on his autographed picture of Davion Griffin. *I don't care who Chloe looks like. I will not be ignored. Who does she think she is?*

His laptop called to him, inviting him back to the familiar--his other home-court, where he dominated over the game, the players, and the objects.

* * *

May and Chloe were on the late side Monday morning. The first bell had rung; the halls were beginning to thin out. May went straight to her first class, but Chloe needed her French notebook out of her locker. She flipped opened her binder to see if they were still there. Yes. Last night, she'd carefully transferred the pink H & H brochures from her purse, and then smoothed them out. *Should I give one to Lily's sparkly gold friend? How do you nonchalantly offer a girl "hope and help?" Does she even know she's pregnant yet?*

The second bell rang.

Crap. Another tardy won't help me in my changing-from-French-to-Spanish case with Miss Marilyn.

A little shot of adrenaline pumped through Chloe as she gave the locker door a quick slam and walked quickly toward Pip's class.

Just ahead, Ty De Veen exited the guys' bathroom and looked straight at her.

Chloe's veins pulsed with fear.

Ty stopped for a split second and glared at Chloe, then ignored her. No small talk. No talk at all. No gesture.

Chloe first felt a small pang of relief, then creepiness. She lagged behind Ty as he walked into Pip's class, then followed suit. She eyed the empty seat in the back row, and headed for it.

Ugh! The thought of eight more weeks in Pip's peekadilly playground made Chloe cringe. The room felt heavy, like it was smothered with poison, designed to choke a person's heart.

"Miss Hudson, you're tardy," said Pip, tapping her pencil on the desk. Miss Pip gave her gum a few chews and stared at Chloe. "You have to go to the office and get a pass," she said curtly. She turned to the class and said something in French.

No probléma. Chloe headed for the office through the empty hallway. She saw Miss Marilyn through the glass doors of the front office. She walked in and stood by the counter. "Hi, Miss Marilyn, I was wondering . . . ."

Miss Marilyn raised a finger in the air, as if to say, "Quiet. I'm listening to the attendance line."

A student's voice spilled out of the recorder. "Amy Emercon won't be in school today, because she is sick. Oh, yeah, um, this her mom."

Miss Marilyn listened to two more, each time making a notation on the computer. She looked up at Chloe. "Hello, Dear. What can I do for you?"

"Well, I was wondering if there was any chance that I could switch from French to Spanish class?" asked Chloe, a bit nervous.

Miss Marilyn gave her a quick smile. She pulled a yellow transfer paper from a stack of plastic trays on her desk. "Sure, Dear. It's no problem at all for anyone who's a friend of Lily Hunt's," she said. "You'll need to finish out the week in French, and then start with Mrs. Esperanza next Monday."

The sparkly gold girl was absent that day, and the next, and the next.

By Friday, when she returned, her beautiful sparkly gold outline had disappeared, and her *déjà vu* heart was now charcoal black with a peekadilly center.

When Chloe saw the girl, her mouth dropped open and she hurt all over. She went into the bathroom, entered a stall, and cried.

* * *

"Stand firm then, with the belt of truth buckled around your waist, with the breastplate of righteousness in place, and with your feet fitted with the readiness that comes from the gospel of peace. In addition to all this, take up the shield of faith, with which you can extinguish all the flaming arrows of the evil one. Take the helmet of salvation and the sword of the Spirit, which is the word of God. And pray in the Spirit on all occasions with all kinds of prayers and requests. With this in mind, be alert and always keep on praying for all the saints." Ephesians 6:14-18

Dropping French cured a lot of Chloe's Dutch problem. Or maybe it was because basketball season started? She couldn't pinpoint what had made life at Jefferson High tolerable, but she was relieved.

Of course, Lily and her possies still occasionally did the locker huddle, shooting eye arrows of disdain toward Chloe. But at least it wasn't every day and between every class. And whenever an arrow was shot her way, Chloe asked her One and Only to protect her and help her deflect it with the shield of faith. *God, I know you love Lily. Help me to love her, too,* she prayed. Then she'd shoot Lily a smile and dart off to class.

℞

Chapter 19

Light adrenaline and excitement wafted through Chloe like the smell of popcorn through the air. She pulled her student ID card from her purse and laid down $2.

"Welcome to the Thanksgiving Gobbler Tourney," said the ticket lady as she plunked a basketball stamp on Chloe's hand.

"Come on," said May, headed for the double doors of the gym. They stood outside of the packed gym, waiting for the end of the National Anthem.

"And the home . . . of the . . . brave," croaked a short, plump girl, whose face was blushed. Thunderous applause filled the gym. Crowded bleachers blended, forming a sea of *déjà vu* colors with twinkles of bright white and a few dots of black.

Jefferson's cheerleaders were center court doing a dance routine with a pyramid-flip finale.

Sparkly gold was flying through the air, looking like a fourth-of-July sparkler being hand spun in a circle. When the music stopped, the gold landed.

Lily! Lily now has sparkly gold? Chloe's heart started to ache. Does she know? *God, please help me to know how to help her.*

"Poop," said May. "Looks like we're stuck in the 'rents section." May gestured Chloe to follow and started walking down the baseline, heading for the Jefferson High section across the gym. "Hurry up," she chided.

"The Jefferson High School Bobcats welcome the Cedarville Lions to the court," bellowed the announcer, his voice two octaves lower and three times louder than the average guy. "And now, for the Cedarville Lion Starters . . ." With each number the announcer called, a healthy-looking teen guy, wearing purple and yellow, ran through a tunnel of cheerleaders, giving high-fives to his teammates.

Chloe and May climbed a tall flight of concrete stairs and squeezed into the front row, politely nudging their two behinds in a space really only big enough for one. Each side was flanked with two amicable mom-types, each video-taping, that didn't seem to mind.

Chloe turned around, scanning the crowd. Down the way and a few bleachers above, her eyes landed on Gary and Candice. Next to Gary was Harding and Alice De Veen.

Gary and Dr. D sat in the middle of the ladies, chatting.

Alice De Veen was wearing a low-cut shirt with Ty's number on the front. She held a compact mirror in front of her face, checking her look. She applied some lipstick and pressed her lips together.

"And now for the Cedarville Lion starters! At Center, Number 11, a 6 foot, 3 inch Senior, Evan Smith!"

Smith. Evan Smith? *Evan?* Chloe's heart took an extra beat. Had she just heard the sweet sound of Letter Jacket Boy's name, or was it a figment of her over-active imagination? She peered at center court.

There he was.

A silence fell over Chloe's mind, muffling the sound of the basketball hysteria around her. She stared. And stared some more. And smiled.

Evan Smith's bright white heart shone brilliantly as he ran out of the cheerleader tunnel, gave his high-fives, and took his place in the line.

The purple and yellow crowd, and his teammates, cheered him on.

His bright white smile was accented by his blond hair, tousled yet clean cut. And those legs.

Okay, I know a nice Christian girl shouldn't gaze upon a guy like he's an amoeba under a microscope, but . . . those legs are the most beautiful . . . and those shoulders. Wow, God, You did a really good job on him! Chloe nudged May, while continuing to look center court. "Do you have any binoculars?"

May shook her head slightly. "Sure. I always have a pair of binoculars handy dandy," she said sarcastically. "Chloe, you're such a goob."

Chloe was mesmerized.

"What are you drooling over?"

"It's him. It's Letter Jacket Boy from Anjou . . . you know, the guy who always comes into the Shoppe? His name is Evan Smith."

"Too bad he's always with another girl," said May.

Thanks for reminding me. Unfortunately, May was right. Since their first encounter, Chloe had counted three different girls with Evan Smith. Each one was super-cute, seemingly intelligent and, worst of all . . . each seemed really nice, like the kind of girl you'd want for a friend or even a kindred spirit.

Evan seemed to like them, too. On separate occasions, he lightly touched the shoulder of each one, opened the door for her, and smiled at her. *But he smiled at me too!* Isn't that a little weird to smile at another girl, when you're on a date with someone else?

May's eyes were super-glued to a certain suited specimen with a Jefferson blue tie. "See the guy in the suit? That's Sam. He's in my English Lit class. We were in the same discussion group for *Romeo and Juliet*. Yesterday after class we had this in-depth conversation about some of the structural and thematic elements. He's the team manager."

"Sounds fascinating," said Chloe. "Where for art thou Mayble?" she teased. 'Tis, Sam I am, O love-smitten one."

"Giddy-up," said May, smiling.

Suddenly the crowd around Chloe and May bolted to its feet, its cheer meter registering HIGH. The announcer called out the names and number of each Jefferson High Bobcat as he trotted on the court, egging on the crowd. Then, a moment of calm, before a thunderous drum roll . . .

"And last, but certainly not least," bellowed the announcer, "starting as Center for the Bobcats, our own . . . #66, a 6'7" Senior, Tyler De Veeeeen!" The announcer's voice sounded like the horn of a barge sailing through a draw bridge open to the sky.

Ty, dust, and peekadilly strutted casually toward the rest of the team, acknowledging the crowd by alternating waves of each hand, like he was on a presidential campaign tour. Before high-fiving his teammates, he turned, posing deliberately for the local newspaper and TV cameras.

The crowd went more-than-wild, as the pep band and cheerleaders chanted, “T-Y’s the guy, T-Y’s, the guy.”

Chloe turned and looked at the crowd. Mrs. D and Dr.D were both standing up, smiling big and repeating the chant. Alice turned to the crowd around her, pushing her open palms to the ceiling, encouraging everyone to stand up and join in.

Ty moved to center court by the referee, while the rest of the Bobcats retreated into a huddle around the coach.

Cedarville’s team broke its huddle and the five starters headed for the circle in the middle, positioning themselves.

Evan Smith’s bright white shone in solitude on the court. He stuck his hand out toward Ty, a gesture of sportsmanship.

Ty stared at his hand, looked up at him and . . . totally ignored him, turning instead to his four teammates who were now polka-dotting the center circle.

Anger bubbled in Chloe. What a jerk! *I hope Cedarville creams Jefferson High.*

* * *

PEEKADILLY wins the jump, sending the ball soaring in the air to #22. Jefferson controls the ball. 22 passes to 66 and now 66 fakes BRIGHT WHITE. Two points for Tyler De Veen!

The crowd goes wild.

Cedarville now taking the ball down the floor. Will they be able to break Jefferson’s man-to-man defense? De Veen is all over Smith. #13 passes to

#18. He looks for an opening under the basket. Passes to BRIGHT WHITE, who drives to the basket and . . . flagrant foul by PEEKADILLY. Can you believe the officials didn't call that one? #66 with a fast break down the court . . . easy layup by Ty De Veen. Two more points for Jefferson.

Cedarville is off to a rough start. Purple possession again. 13 looking for the opening in the keyhole. PEEKADILLY is all over BRIGHT WHITE in the paint. #13 fakes and shoots. De Veen with the rebound. Will he pass to his teammate under the hoop? No. He drives it down the court in a dribble series, and despite strong coverage from #11, another two points for PEEKADILLY on a shooter's roll.

Halftime.

Jefferson is clearly in control of this game. #66, De Veen, bringing his usual dominance to the court. Cedarville's Smith seems to be a bit off tonight.

* * *

A janitor wearing a bright blue Jefferson High polo started pushing an oblong mop over the gym floor. He pushed with one hand and snapped his finger on the other one to the rhythm of the pep band.

Chloe breathed in the smell of popcorn and hot dogs wafting through the air.

"We gotta get down by the action for the second half," said May. "I gotta pee. Can you get me some popcorn? I'll get us seats in the student section and meet you there."

Better seats, better view. Sounded good. Chloe fell into a herd of parents heading down the steps to the cafeteria and found the back of the concession line.

The line ebbed slowly toward a cubby hole where athletic boosters were serving up a variety of snacks. Until the popcorn machine broke. The line came to a grinding halt as one frantic dad worked feverishly to restore it.

Chloe scanned the cafeteria. All sorts of *déjà vu*. Across the way, she saw Gary and Candice visiting with Dr. D and Alice De Veen. Then she saw a big splotch of bright white.

Three girls, all of whom looked vaguely familiar, were huddled together. Their bright white *déjà vu* hearts made them look like a heavenly spotlight was shining on them.

Chloe did a double-take. *Do I know them from somewhere?*

One of the girls happened to look Chloe's direction, then turned back to the huddle and whispered something. All three looked at Chloe simultaneously and smiled. Then, as if they caught themselves in their extremely-obvious-staring bout, they turned back to each other, ever so nonchalantly, and giggled.

Did I just imagine that? Chloe turned around, looking behind her. Maybe they're looking at something else? Maybe some poor schlep behind me dropped a soda down his front? *Maybe they recognize me from my famous photo shoot!* Yeah, right, Chloe. Or maybe, they haven't seen a tall brown girl?

An inkling of self-consciousness sprung inside her. She turned around, then checked her outfit. She pulled a compact mirror from her purse and checked her look. *Maybe I have drool on my face from when I was looking at Evan Smith?* Nope. *Oh, well, 'Tis nicer to be gawked at by smiling bright whites than stinging black peekadillies.*

She looked over at the girls who were looking at her again. A small flutter went through her as each of their faces attached to a Shoppe memory in her mind. These are the girls that Smith brought into Anjou!

All three girls were pretty and fairly tall. Each was dressed cute and fashionable, except for the two weird spirit badges pinned to their sweaters.

As Chloe watched, a mom and dad type joined their circle, each donning their own bright white hearts accented with large buttons. The mom looked to be older, like in her sixties, and very classy. The dad was tall and looked just like an older version of . . .

Evan Smith! Duh. This was his family! The girls who were always with him were his sisters!

O Happy Day!

"What can I get you, Miss?" asked a plump parent, munching a candy bar from the concession hole window.

Chloe was slightly startled, her heart pounding. "Um, I guess I'll have a Snickers Bar," she said. She handed over a buck and quickly tore the wrapper open. She took a huge bite, hoping to chew off some jitters. She turned toward the gym door, hearing a pleasant voice behind her.

"Excuse me. Is your name Chloe?"

Chloe's face blushed as she chewed furiously, imagining she looked like a cow chewing its cud. *Oh, man, a year ago, I didn't even know what a cud was!*

There, standing before her, were Evan Smith's three sisters.

Chew, Chloe, chew! She tried to make a pleasant expression while she finished, holding up her pointer finger to signal, "Just a second, I'm almost on the last cud cycle." She swallowed hard, sending a noticeably large mound down her gullet. She wiped the edges of her mouth. "Yes, I'm Chloe," she sputtered.

"I'm Sue Smith. These are my sisters, Sarah and Grace." Each girl extended her hand to Chloe.

Chloe reciprocated, her diamond ring glistening and matching their *déjà vu* hearts. Her eyes zeroed in on their buttons. Of course. In the center of each one was a picture of Evan and a small lion footprint with the number 11 written inside of it. "Nice to meet you."

"You work at Anjou Fine Chocolates, don't you?"

"Yes. I think I've seen you in the Shoppe before," said Chloe.

"Our brother keeps dragging us in there," said Sue, laughing.

"And I'm allergic to milk, so I can't even eat chocolate!" Sarah added.

Little cupids put drops of thrill on their arrows and shot them through Chloe's heart. Smiling big, she pointed to the button on Grace's chest. "Your brother is Evan, right? I've seen him come in before, but I've never actually got to talk to him."

"Precisely why we came over here," said Sarah. "Look, our whole family is going out for pizza after the game. Would you think it's too weird to come out with us and our parents? Evan doesn't know we're asking you. He probably doesn't even know you're here, but I'm fairly confident he won't mind if we ask you."

Yes, yes, yes! "Yes, that sounds like fun," she said, trying to appear charming and elegant. *Hot dog! This is like finding the immunity idol on Survivor!*

"Great. We'll meet you at the exit after the game. What's your cell number?" said Sue.

* * *

Chloe heard the buzzer inside the gym as the cafeteria cleared out. She looked through the student section for May.

May stood up waving her arms, looking slightly annoyed.

Chloe scurried through the crowd toward her.

"It's about time. Where's my popcorn?"

Chloe's face beamed. "Sorry, I forgot." She handed May the rest of her candy bar. "Here."

"What happened to you?"

"Guess what? Evan Smith's sisters just introduced themselves and invited me out with their family after the game!"

Chloe saw May respond, but she couldn't hear her.

"T-Y's the guy! T-Y's the guy!" the crowd yelled, deafening everything else.

Oh, gag me. Chloe watched the game, secretly cheering inside for Evan and his team. On one foul against Jefferson, she accidentally started clapping, inviting a heaping helping of angst from the students around her.

"Watch it, Chloe," whispered May.

* * *

"This is Jed Turner and Jake Toppen from WLP Sports Radio here at Jefferson High School, where the Bobcats are beating down the Cedarville Lions."

"Jed, what do the Lions need to do to get back in this game?"

"Well, Jake, being down 16 points, they've got their work cut out. Their center, #11 has *got* to get defense going against Jefferson's De Veen."

“Well, the four inches of height is pretty hard to beat.”

“You’re right. And De Veen is just an amazing ballplayer. When he’s on, he’s just about unstoppable. That’s why I.U.’s Davion Griffin signed him last year as a junior. De Veen brings it every time. He’s definitely NBA material. In fact, the question is how many years he’ll even play for Griffin before going pro. Really, he just blows the competition out of the water.”

“Agreed, but what do you say about De Veen’s fouls? Clearly, the refs are overlooking a lot of violations. Take the one in the first quarter against Cedarville’s Smith. What gives?”

“Well, Jake, Jefferson does seem to have the home court advantage in this game, in more ways than one. I do think De Veen’s temper is a concern for Davion Griffin. He’s like a bubbling volcano, and that can bring a whole team down.

* * *

With 1 minute, 13 seconds left on the clock, the volcano erupted. Cedarville’s #11, Evan Smith, lay on the ground, his nose bleeding. After a few minutes, one of Cedarville’s assistant coaches arrived with an ice pack and escorted him to the locker room. The visitor’s section applauded for him.

“Foul’s on Jefferson’s #66, Ty De Veen,” said the ref. The student cheer section booed and made hissing sounds.

One of Cedarville’s guards approached the free-throw line and sunk two. But it was too little, too late. Final score: Jefferson 63; Cedarville 41.

* * *

After the game, Chloe stood by the gymnasium exit, craving pizza and filled with disappointment. Her phone buzzed with a text. No surprise.

CHLOE--SUE SMITH HERE. SORRY TO CANCEL TONIGHT. WILL TELL EVAN TO CALL YOU.

May was down the hallway, talking with Sam.

Out of the corner of Chloe's eye, she saw the sparkly gold rah-rah holding on to the arm of Mr. Creeper-Jerk-Dream Crusher.

They looked at her and glanced at each other, snickering.

Urrh. Chloe's blood temp went up several degrees. *I don't like them! I can't stand Ty, and I don't like Lily. They are my enemies.*

Chloe heard a voice within her spirit.

THEY ARE NOT YOUR ENEMIES. YOU DON'T HAVE TO LIKE THEM, BUT YOU DO HAVE TO LOVE THEM. LET ME FIGHT FOR YOU!

A reflection of Lily's sparkly gold shone through the glass door of the school lobby.

Sparkly gold. My brother . . . or my sister.

CHLOE, I WANT TO WORK THROUGH YOU TO SAVE A GENERATION. USE YOUR WEAPONS OF FAITH AND LOVE.

What? Weird.

Chloe felt a finger tap on her back shoulder that made her jump. She turned around to see May, who gave her a hug.

"Sorry about your night, Sweetie," said May. "You want to go out for pizza with Sam and me?"

"No, thanks. I'm not hungry." *At least not for pizza. I think I'll check Facebook tonight.*

℞

Chapter 20

On Monday, Chloe opened her folder, jotted a quick note, then put the cap back on her pen. She looked up and down the empty hallway by the lockers, then stuffed the pink H & H brochure through the slit of Lily's locker.

* * *

Waiting is hard, especially for said romantic types prone to infatuation.

On a Friday night in early December, Chloe came home from work to find a beautiful pine tree from Gary's woods standing tall in the great room.

More than ten feet of emerald green shone with thousands of white twinkle lights, reminding Chloe of miniature bright white *déjà vu* hearts.

"Want some hot chocolate for decorating?" said Gary.

"No, thanks," said Chloe, throwing clumps of tinsel on the middle section. She nonchalantly checked her phone again for the eighth time today. Why hasn't he called already? *I mean, this guy comes into the Shoppe supposedly to see me--and I'm sure his sister gave him my number--and then he doesn't even call me in the next two weeks? And why doesn't he have a Facebook account?*

"Do you think I should call him? I think I found his home number in the phone book. There's an Evan Smith, Sr., who I think is his dad," said Chloe.

"You mean the guy from Cedarville?" Gary unfolded the stepladder and propped it next to the tree. "Nope."

"Nope?" Chloe put her hand on her waist. "What's that supposed to mean?"

"It means, I don't think you should call him. If he's interested, he'll call you."

"Well, why isn't he calling?"

"Maybe he's busy or---"

"Or what?"

"Or, he's not interested."

"Well, if he's not interested, why did he keep coming into the Shoppe? His sisters said he liked me."

"Chloe, who knows? I just know guys like the pursuit, okay? They don't want a girl trolling or chasing them."

"Well, how do you know that?"

"Hmmm. Let's see." Gary made a goofy face and scratched his head. "Maybe because I'm a guy."

"Well, maybe you feel that way because you like hunting."

Gary looked like he was pondering the thought, then shook his head slightly. "I don't think so. No guy wants to feel like a bound sacrifice being dragged to the altar. That's one of the things I love about Candice. She never chased me."

Oh, but she reeled you in. Chloe did an internal huff laced with frustration.

CHLOE, I WANT TO BE YOUR FIRST LOVE.

You mean you want me to chase you?

YES. YOU WILL SEEK ME AND FIND ME, WHEN YOU SEEK ME WITH ALL YOUR HEART.

* * *

"Praise the LORD, O my soul; all my inmost being, praise his holy name. Praise the LORD, O my soul, and forget not all his benefits--who forgives all your sins and heals all your diseases, who redeems your life from the pit and crowns you with love and compassion, who satisfies your desires with good things so that your youth is renewed like the eagle's." Psalm 103:1-5

"Reading a love letter written to you is *so* romantic! And being awakened every morning with the words, 'I love you, Chloe,' or with poetry! Like today, before my alarm clock went off, He whispered to me, 'When I awake, I am still with you.' Or sometimes He wakes me up in the middle of the night and tells me a secret!

And He even gives me little romantic gifts, like a red cardinal perched outside of my window and rose caramels in the dud box that aren't even duds!

And to think that my Lover wants to be with me all the time. And that He gets jealous for my love, and loves me *so* much that He died for me.

And now we're in the midst of an adventure!"

Chloe basked in the warm December sun beaming down on her. She kissed her mom's grave, cool to her lips. "Mom, I'm falling in love."

* * *

The day before Christmas break at Jefferson High was customarily a blow-off day, and this year was no different. Classes were being shortened in the morning, so that "clubs" could meet. During the afternoon, the entire student body was scheduled to watch the drama club's production of "A Christmas Carol."

May checked her look in the rearview mirror. Her pickle was one of the first parked this morning in the high school lot.

"Don't you have to be an athlete to join the Fellowship of Christian Athletes?" Chloe asked May, snickering.

"Well, the President of the Club said no. And besides, I've been running a little bit each day, because I'm going out for track in the spring," said May.

"Sure," said Chloe, smiling. "And I'm sure the fact that Sam is the president has nothing to do with your new interest in athletics and Christian fellowship?"

"Jinkies," said May laughing. "Of course not." May fluffed her hair and put on a thin layer of lip gloss, then tossed it back in her purse. "Okay, Miss Uninvolved-In-Any-Clubs, are you coming in, or do you want to wait in the pickle until the first bell?"

"I'll come in, too," said Chloe.

May and Chloe walked in the foyer and toward the gym. They stopped in front of the trophy case. "Save me a seat at the play, if you get there first, and I'll do the same. Have a good one," May said, walking toward the weight room where the FCA meeting would be starting.

"You, too," said Chloe.

The life-size cut-out of Ty De Veen hovered close to the case.

Good thing I don't have a marker with me, Chloe thought, resisting the urge to put artistic touches of-the-mustache-kind on Ty's cardboard body.

Chloe browsed the case, her eyes landing on the basketball picture with Gary in it. Nice suit, Gary. And mullet haircut. Chloe laughed as she stared at the picture. *I love Gary. He's kind of turned into my dad.*

AND I'M YOUR FATHER, CHLOE.

Chloe continued looking at the picture. So that's Davion Griffin, the big I.U. Coach who recruited Ty? *Do I really look like him?* Lily had mentioned that once. And for some bizarre reason, Creeper Ty had once asked me if my middle name was Griffin or Davion. Fortunately, he had never heard of the name Rahab, or he may have taken it as a come-on.

Chloe's reflection off the case caught her attention.

Is my mascara smeared? She walked down the locker hallway, made a quick stop to drop off her book bag, then headed for the girls' bathroom. She walked in and set her purse on the counter.

The sound of someone throwing up was coming from the stall.

Should I say something? What's protocol? *It might be one of the pink-headed Emos hungover, and I really don't think she will want my help!* And really, how can you even help someone who is puking, unless you're bringing her a bucket or handing her a tissue? If she's already praying to the porcelain, there's really not much you can do for her.

Chloe flaked a piece of mascara from her eyelid with her fingernail, making her diamond glisten in the mirror. She quietly turned on the faucet, dampened her finger and cleaned the black smudge under her eye.

Now the sound of dry heaving.

"Are you okay?" Chloe said, turning toward the stall. "Can I help you somehow?"

A girl coughed and then flushed the toilet. "No, I think I'm okay now, but thanks." The door on the stall opened and out walked . . .

Sparkly gold Lily. Chloe sucked in a quick breath. *God, please give me your words.*

Lily's face was pale and depressed. Her small peekadilly heart was covered with thick black, reminding Chloe of a cordial cherry being suffocated in chocolate. Underneath the beauty of sparkly gold was her thin layer of dust.

"Lily, I'm so sorry you're sick," said Chloe, nervously, but with compassion. "Is it morning sickness because of the baby?" *Oh no, did I just say that?*

Chloe gulped hard. It's almost never good to ask someone if she's pregnant. Let alone someone who can't stand you and has no idea that you see sparkly gold all around her and black and peekadilly on her heart! Chloe's heart raced anticipating Lily's reaction.

Which was nothing like Chloe expected.

Lily melted. And cried. Words tumbled from her mouth at warp speed.

Does she remember she's talking to the girl whom she's hated for the last semester? But she keeps calling me Chloe!

"Chloe, I'm so scared. I don't know what to do. First of all, I can't believe it! I've been on the pill since eighth grade and I *always* make Ty use protection, so how did I get pregnant? For a second time! And the first time . . ." Lily brought her hands together, touching her fingers to a point at the top of her nose and wiped under both of her eyes. "The first time I used that RU486 stuff to end my pregnancy. Ty got it from his dad."

Dr. D? But I thought doctors take a hippocratic oath to never harm life?

Lily pressed her lips together. "Chloe, it was terrible. I can't get the image out of my mind." Lily hugged Chloe. "Chloe, how am I ever going to get that out of my mind?"

Chloe hugged her back for a long time without saying anything. "Lily, I can't know what you're going through, but I know where you can get help--for you and your baby. I have a friend who works at the---"

"Hope and Help Center?" Lily interrupted. She pulled the pink brochure from her back jeans pocket.

"Yes." Chloe pulled out a tissue from her purse. "And I'll help you, too. My mom told me about when she had an abortion and how she was healed."

Lily blew her nose and looked puzzled. "But your mom had *you*, right?"

Chloe pressed her eyebrows together. "Well, yes. It was before me."

Noise from the hallway outside of the bathroom indicated that first period would be starting soon.

Lily looked Chloe in the eye. "Thank you." She paused, then said, "Could you not tell anybody yet? I have to tell my parents. They're gonna kill me."

Chloe reassured Lily. "I won't tell anybody. And I'll pray for you."

"Thanks. Hey, when you talk to God, could you ask him to lay off on the morning sickness?"

℞

Chapter 21

When you lose a loved one, every holiday is bittersweet. The ghost of Christmas Past, or Easter Past, and especially Mother's Day Past, floods your mind, making it hard to focus on experiencing the present. But today is where life is lived.

During Christmas break, Chloe hung out with her One and Only, did a lot of stuff with Gary and Candice, and worked at Anjou, wondering if Evan Smith had moved, married, or fallen off the face of the earth.

At 7:30 on Saturday morning, May's green pickle drove up Gary's drive, freshly plowed of new snow. Chloe darted across the porch and hopped in.

"I can't wait until you get your stinking license," said May. "You know how much I look forward to sleeping in."

"I know. I'm sorry to ask you, but I promised Marg I'd help her at the center for an hour before it opens. May, the H & H Center helps so many people. They save lives--babies *and* women. I want to be a part of it."

"Well, next time you want to help save lives, couldn't you do it in the afternoon?"

"Yes," Chloe conceded. "And, by the way, I'll be driving *you* to school on February 14. Only 57 days from now."

May pulled into the parking lot of the Hope and Help Center. "There's Large Marg waiting for you," she said. "She's taking you home, right?"

"Yes. Thanks a lot, May. Sweet dreams when you get home."

Marg stood inside the glass door, her bright white heart beckoning Chloe. She unlocked the door, let her in, and locked it behind them. "Morning, Child," she said, giving Chloe a hug.

Mid-hug, Lily pulled her white sports car into the parking lot. She looked around and looked toward the door where Marg waved at her. She darted out of her car and jogged to the door.

"Come on in, Child. I'm Marg. I'm glad to meet you."

"Nice to meet you, too," said Lily. "Hi, Chloe."

"Let me show you girls around," said Marg. She sauntered down the hall, explaining how the building used to be a restaurant, but was gutted and totally renovated. Everything looked clean and new and smelled like baby powder.

Down the one hallway, several small rooms were fashioned into quaint miniature living rooms. Each had a chair, a love seat, nice furnishings and a table with a box of tissues.

"This is where our advocates meet confidentially with our clients," said Marg with a measure of compassion that looked noticeable to Lily. "Lily, you and I can talk here in a little while, or in my office if these get filled up when the Center opens. Sometimes we have girls waiting to come in on Saturday morning."

Across the hall was a medical examination room that looked more like a family room than a doctor's office. Across the large room was a sprawling countertop, with a sink, several live plants, and framed, colorful pictures of butterflies.

A small, black velvet trunk held several tiny figures of various sizes. The "twelve-week-old" figure looked exactly like a miniature baby with tiny fingers, toes, and a doll-like face. In the corner of the room, closest to the door, a female examination table, made of light peach leather, lay diagonal to form a triangle with two chairs against the wall. A small machine with a TV screen was on a cart with rollers.

"Is that an ultrasound machine?" asked Chloe.

"Yes, Child. Remember last summer, I told you we got an anonymous donation from some gal's estate? This is what we bought." Marg went over and pulled her hand across the top of the screen, like she was a Price-Is-Right girl modeling a grocery item. "This here is our medical room where we do pregnancy tests, ultrasounds, and STD and STI testing. That door leads directly to the ladies' room, so we can take the urine samples in here, instead of walking them down the hallway."

Chloe saw Lily flinch when Marg mentioned STD's. Poor Lily. *She'll soon find out about that too. I wish she didn't have dust.*

Marg started down the hallway again, Lily and Chloe following her. "This is the main office where we do all the computer stuff and where our paid staff works." Marg pointed down the hallway. "Down at the end is a kitchen, and on the left is our training room for our parenting classes." Marg walked in the office and continued to the back. An expression of pride filled her face. "They gave me my own office a few years ago, when we moved to this building. They said I'd volunteered more hours than anybody in H & H's history." She opened the door and flipped on the light switch.

Marg's office had a small desk in the corner, neatly organized with a pencil box, a vanilla-scented candle, a box of tissues, and a box of Anjou Chocolates. A love seat sofa with a contemporary upholstered design was flanked by two black end tables, each with a small lamp. One wall consisted completely of shelves from ceiling to floor. On the shelves were hundreds of small pictures. Some were 2 x 3 inches. Others were 4 x 6. Most of the pictures were of teen girls, plus a few women who looked to be in their twenties or thirties, and some were of newborn babies.

Marg took the lid off the Anjou box, offering Lily and Chloe a chocolate. "You two look impressed by my gallery of photos. That's 30 years of lovin' like Jesus does. I mentored each one of those girls. I helped them know they had a future, and I stood by them, when they let me. Mostly, I just told them how much God loves them and how He always helps somebody when they make a redemptive choice."

Lily's pale face flickered with interest. "What's a redemptive choice?" she asked. She nibbled the chocolate maple cream in her hand.

"When you stop where you're at in your situation--no matter what the circumstances--and you say, 'God help me! I'm sorry for what I did. I'll do whatever you want me to from here.' Then He works in your life, and takes your crummy mistakes and turns them into something for your good, and His purposes."

Like He did with Mom's life.

"That's what hope is," said Marg, scanning her photo gallery. "I still pray for each one of them."

Chloe beamed with admiration as she watched Marg pour out a few stories of some of the girls.

"These girls all said I could share their stories. I always asked them before I took their picture. That's part of a redemptive choice, too. You can use your story to help somebody else, because you've been there." Marg picked up a picture and gave a short anecdote of the girl's situation and how it turned out.

Lily looked from shelf to shelf and picked out a picture.

"This was a girl who chose to have an abortion. I met with her several times, and then she never came back. Until ten years later, when she was 27. Said she had never recovered . . . emotionally or physically. But, praise the Lord, she found Christ's forgiveness through a post-abortion Bible study offered here at the H & H Center. He healed her and restored her life. That's what the Great Physician does."

Chloe looked at Lily, who seemed enthralled with Marg's stories. Hadn't Lily ever met someone who cared? *Lily sees Christ shining through Marg!*

Marg's bright white heart shone brilliantly, right through her extra hundred pounds or so, beaming Christ's love to Lily's *déjà vu* heart.

Lily perused the shelf again, like she was looking for a choice piece of produce. She plucked one of the baby photos from the top shelf and handed it to Marg. "What was this little person's story?"

Marg smiled. "That little guy got adopted by a family that ached for a little one. He was left at the hospital emergency room when he was just a few hours old."

"Left?" said Chloe, a bit shocked.

"Was the mom arrested?" said Lily. "What kind of a person just leaves her newborn baby?" Lily's tone dripped with judgment. "My dad runs the new hospital, and I don't think you can just *leave* your baby."

"Well, Child. It is legal in Indiana. It's called the Safe Haven Law.[5] And we don't know what the mom's story was, but at least she was brave enough to do what she needed to do to keep her baby safe. And this little guy was a huge blessing to this couple who wanted children so badly, but couldn't have them because the gal got chlamydia as a teen."

Lily looked sheepish. She quickly plucked another picture from the shelf, 2" x 3", and handed it to Marg.

Marg glanced at it and cupped it between her hands. "Sweet Lisa."

Lisa. Mom's name always brought a sensation of love to Chloe's heart.

"I met Lisa by the fence at the abortion clinic in Dodge. February, I think. There was a blizzard on the way, and I almost didn't go to the fence to pray that morning, but I felt God sayin' to me to go. Nobody else came. I was the only one that day. When Lisa got out of the escort car, our eyes locked. She had the most beautiful blue eyes. I smiled at her and said I was praying for her and her baby, and I wanted to help her, but she went into the clinic anyway. The wind was howlin' outside and it got freezin' cold, but I kept praying the whole time. Then, about a half hour later, all the sudden Lisa comes running out the front door, barefoot and in a blue paper gown, screaming and crying. She ran right into my arms and said, 'Please! Will you help me? I think I just heard God talking to me, and telling me not to abort my baby.' I took her back to the center--we were at a different location then--and cleaned her up and gave her some slippers and a big fluffy white robe. She told me how her mama had forced her to have an abortion when she was fifteen."

Chloe was listening intently. "At that same clinic?"

"No, Child. The Dodge clinic was brand new back then. Before, the nearest clinic was in North Bend, Indiana. When they built this clinic, the abortionist would come to Dodge every Saturday to do abortions."

North Bend? Lisa? Chloe's stomach began to churn.

"So, what happened?" said Lily. "Did she have the baby?"

Marg got a sad look. "I don't know. I met with her several times, and I know she fell in love with Jesus, but I never heard from her again. That's okay. I'm just supposed to plant seeds. It's up to the Holy Spirit to water them." She handed the photo back to Lily. "Oh, isn't she beautiful?" said Marg. "She kind of looks like you."

Chloe stuck out her hand to intercept the picture.

Marg glanced at the picture again, then at Chloe, before handing it to her. "If that don't beat all. She kind of looks like you, too, Child."

Lily grabbed the picture from Marg's hand before Chloe could. "She does. That's amazing. It's like looking in a mirror." She turned toward Chloe. "Check it out."

Chloe looked down at the picture and her knees weakened.

There, in the center of the small, black picture frame was her very own mother. And the reality that Mom had planned on aborting her.

* * *

"Though my father and mother forsake me, the LORD will receive me." Psalm 27:10

Chloe was silent on the ride home, despite Marg's promptings.

"Child, you sure you're okay? You sure you don't want me to get you some lunch before I drop you off?"

"No, thanks, Marg."

The house was empty. Good.

Chloe ran through the great room toward the loft, accidentally bumping Gary's card table and putting his half-finished puzzle in disarray. She ran to the loft and pulled a hat box from under her bed and pulled from it a stack of Mom's letters. She ran back downstairs. She grabbed the quilt hanging on the back of the sofa and snuggled it around herself, falling into Gary's La-Z-Boy chair.

She leafed through several of Mom's letters until she found the one she was looking for. She quickly scanned the letter, her eyes falling on, "Here is part of my story. Some things are left for eternity." And on, "He rescued you!"

How are you supposed to feel when you find out that your mom almost ended your life? Or she made you get an abortion, like Grandma Hudson and Marg's mom did? Or she didn't want you? What do you do with *that*?

Chloe sat silently, her mind racing. Marg's words swirled in her head, mixing with her conversation with her One and Only.

What do I do with this, Lord? . . . I have to make a decision in my mind to choose love and forgiveness, and let God judge the sin . . . May your unfailing love be my comfort . . . Do not reject me or forsake me, O God my Savior.

I LOVE YOU, CHLOE. I WILL NEVER LEAVE YOU OR FORSAKE YOU.

Gary's truck drove up the driveway.

Does Gary know?

Gary walked in and peeled his flannel jacket off, tossing it over a dining chair. "Hey, want a fire?"

Chloe took a deep breath and swallowed it back down. "Did you know about Mom's abortions?"

Gary looked dumbfounded. He stood silently staring at Chloe, like someone had just shot him and he was waiting for his body to react. "What?" A look of deep concern came over his face. "What are you talking about?"

Chloe relayed the story from Mom's letter and Marg's picture.

Gary silently saturated the stories into his conscious, his face looking fully absorbed in what his mind was experiencing. "I just knew your mom was pregnant with you," he finally said. "Chloe, your Mom and I were reeling with the death of our parents on New Year's Eve."

"From the drunk driver, right?"

"At first your mom was so angry. Then, one day she came home, and she was a new person. That's when she told me she met someone. 'I met Christ,' she said. 'Gary, He rescued my baby! I heard His voice.' Your baby?" I was shocked. "I mean, she wasn't showing or anything. She'd been crying a lot during the previous two months, but I thought it was because of our folks. From that moment on, she *was* a new person, Chloe. She was so excited about life, about the Bible, about . . . you."

"She was?" A flicker of warmth glowed in her. "What about my dad?"

"Well---" Gary looked like he was about to spill, then stopped himself. "He never knew."

"How can a guy not know?"

"Chloe, it was your mom who didn't know. Apparently it could have been any one of a lot of guys."

"So she really didn't know who my dad was?"

"Well, once you were born, it was kind of obvious."

"Obvious? Why?"

"Well, there was only one black kid in the whole county. He played---"

"Let me guess," Chloe interrupted. "Basketball."

"Yes. Davion was the star player of the team. I was the manager back then, and we were friends. He was a foster kid who came to our middle school when he was in eighth grade. By the time he was a freshman, he already had recruiters looking at him to play college ball. He went to I.U. and entered the NBA draft when he was a junior. He played for the Bulls for about ten years, until he got injured. Then he went back to I.U. as the Head Coach."

Where he's still the head coach.

"Yes. Your dad is Davion Griffin. He was already down at I.U. by the time you were born."

"So he just ditched me and Mom, and went to Bloomington? He never loved me?"

"You can't love someone you don't even know," Gary said, defensively. "Your mom never told him. I didn't think that was right. I always wanted to tell him, but she made me swear not to."

"So, to this day, he doesn't even know he has a daughter walking around the planet?" said Chloe.

"I don't think so."

CHLOE, I KNOW YOU AND I LOVE YOU. I AM YOUR FATHER.

℞

Chapter 22

The Dutchman was clearly not happy.

Panic began to trickle into Chloe's bones as she slowed the pace of her walk to Spanish class. Should she turn and go the other way? Or pretend she didn't see him? Run into the girls' bathroom?

He walked quicker, directly toward her. He switched his book from his right hand to his left, approaching her. He pressed his large hand into her shoulder, breaking her stride and pressing her against the locker behind her, hard enough to make it clang. "Ve need to talk," he said, in his Dutch accent.

Adrenaline pulsed through Chloe's veins. "O . . . K." *When I am afraid, I will trust in you! When I am afraid, I will trust in you!*

Ty's squinted gaze penetrated Chloe's eyes for several seconds, as if he were calculating his words. Finally, in an eerily quiet voice, he said, "Chloe Hudson, you are *not* going to screw vith my future, so you better @#*!*# butt out." Ty poked his index finger deeply into Chloe's collar bone to punctuate his threat. “Stay. Away. From Lily.” He glared at her, waiting for her response.

Her heart was pounding like crazy, but she steadied herself and set her jaw. Her bright white heart penetrated Ty’s peekadilly heart, like a roaming light on a watch tower, shining on an escapee in the prison yard. She glared back at him, stoic. “I . . . am *not* afraid of you,” she said confidently.

Ty glared back at her, appearing slightly taken back, then smiled coyly. He resumed his strut down the hall, catching up with some of the other basketball players.

Chloe felt a flash of hot, then cold, and her legs felt like wet noodles. *When I am afraid, I will trust in You! The Lord is my light and my salvation, Whom shall I fear? The Lord is the stronghold of my life. Of whom shall I be afraid? The Lord is my . . .* She kept saying the verses over and over until she could breathe normal again.

* * *

Ty De Veen

The bell rang just as Ty De Veen swept through the door of Pip’s French class and plopped into the front seat.

“Class, I’m handing back your first exam for the new semester,” said Miss Pip. She walked around the room, placing papers facedown on each desk. “Several of you boys might want to consider staying after school for some one-on-one tutoring,” she said flirtatiously.

Behind him throughout the classroom, Ty heard the repeated sound of a paper flipping, followed by moans and whispered expletives. Next to him sat

Max Chapman, his teammate on the Jefferson basketball team, who apparently wasn't learning any French either.

Max looked over at Ty and shook his head. "@#!@. He's gonna bench me."

Last week at practice, Coach Hinsley gave a sermon about how the five starters on the team were supposed to be leaders, in every way, including academics.

Screw him. I'd like to see him bench me. Without me, the team doesn't amount to squat. Without me, they won't even make it past sectionals.

Walking to the front of the room, Miss Pip lost her grip on the last paper in her pile.

It floated to the floor, like a glider, landing in front of Ty's chair.

Miss Pip smiled and looked into Ty's eyes, teasing him. She carefully bent over, holding her stance.

Ty's heart pounded out of his chest. He held his gaze as beads of sweat formed on his flushed brow. Immersed in a dark corner of his mind, he forced Pip to a place where she no longer teased. He gave it to her--again, and again, and again. And there was no mercy, even though she pleaded for her life. *I hate her. I hate Chloe. I hate Lily. I hate all of them.*

Reaching for his cell in the back pocket of his Fitch jeans, he quickly left the room and ran to the guys' bathroom. Entering the handicapped stall, he slammed it and locked the door behind him. With frantic fingers, he logged into the first site on his Internet Favorites, and filled himself with filth.

* * *

"You either do it this weekend, or I'm telling Miss Marilyn," said Ty.

"Tell her what?" said Lily.

"Why you're getting fat." Ty shot a mean look at Lily. "Jefferson High School doesn't vont its head cheerleader to be *fat*, especially going into tournament time. Got it?" Ty took out an Rx form from his back jeans pocket, folded it in half and tucked into the top part of the Lily's cheerleader V-neck top.

Lily's face turned red, and she looked both angry and sad. "The whole universe doesn't revolve around your stupid basketball. I told you, I don't know what I'm doing yet."

"Haf you told your parents?" Ty asked.

"No, not yet. I'm going to this weekend." Lily searched Ty's eyes, hoping for a glimmer of compassion. "Tyler, have you ever thought about us . . . maybe . . . well, you know, like keeping the baby?"

"No," Ty said curtly. "No way. First of all, I hate kids. Second of all . . . Lily Hunt . . . I'm never getting married. When I graduate, I'm getting the @#!@ out of here and playing ball at I.U." Ty glanced down at the pooch on Lily's cheerleader skirt, "And *zis* is not going to ruin my career."

Lily took the Rx from her shirt. "Well, I'm never doing this again." She held it in the air in front of Ty and tore it in two. "And the lady at the Hope and Help Center told me that it's illegal for your dad to be writing prescriptions for girls he hasn't even seen."

Ty absorbed Lily's words, then softened. "Well, okay. Just go and see my dad. He'll do it for free, the other way." He touched her arm and gave her a nice look.

"I don't know," said Lily.

Ty flared, squeezing his hand away from Lily's arm. "You either see him, or we're done." Ty paused, thinking. “No. We’re already done. You’re on your own.” He walked away, toward the school office.

℞

Chapter 23

'Twas not the Valentine's Day that Chloe dreamed of--the one involving a certain Evan Smith, who had apparently come down with a severe allergy to phones, but still it was good. Getting a driver's license is a *big* deal!

Free at last! Thank God almighty, I'm free at last! Chloe laughed internally at her melodrama, as she and Gary got into her VW bug.

Confidently, she pulled the blue bug out of the license branch lot, heading toward Gary's house. "Okay with you if I run errands today?" she said.

I'll bring Lily her present. Then *drive* to the mall. And *drive* back home. And then *drive* to work!

"You have your phone, right? Thanks for the ride," Gary said, going into the house.

Chloe idled the engine in the driveway and pulled her cell phone from her purse. She glanced in the back seat to make sure Lily's gift was still there.

Inside, one of the leather Bibles from Mom's wedding was tucked between white iridescent tissue paper and a note to Lily that Chloe had agonized over. " . . . so here is God's love letter to you, Lily. Fall in love with Him. Love, Chloe."

Chloe sent May a text. HAPPY VALENTINES! I'M LEGAL! GOT MY LICNSE 1 HR. AGO.

CONGRATS! May responded. R U DRIVING US TO SCHOOL MON?

YEP. HAVE FUN ON YOUR DATE 2NITE WITH SAM I AM.

K! CAN'T WAIT :) LOVE YOU.

YOU 2.

Chloe tossed her phone back in her purse, when it buzzed with a new text. *Lily. Good. She was going to text me directions to her house.*

R U BZY RT NOW?

WHATS UP?

I HAVE SUM PILLS

WAIT! PLS WAIT. WHERE ARE YOU?

IM ALONE

STAY THERE. IM GOING TO CALL YOU.

Chloe frantically clicked the buttons on her cell phone. *Please answer, Lily.*

"Hey, Chloe," Lily said, sounding like she was drunk. "How's my cutie little black friend?"

"Lily, where are you?"

"At the mom and pop's house," said Lily, laughing softly. "It's really more of a mansion," she said, slurring her speech.

"I'm coming over, okay? Tell me where you live."

For the next hour, Chloe talked to Lily on the phone, coaxing directions, while driving around Dodge. As she turned into the driveway of a place that resembled the White House, she heard the sound of a woman in the background.

"Lily! What are you doing? How much of this did you drink?"

"Hey, Mumsy Pie, Happy VD," said Lily, laughing. "I'm gonna be a mumsy, too."

Chloe heard commotion in the background and then, "Who is this?" said the woman into the phone.

"My name is Chloe. I'm a friend of Lily's. I've been talking to her for the last hour, while trying to find your house. I think I'm in your driveway now."

Chloe saw a curtain pull back in one of the upstairs windows.

"Chloe? I've never heard Lily mention you."

"HIIIIIIII CHLOEEEE!" Lily howled in the background.

"Is she okay?" said Chloe. "Can I come in? She said she had pills."

More commotion, then quiet.

"I'm her mom, and I'm here now. I'll take care of her."

"Please, can I come in? I have a Valentine's Day present for her."

"Just leave it on the doorstep. I'll have Lily call you."

Click.

I guess sometimes all you can do is pray. Chloe cried out to her Best Friend about Lily, her baby, and the Hunt family, as she carefully placed the gift on their welcome mat.

* * *

Driving a stick shift has its challenges. At 9:17 a.m. Chloe pulled her VW bug into the H & H parking lot. Marg's four-door sedan, and Lily's corvette were parked in the lot. *I hope I'm not too late.* Chloe rushed into the lobby and tapped on the glass window by the front desk.

The receptionist opened it and smiled. "You're here to see Marg this morning, right?"

"Yes. And my friend. I'm sorry I'm late."

"They're probably just getting started. Nurse Nelson was a few minutes late, too." She motioned toward the hallway. "Just tap on the door of the exam room. It's the third door on your right."

Tap. Tap. Tap.

Marg slowly opened the door, stuck her head out and smiled big. "Hey, Child. We were hopin' this was you. Come on in."

Lily was lying on the exam table in a blue paper vest that opened in the front, under a white sheet. "Hi, Chloe. This is my mom."

A classy-looking woman stood up and extended her hand. "Chloe. I'm Carol Hunt. I understand you've been a really good friend to my daughter. Thank you."

"And I'm Nurse Nelson. I'll be doing the ultrasound today," she said, flipping a switch up and on.

The machine sounded like the fuzz of a radio when tuning into a station.

"If I'm not mistaken, I think you're the 100th ultrasound that I've done on this machine since we got it last year," said Nurse Nelson.

A big smile filled Marg's face. "And the 95th life to come from it," she said.

"This might be a little cold," said Nurse Nelson. She squirted a clear, gel-like substance on Lily's stomach and spread it around. Carefully and tenderly, she moved the wand around the top of Lily's stomach.

Chloe watched the amazement in Lily's face as she looked at the screen and smiled.

Marg poked Chloe. "It's always amazing. Seein' this tiny little baby that nobody except God Almighty has ever seen."

Chloe looked at the screen for herself and was definitely amazed. Before she could zero in on Nurse Nelson's words, she saw . . .

Colors. My déjà vu colors! ALL of my déjà vu colors! Small bursts of each color were lightly exploding around a tiny body, just the way Chloe saw throughout her childhood whenever a camera flashed. Even veranda! *I haven't seen veranda since I saw my own veranda heart, before accepting Christ.*

Chloe watched the screen as faint traces of dust, veranda and peekadilly created a haze of *déjà vu* color around the baby's tiny body. *Sin. We are each born with sin, because of Adam and Eve's disobedience.*

"This is the head," said Nurse Nelson, pointing to the screen. "Here are the eyes." She gave Lily time to absorb each description. "See the little foot and toes on the fetus?"

"Fetus?" asked Lily.

"Yes," said Nurse Nelson, smiling. "Fetus comes from the Latin word for *little one*."

Lily let out a soft gasp."Oh, my," she said, staring intently as the tiny body danced across the screen. "Hi, little one." Mesmerized, she continued her gaze, smiling. "What's the little hiccup on the screen?"

"The baby's beating heart."

Chloe stared at the screen, too, feeling surreal. A wave of emotion bubbled deep inside her, flooding her soul. Had she ever felt *this* emotion? It vaguely reminded her of a cross between her first glimpse of the Grand Canyon and the first time she saw the Mona Lisa in person. Seeing the little body on the screen felt like . . . something sacred . . . a mixture of awe, wonder, and secret holiness. Was this the feeling somebody had when they saw Jesus perform a miracle? What would it be like to see a person who couldn't walk, just get up and walk?

Is this what a strong, motherly instinct feels like? Isn't it inexplicable? How can you love someone so much, that you've never met? Someone who has taken up intimate residence inside of your body? A precious gift tucked secretly inside of you by the Creator of the Universe . . . .

Chloe sat quietly, allowing the feeling to emerge fully. When it had, she felt . . . incredibly sad. *What if I never experience having a child inside of me? What if I never get to be a mom? Lord . . . please, Lord . . . please, let me be a mom someday.*

CHLOE, I AM ALWAYS WITH YOU. I WILL NEVER LEAVE YOU. SOME MOTHERS ADOPT THEIR BABIES, JUST AS I ADOPT ALL OF MY CHILDREN.

A strong *déjà vu* feeling overcame Chloe, bringing her back to the same place where this tiny baby was, where she remembered first seeing her colors, and feeling sadness, and then inexplicable joy.Where she danced and somersaulted to the music of Pachelbel's Canon in D, and where she heard her mother's words change over time from, "I'm sorry, little baby," to "I can't wait to meet you and hold you and love you." And where she distinctly heard her Creator, her One and Only, speaking into her soul.

FOR I CREATED YOUR INMOST BEING. I KNIT YOU TOGETHER, CHLOE. YOU ARE

FEARFULLY AND WONDERFULLY MADE. ALL THE DAYS ORDAINED FOR YOU ARE WRITTEN IN MY BOOK.

"Child!" Marg poked her elbow into Chloe's arm. "Quit spacin' out. You're missing this."

Ouch. Chloe straightened in her chair and tried to look attentive.

"Let me see," said Nurse Nelson, as she moved the wand carefully, positioning it on the midsection of the baby's tiny body. "I'm pretty sure I know. Are you sure you want to find out?"

Lily looked over at Chloe. "Do you think I should find out?"

Find out what? Chloe felt like a student caught spacing out in class when the teacher asks a simple question. "Um, sure."

"See that?" said Nurse Nelson, pointing to a teeny-tiny appendage on the screen with her finger.

Everyone leaned in.

"It's a boy."

* * *

Marg and Chloe stepped into the hallway and walked toward Marg's office.

"Do you think she'll keep the baby?" Chloe whispered to Marg.

Marg ignored her question momentarily, walking through the lobby and smiling at a few girls who were waiting.

Chloe followed Marg to her office.

Marg shut the door behind them.

"Can't know for sure, but I do know that a lot of girls choose life for their little ones, when they see them on an ultrasound. They see that what is growing inside of them is not a mass of tissue, but a tiny life that wants to be born," said Marg. "Before we got that ultrasound machine, it was harder to convince girls of that. But, you saw it. The ultrasound doesn't lie. It makes it crystal clear that there's a baby inside, and it also shows if the fetus is alive."

"You mean sometimes the baby isn't alive?"

"Child, almost one-third of all pregnancies end in natural miscarriages. In fact, a lot of ladies don't even know that they were ever pregnant. For others, it's just heartbreaking, because they've lost a little one that they already love and hoped to meet," said Marg. "Think about a girl who has an abortion, and never knows if her body has already naturally miscarried. She'll go through the emotional trauma, physical pain and lifelong thoughts . . . ."

Chloe began to bubble with emotion as her eyes scanned Marg's photo gallery, landing on the picture of Mom. *All the days ordained for you were written in your book before one of them came to be.* Chloe lifted her hand to the shelf and pulled down the small picture of her mom and handed it to Marg. "That was my mom."

Marg was silent for several seconds, then gave Chloe a huge hug. "Oh, Child. Praise God! He rescued you! What a blessing you are. He's got a great purpose for your life."

Chloe returned the hug, feeling a sense of warmth, acceptance and strangely . . . purpose. *I was born for a reason.*

YES, CHLOE. YOU WERE BORN TO WORSHIP ME . . . AND TO HAVE FELLOWSHIP WITH ME . . . AND TO GROW TO BE LIKE CHRIST . . . AND TO SERVE AND LOVE OTHERS. . . AND TO BE ON MISSION WITH ME IN THE WORLD, FIGHTING SPIRITUAL BATTLES WITH LOVE, AND SPREADING MY

MESSAGE OF FORGIVENESS . . . AND RESTORATION . . . AND LIFE.

I love you, God. I'll do whatever you want me to do and go wherever you want me to go.

CHLOE, I WANT TO USE YOU TO SAVE A GENERATION.

℞

Chapter 24

"Please, Chloe," said Lily. "I have to get his signature."

"But, don't you want your parents to come with you?" said Chloe.

"It's just so awkward . . . you know, Ty's dad, working for my dad at the hospital. Please, Chloe. It will only take thirty seconds. Ty said he would sign the papers at 2:00 tomorrow."

"What papers?"

"Adoption papers. I've decided to place my baby for adoption with a loving family. Ty has to sign off on his parental rights."

"But I thought your mom wanted you to keep the baby?"

"She did. She does. But my dad freaked. He said this would ruin his precious reputation in the community. They've been fighting about it for the past two weeks. Their marriage isn't all that great to begin with, and, besides, I just want to move away and go to college and start over.

"Okay, I'll go with you," said Chloe.

"Can you drive? It's getting hard to fit behind the steering wheel in my Corvette," said Lily.

* * *

Chloe flipped on her turn signal and waited to turn into Great Scarlet Subdivision.

"He lives on Scarsdale Drive. It's in the back. They have a few acres on the end of a cul-de-sac."

Chloe followed Lily's directions, which brought her to a paved driveway that extended into thick woods. At the end of it, the driveway curled into a circle around a large stately, fountain in front of a three-story brown brick mansion, with arched double oak doors. The home looked new, perhaps built in the last couple of years.

Chloe parked her VW bug in front of the entrance.

"Thanks for coming, Chloe," said Lily. "I'm hoping this is the last time I ever have to see Ty De Veen. Well, at least talk to him. I can't very well go to Jefferson High School without hearing about Ty and basketball."

Lily rang the doorbell and waited.

Alice De Veen opened the door and feigned a smile. "Hello, Lily," she said curtly. She turned to Chloe. "I didn't know Jefferson had any black kids right now."

Nice welcome.

"This is my really good friend, Chloe," said Lily. "Um, so is Ty here? This will only take a few minutes."

"Come in. He'll be back in awhile," said Alice. "Does your friend want to wait for you in the car?"

Lily's face registered frustration. "No. She's with me." Lily stepped into the foyer and Alice immediately began to close the door.

Did she just try to shut the door on me? Chloe followed Lily into a huge open living area, sparse of furniture. She looked into the dining room, which had an oak dining table that clashed with the room's cherry woodwork.

Moments later, Dr. D entered the kitchen and gave a hearty greeting. "Hi, Lily," he said. "Good to see you." He turned to Chloe. "Well, hello, Chloe. What a nice surprise. I didn't realize you and Lily were friends." Dr. D went to the refrigerator and pulled out a pitcher of iced tea. "Would you girls care for something to drink?"

"No, thanks," they said in unison.

"Hey, Chloe, you have to see your uncle's fine work in our trophy room." Dr. D motioned for the girls to follow him.

Mrs. D huffed. "Harding, we'll meet in the office *right* after."

"Will Ty be back then?" said Lily.

Mrs. D didn't respond.

Dr. D led the girls down a large hallway with arched oak doors on each side. He opened one of the doors and flipped a switch. "Go aheadt, und take a look, Chloe. Your uncle probably did seven or eight of those pieces," he said, warmly.

Lily stuck close to Chloe's side.

A shiver went up Chloe's spine. She was pretty sure she'd never get used to taxidermy, or Dr. D. Was she the only person in Dodge who got creeped out by him?

The room looked like something straight out of Alaska. Except for the wall of glass shelves with basketball figurines, trophies, and banners from

Jefferson and North Bend High School, Indiana University, and the Chicago Bulls.

Chloe stared through the glass at a framed 8 x 10" picture of Davion Griffin. *Davion Griffin. He doesn't even know I exist.*

Dr. D talked incessantly about where he bagged each of his taxidermy animals.

"Come on, Harding," said Alice impatiently, from the hallway.

"Oh, good, Ty must be here," said Lily.

Dr. D waited for the girls to go into the hallway, flipped the switch off, and pulled the door shut behind him.

Alice called from the room across the hall. "In here." She sat by a table and invited everyone else to have a seat. "Come in, girls. This is private. Those are all one-way," she said, pointing to the wall. "No one from the outside can see in."

Lily entered and sat next to Mrs.D. Dr.D held the door open for Chloe. "Ladies first."

Chloe walked in and looked around.

An entire wall of windows, two stories high, similar to those in the trophy room, made up the back of the room with thick heavy woods outside. At the base of the windows was the makings of a small clinic with a sink, an ultrasound machine, and an examining table. Mounted on the wall was a plastic container labeled "biomedical waste."

Chloe's heart raced and beads of sweat began to form. *Dr. D does abortions here?*

"Here. Haf a seat, Chloe," said Dr. D. He motioned Chloe to the empty seat across from Lily.

A darkness hung in the air, even though the room was fully lit.

Lily looked uncomfortable but not that surprised. "When is Ty going to be here to sign?"

Dr. D looked surprised. "What is Ty signing?"

"I'm placing the baby for adoption. It's a really nice family. He needs to sign away his parental rights."

"This is Ty's baby?" said Dr. D. "Alice, you didn't tell me that."

Alice's anger flared, then she calmed herself and said gently. "Harding, you know that is irrelevant." She turned to Lily and placed her hand on Lily's forearm. "Lily. Harding is very skilled. He's done thousands of these. He can help you--today. You could probably even cheer at the sectional game next week," said Alice, looking intent.

Chloe was stunned. Her mouth dropped open. She tried to form words but her brain was firing chaotically and frantically.

Dr. D placed his hand on Lily's other forearm. "Lily, this will relieve your stress. No young lady deserves to be unhealthy, and your emotional and psychological health could be at stake. I will restore your future. I will make it superb again."

Dr. D's words triggered a stronger-than-strong *déjà vu* feeling inside Chloe. Her throat got dry. Her body felt chilled, then she broke out into a sweat. That voice. *I know that voice.* North Bend. Mom. Sixteen--no, seventeen years ago . . . .

* * *

In unison, three colors mocked, "Our painter *hates* you."

Her heart trembled.

One of the colors attacked her. "I will kill you," it said, pressing on her tiny frame.

I WILL DIE FOR YOU.

Another color joined in the attack. "I will steal your future."

I KNOW THE PLANS I HAVE FOR YOU . . . PLANS TO PROSPER YOU AND NOT TO HARM YOU, PLANS TO GIVE YOU HOPE AND A FUTURE.

The third color lurked in the heavy darkness, watching and waiting. "I will destroy you," it whispered.

I WILL RESCUE YOU.

An eery silence . . . then, a humming sound.

A pang of pain, but nowhere to go. *Help me!*

A voice. "Good afternoon, Miss Hudson."

"We're ready, Doctor."

"Superb."

More pain . . . stronger. *Someone, please help me! Help me, Mama!*

"I'm not sure about this," says a familiar voice.

"Miss Hudson, no young lady deserves to be unhealthy. Your emotional and psychological health could be at stake. I will restore your future. I will make it superb again."

"No! Please, wait. I'm not sure."

Commotion. Screaming.

"Let me go!"

Flight.

Silence . . . Crying . . . Prayer . . . .

Peace . . . Praise . . . Purpose . . . .

I LOVE YOU, CHLOE.

* * *

"It's just tissue," barked Alice. "The fetus won't feel it."

Chloe tried to speak, but felt like she was in a coma, watching everything around her, and yelling to an outside world that ignored her cries. *The baby will feel it! I remember feeling it.*

"And Lily, you won't feel it either. We'll give you anesthesia, for *free*," said Alice.

"Alice," said Dr. D bluntly. "If she doesn't want the procedure, I'm not going to force her."

Alice flared again. "Harding, do you want this to ruin Ty's scholarship? He *needs* that scholarship. Remember? Remember all the debt from your stupid exotic hunting trips? You can't keep doing these procedures for free."

Now Dr. D flared. "How about the debt from all your plastic surgeries? What about that?"

Alice opened her palms in front of her, like she was pushing something, and as if to say, "Enough." She turned to Lily. "Lily, we don't even know this is Ty's. In fact, Ty is not the kind of kid who goes sleeping around, especially with a slut like *you*."

Tears began to form in Lily's eyes.

Chloe choked, then coughed. She pushed her chair back quickly. "Lily, come on. We have to go."

"But, Alice, what *if* this is our grandchild?" said Dr. D, as Lily and Chloe darted out the door down the hall.

Chloe grabbed Lily's hand and ran across the granite foyer. She flung open the double doors and rushed out, opening the door for Lily and then dashing around the car to the driver's seat.

Once Lily shut her door, Chloe hit the lock switch and cranked the stick into first gear; second gear by the time they'd circled the fountain.

They sped away, listening to Alice De Veen shout obscenities behind them.

Minutes later, Lily's phone buzzed with a text from Alice De Veen that said, TY WILL NOT SIGN.

℞

Chapter 25

Whoever coined the term March Madness must have been a psychiatrist. Could people really get this emotional about basketball? And the term Hoosier Hysteria? Absolute confirmation that people from Indiana must have some sort of basketball lobotomy performed on them at birth.

May had fallen victim too, partly because of a certain FCA President named Sam. The week of the big sectional game, she and Sam coordinated their school-spirit-wear daily. On Monday, they painted their faces into puzzle pieces interlocking like BFF necklaces. Tuesday, May wore solid white; Sam wore solid blue. On Wednesday they won the spirit award for best cartoon characters with their rendition of Velma and Scooby Doo. Thursday was matching hat day. And Friday? Today, Sam wore a suit and a tie, since he was the team manager, which won him the hottest-and-nicest-guy award in May's book.

It was predicted throughout the region that the great Ty De Veen would lead the Jefferson Bobcats to the state championship in Indy.

If Chloe heard about him one more time she might barf. Lily needed his signature to proceed with the adoptive family, and the jerk wouldn't give it to her. *How fair is that? He won't own up to being a parent, or pay child support, but he won't let her make a redemptive choice, and bless someone else who desperately wants a child?*

Not that Chloe thought what Mom did was right either. *I mean, was it fair to Davion Griffin not to even tell him that he was my dad? Maybe he would have made a redemptive choice, if Mom had given him the chance? Maybe he would have been part of my life?* It's just so complicated!

Chloe prayed for Lily every day and held her breath every time she saw Lily arrive at school. Would her sparkly gold still be with her? She wouldn't visit Alice De Veen on her own, would she? What if someone forced her to? What if Ty kidnapped her or something? Chloe's main prayer was that Lily would someday show up with a bright white heart.

May and Chloe waited for Lily by the gym doors. They were her only friends nowadays. Her cheerleader buddies and even Miss Marilyn had ditched her once they found out she was pregnant. *I still don't get that.*

"Did you see Lily at all today? She's still having morning sickness, so she comes in late some days," said Chloe.

"Nope. Didn't see her," said May.

Students funneled into the gym as the Jefferson High School pep band jammed to the school fight song. The basketball players were seated in a row, center court.

Chloe looked up and down the hallway, searching for Lily.

"Chloe, I have to go," May said, looking at her watch. "Sam and I are announcing the party details for the victory party on Saturday. He wanted to go over it with me beforehand."

"Okay, I'll meet you at the car afterward," said Chloe. She pulled out her phone and sent Lily a text. "ARE YOU AT SCHOOL?"

Lily responded. "NO. DR PUT ME ON BED REST UNTIL BABY IS BORN."

"WOW. OK. CALL ME."

Chloe leaned against the door, looking at the gym. *Don't know if I can stomach a half an hour of T-Y, The Guy.*

"Welcome, Bobcats!" said the principal. "Today we're getting psyched up for the first round of the Indiana High School Athletic Association Boy's Basketball Tournament. Let's show our school spirit and cheer on our team to a victory! Then we'll party, party, party! Well, I mean, we'll celebrate. Here to tell you about the victory party being planned are two members of our Fellowship of Christian Athletes. Please give them a warm welcome!"

Sam and May walked to the podium, as the crowd cheered. Everyone, except Ty.

Chloe smiled. *Their bright white hearts are cute together.*

May looked great. Was it the fact that she hadn't eaten a donut for four months or all the training for track? She wore a Bobcat blue sweater tucked into jeans that were on the loose side, with sterling silver jewelry and a black belt. She was svelte and slender and exuded a healthy glow.

May was truly happy lately! And so were her parents. Apparently, they really liked it when Sam came to their front door and asked permission to take May on a running date.

During basketball season Sam was the team manager, but during track, he was a star runner. May could be this year, too.

"Hey, Bobcat Fans," Sam began. "The Fellowship of Christian Athletes is honored to throw our victory party, immediately following our win tonight!"

The crowd cheered.

"The Hogans are a sweet old couple who have graciously offered the use of their place while they're in Florida. The cheerleaders will hand out directions on the way out of the pep session," said Sam, before turning to May.

"There's going to be a bonfire and hayride and s'mores and fireworks," said May.

"Everything will be chaperoned and it's dry. Got it? No alcohol. No drugs. Just fun. All right, go Bobcats!" said Sam.

Most of the crowd cheered, except for a few boos.

Ty looked slightly up in the air, like he was rolling his eyes and then he locked them on . . .

Me. Is he looking at me? Chloe watched center court and then turned away, scanning the gym, before looking back at him.

He stared some more. More like a glare. Like a blow torch melting an icicle.

His peekadilly heart shouted silent obscenities at Chloe's bright white heart.

Her heart raced. She felt like a lone gazelle being eyed by a hungry lion. *It's better when he ignores me. But, God, You have armed me with strength for the battle.*

Ty locked his eyes on hers and mouthed the words, "@#!@ you!" Then he stood and smiled, engaging the crowd.

* * *

Chloe straightened her black beret and smoothed her Anjou apron. She punched the time clock and headed for the prep kitchen. Yay. She could space off into her own little world tonight while making sundaes and coffee drinks. Maybe she'd get lucky and Namby would make her work late tonight so she could ixnay the whole game-nay? Her heart thumped as she thought about the victory party afterward, knowing a certain *déjà vu* Dutchman would probably be there. What if? But, there's safety in a crowd, right?

May punched the time clock right after her. "So, Chloe," said May, "we're bookin' out of here ASAP tonight, right?"

Dread oozed through Chloe's bones. "May, couldn't I just drop you off at the game? You could go to the party with Sam, right?"

May looked disappointed. "Sam has to stay after the game. I'm supposed to be one of the first ones to get to Hogan's Farm to make sure everything is all set up. Sam's going there after school and he's going to leave me a list of what we need to do right when we get there." May looked at her friend's eyes. "Chloe, don't worry. Sam said Ty probably isn't even going to be there because he doesn't like dry parties. It's going to be really fun. You can hang out with Sam and me."

Chloe felt the words "third wheel" stamped on her forehead.

"Please. You're my best friend, and this is the first thing at Jefferson I've ever gotten involved with. I *want* you at this party."

May is my best friend. I should be there for her. "Okay, but if Ty shows up, I'm leaving," said Chloe.

May's face beamed with excitement. "Trust me. It's going to be a blast!"

Namby walked through the time clock area and stopped to look at May and Chloe. He looked at his wristwatch. "Girls, is it 4:05?"

Translation. "You're late. Get to your work stations in the Shoppe right now."

"And, Chloe at 6:00, you're on a special job. Here's the detail sheet," he said, handing her a Nambygram. "One of our new recruits will take your spot on the floor."

Chloe heard May mutter under her breath as she headed to the Shoppe.

Chloe tucked Namby's instructions into her apron and hurried to the prep kitchen. She tidied the back area until the machine spitted out a "to go" coffee drink order. Confidently and carefully, she executed each step of the preparation process, topped it with whipped cream and placed a lid on it. She walked it to the front counter, where the customer stood.

May was pulling chocolates from the case for his order.

Chloe started to hand the drink over and stopped.

A tall black man who looked to be in his early thirties, dressed in a business suit, smiled at her, waiting to receive the drink. An outline of dust surrounded him and he had a peekadilly heart.

Davion Griffin?

Davion extended his hand to receive the drink and paused. He gave her the same kind of look that someone gets when they're trying to remember something, or they recognize something, but they can't pinpoint from where.

Chloe felt . . . confused. She didn't know what she felt. Maybe curiosity? Yes. Connection? No. Davion Griffin was a complete stranger. Chloe's mind raced back through her childhood as she remembered all of the lines that she'd rehearsed for the day she might meet her biological father, but none of them fitted this moment.

After May and the customer exchanged some pleasantry conversation about tonight's big game, Davion Griffin said, "Thank you," turned around and walked out, limping.

Chloe mentally followed Griffin's dust outline out the door and watched him get into a cream car with crimson I.U. detailing. *Dust. Did he give my Mom an STD, or did she give him an STD? Did he ever wonder about me? No, how could he? He never even knew I existed! But Ty knows about his baby, and he doesn't even care!*

CHLOE, YOUR PARENTS MAY NOT HAVE PLANNED YOU, BUT I DID. AND I HAVE A PLAN FOR LILY'S BABY, TOO.

May nudged Chloe, motioning to go back to her station and make the sundae she just typed into the register.

Chloe retreated to the prep kitchen and worked mindlessly, but in deep thought about the story of her life and how she'd been reading it lately. And how she was learning to fight spiritual battles every day by following her Commander! The more she memorized the fighting Psalms, the brighter white her heart would get, and the more she felt armed with strength for the battle. And the really strange part to her? It was all extremely romantic!

At 6:00, when the new girl took her place, she pulled out the instructions for her special project: For Dodge Purity Ball Association: 250 Milk Chocolate Heart boxes. Fill with a variety of milk, dark and white soldiers.

* * *

Chloe's bug circled the Jefferson High School parking lot, searching for an empty space. It looked like the entire city of Dodge was at the big game. "I'm sorry we're late, May," said Chloe. "I was barricading soldiers as quickly as I could."

"I know," said May with a hint of frustration. "But, let's hurry. Maybe we can still catch the half-time stuff." She waited for the bug to park, darted toward the school, slamming the door shut.

"Hey, wait up," Chloe said, pushing the lock on her key fob. Within the first ten steps of her trot, she learned her new sandals only rated about a "2" on the practical scale, because they kept falling off her feet. But they were cute and pink with sequins, and it's not every day that you find shoe apparel that looks cute on Size 11's!

May stopped and turned around. "Why did you wear that?" she said annoyed. "You're supposed to wear Jefferson blue and tennis shoes, not Pandora pink and Barbie boots."

"Sorry." Chloe slipped off her sandals, clasped them in her hands and caught up with May, doing a combination of trotting and tiptoeing.

They hurried past the admission table, which had already been abandoned, toward the gym. Loud cheers and applause poured out.

A pang of disappointment went through Chloe. *Last time I was at a basketball game here, I saw*

Evan Smith. If only we were playing Cedarville tonight. Shoot. I wonder whatever happened to him?

* * *

As predicted, Jefferson High creamed the opposing team to take the Sectional title. Every player, the coaches, and Sam, climbed the ladder and cut down part of the net down as a keepsake. Ty was interviewed by the all the local TV stations and strutted around, soaking in the notoriety, like a proud rooster.

* * *

The Hogan residence was a good place for a victory party. The farmhouse and matching barn had been renovated from old-boring-farmhouse to pristine Shaker motif. A large open field provided lots of space for parking. The barn had large double doors that were open to the night. The FCA had strung white twilights throughout the barn and in the large trees surrounding the property. It looked like Shaker Disneyland.

May and Chloe were the first students to arrive after the game, and to May's pleasant surprise the chaperones had already completed Sam's To Do list. The bonfire was already roaring and multiple trays of graham crackers, marshmallows, and chocolate bars sat on card tables.

The kitchen had been stocked with every kind of chaperone-friendly beverage you could think of--hot chocolate, cans of soda, a coffee drink station and bottled water, all courtesy of the Booster Club and one of the local church youth pastors.

Chloe breathed deeply, inhaling the scent of cinnamon mixed with vanilla as she wandered through the empty house, admiring the decor. It reminded her of a Bed and Breakfast she and Mom had stayed at in Pennsylvania. Narrow hallways.

Lace curtains on the windows. Oak floors. Closets with skeleton keys placed on the rim above.

Outside, the sound of car doors were slamming.

May ran from the kitchen. "Everyone's here. I'm going out to find Sam. Want to come?"

"No, I'm fine."

"Okay, meet me at 11:45 to get ready for the fireworks, okay?"

Within moments, the house, barn, and open spaces were packed with celebrating teens.

For the next hour everyone had a blast, including Chloe.

She hung out by the bonfire, warming her feet, cold from her sandals. She could talk to girls all day long, but guys? *I still have a slight speech impediment, but I'm definitely improving.*

And, this very night, Chloe discovered a new calming mechanism. Eating toasted marshmallows. Every time she found herself getting nervous while talking to a guy, she toasted a marshmallow and ate it. It was working! With every toasted glob of goo, she met a new kid from Jefferson, whom she'd never seen before. A lot of them had bright white hearts that matched their marshmallows. *May was right. This is a great party.*

Sam introduced her to some of the guys on the basketball team who were surprisingly nice.

Chloe fluttered around like a talkative social butterfly. *Wow, this is great practice for when I meet Mr. Right someday.* During one conversation, a guy wiped above his lips. "You have some marshmallow on your face," he said.

A blush of embarrassment went through Chloe. "Oh, thanks," she said, excusing herself. She went inside the back kitchen door and inched her way through the crowded living room toward the hallway with the bathroom. As she got close to the front door, the flow of people came to a standstill.

"Chloe Hudson!" she heard muffled through the voices.

Thankfully, the words didn't have a Dutch twang. She looked around to see which one of her new friends was calling her.

One of Ty's buddies from French class smirked at her and squared himself in front of her. His peekadilly heart radiated from his hulkish body, beaming into Chloe's face.

Dawson? Derek? What was this guy's name again? Like chewing gum on the bottom of a shoe, this guy was always stuck to Ty, hoping for some of his popularity leftovers.

"Chloe, we're playing a game. You want to play?" said Derek.

Nausea swept over Chloe. She feared she might throw up marshmallow fluff. "I-I-can't," she mumbled, her voice staggering. "I'm just leaving."

"But good little girls like this game, Chloe," said Derek creepily, putting his oversized hand on her shoulder.

Chloe began to move toward the door, but was blocked by his hand.

He leaned in close to Chloe's face and whispered, "Heaven."

His putrid beer breath filled her nostrils.

"A good girl like you will like seven minutes in heaven, won't you?"

Chloe's heart pounded. *When I am afraid, I will trust in you! When I am afraid, I will trust in you!* She frantically recited the verse over and over in her head at lightning speed. She lifted her hand and moved Derek's paw off her shoulder.

"Oh, I see you have your little purity ring on tonight." He grimaced. "Does that mean you won't give me any tonight? Come on, Chloe. I promise it will be like heaven. What do you say?"

"When I am afraid, I will trust in you," tumbled loudly from Chloe's mouth. *Oh, crap.*

The words sent Derek into a howl of laughter. Two other gimpy hulks joined him, surrounding Chloe, like they were guarding her, three on one. They formed a triangle that moved to the foyer, bouncing Chloe in the middle, as if she were the silver ball in a pinball machine.

"May!" Chloe screamed. "Sam!"

"Okay, get the door," said Derek.

Suddenly, Chloe's body was thrust into darkness. She heard the clang of clothes hangers and felt something like wool brush against her face. She sensed an eerie presence, one that had taken a bath in Fitch cologne. A hot breath on her neck whispered, "Chloe." *Ty!* Chloe frantically reached for the door knob, but felt a sweaty oversized hand smother it, and another one cover her mouth.

"Help!" she screamed to no one who could hear.

Ty grasped her sweater at the neckline and ripped it down the front, laughing. He tried to tear off her jean jacket, then reached for the zipper at her waistline.

Chloe flailed her two fists, punching into the blackness of the closet, hoping to get him in his privates or his face. She felt her ring hit something and then silence . . . She reached for the door knob and screamed again.

Ty grabbed both of her arms and squeezed them profusely and banged her back against the door. "You're gonna like this, you little . . . ."

All of the sudden, the door burst off the hinges.

Chloe fell backward, crashing into several teens on her way to the floor. Dazed, she looked up to see the room spinning, then her "fight or flight" mode kicked in. She scrambled as quickly as possible to her feet and ran. Out the front door. Down the driveway. As fast as she could. Past a black Hummer. She felt gravel cut into the softness of her bare feet.

In the faint distance, she heard Dutch expletives being hurled at her as fireworks began to explode in the sky. In between a crowd's "ooh" and "ah," she heard a car door slam. Then "oohs" and "ahs" again.

Adrenaline coursed through her veins. She ran east, toward home, like an endangered species running from a poacher. *What if he follows me home? I pray to you, my Protector! Help me!*

Her heart pounded furiously, to the beat of her flight. *He makes my feet like that of a deer. . . He rescued me from my powerful enemy, from my foes, who were too strong for me.*

The darkness of the night enveloped her, but the light of the moon lit a path for her. She kept running . . . finally intersecting with the road that led to Gary's house and making the turn toward home.

Looking into the distance, she saw the big tree, she and May's big tree.

It stood stalwart in the night, bringing her a momentary sense of relief.

Then quietness surrounded her.

She slowed to a trot, reaching into her pocket and dialing Gary's landline. *Please, be home! Please, be home!* Her body shook as she fumbled to press in the numbers. As she got close to the tree, she stopped and stepped . . . *Ouch!*

Chloe felt something sharp slice through her right foot. Intense pain shot through her entire body, like a bottle rocket being launched into space.

Gary's landline was ringing. And ringing. *Please, be home!*

Then . . . .

An engine revved like thunder behind her. A pair of extra bright lights penetrated the darkness like a laser cutting through bone. Something began barreling down the road, going from zero to lightning speed within seconds.

Startled, Chloe dropped her phone. Paralyzed, she watched as the light became increasingly bigger and brighter. Then the sound of a horn killed the silence of the night, intensifying with proximity. The lights were heading right for her at warp speed!

A surge of adrenaline numbed the pain in her foot. Her feet propelled her toward home, even before her numb brain could direct them. She looked straight ahead, running the race of her life!

In the faint distance, she heard a thunderous crash. Glass breaking. The constance of a horn bellowing in the night. She stopped and turned, but saw only blackness. What if Ty was now on foot? His behemoth body could run surprisingly fast.

Light headed, and her foot bloody and throbbing, she pressed on until she felt welcomed relief at the sight of Gary's driveway. She darted through the porch, leaving a trail of blood behind her. Grabbing the key from under the mat, she quickly unlocked the door, slammed it behind her and locked it.

No one was home.

She grabbed a dish towel and moistened it with cool water, hobbling to the chair and gently wiping her foot.

Under the dirt was an inch-long, centimeter-wide gash that had a heartbeat of its own.

Now would be a good time for Gary to have a cell phone! She hobbled to his phone hanging on the wall and dialed the only number she knew by heart.

Busy. She tried again. *Please pick up, Mrs. Hicks*. Busy again.

Minutes later, she heard the sound of a fire truck and an ambulance barrel down the road outside.

She clicked the receiver down to try again and the phone rang, startling her. She dropped the receiver, so it hung toward the floor. She picked it up again and noticed . . .

My ring! My ring is gone!

"Gary? Gary?" a voice called from the receiver.

"Hello," Chloe said weakly.

"Chloe! Are you okay?" said May.

"I have a really bad cut."

"Sam and I will be right there."

* * *

In the Dodge Memorial ER Room, Chloe was feeling light-headed. She lay her head back on the gurney, trying to stay alert, but zoning in and out.

A nurse came in and poked her forearm and did something to her foot.

When I am afraid I will . . . .

And she was out.

* * *

"If I remember right, this happened last time Jefferson won the sectional," said a robust nurse from behind the central nursing station. "Drinking and driving again. What a waste of a life."

In the waiting room, Gary, May, and Sam looked intently at each other. Gary got up and walked over to the nurse. "Excuse me. Did I just hear you say that someone was killed tonight?"

The nurse looked back at him, like she'd stuck her foot in her mouth. "I'm sorry. I'm not allowed to talk about that. Only with kin. And we haven't been able to get hold of doc . . ." The nurse caught herself again.

"Well, when can I see my niece? Is she okay?"

Another nurse approached the station. "Oh, I think she'll be fine. She's got a bump on her head, and she lost a lot of blood, but we're getting some fluids in her now. Is her mother here yet?"

"No," said Gary, shaking his head. "I'm her guardian."

The nurse hesitated. "Well, based on her clothing when she came in and the bruising on her arms, we may need to do a rape test."

"A rape test?" Gary said, two decibels louder and laced with anger.

Both nurses looked behind and beyond Gary at the couple just rushing in.

"Dr. De Veen," said the nurse, gasping.

"Where is he?" said Alice De Veen.

The nurse got up from her desk, a sad look on her face.

"No!" said Harding De Veen, burying his forehead in his hands.

"I *said*, where is my son?" screamed Alice De Veen.

"Mrs. De Veen," said the nurse, placing her hand on Alice's shoulder. "Won't you two please come with me?"

Harding De Veen looked up, his face puffy and red, and noticed Gary.

Gary gave him a look of compassion. "De Veen, I'm here for you, if you need me."

* * *

"Chloe."

Chloe could faintly hear Gary's voice.

"Chloe," she heard again.

Her eyes fluttered open. *Where am I?*

Fluorescent lights were shining above her, and then Gary's face partially filled her field of vision.

"Hey, there," he said, putting his warm hand on hers. "How are you doing?"

Chloe felt like she was still in a state of surreal bewilderment. She looked around her, trying to recall what had landed her in this bed. Her throbbing foot reminded her of some of the details.

"They stitched your foot," said Gary quietly. "They said you'll be on crutches for a week or so."

A surge of unexpected grief came over Chloe. *I miss my mom . . . I want my mom. Please, help me, God.* She loosened her hand from Gary's to touch her ring, but her hand was naked. *My ring. My ring is gone.*

Her heart cried inside of her. *The Lord is close to the brokenhearted and saves those who are crushed in spirit.*

"Chloe, the nurse wants to know, if she needs to do a . . . ." Gary stopped.

A what? Chloe tried to scoop together some coherence. "A what?" she said.

Gary's expression was a mixture of confusion and grief. "A rape test," he said, softly.

A rape test? Chloe's eyes popped. *Was I raped?* Her mind raced through the details of the night---the game, the party, the closet . . . running for my life . . . the tree . . . my foot . . . the sound of the ambulance. *I don't think I was . . .* "I--I don't think so."

"But the nurse said you might not remember. She wants to give you a rape test and emergency contraception, just in case."

A strength and awareness bubbled inside of her. "No. I don't need that," she said. "I don't want that."

The nurse pulled the curtain back and came to the bedside, looking compassionate. She clicked the switch on Chloe's gurney, bringing her to the upright position.

"She doesn't want it," said Gary.

"But what if she's pregnant?" said the nurse.

Chloe lay there absorbing everything around her. *What if I'm pregnant? But I haven't had my period yet, so I can't be pregnant! But what if I was pregnant? What if I am pregnant? What if Ty De Veen raped me? Not every baby is planned, but every baby is a gift. Every baby is a sparkly gold gift. My baby would be a gift . . . Does that mean I want to be pregnant? No. . . No. I don't want to be pregnant. But if I am . . . .*

"Chloe," Gary said, interrupting her thoughts. "The nurse thinks we should."

Chloe opened her eyes big. Her heart began to pound faster. She looked at the nurse. "Could you please bring me a mirror?"

"A mirror?"

"Yes," said Chloe, somewhat frantically. "I need a mirror."

Both Gary and the nurse looked puzzled.

The nurse left and returned twenty seconds later with a handheld mirror.

Chloe closed her eyes, calming herself. She held the mirror up to her face. *Will there be sparkly gold? Will there be a dust outline?*

She opened her eyes slowly and saw . . . .

A bright white heart on her chest. No sparkly gold. *I'm not pregnant.* No dust. *I don't have an STD.* She let out a sigh of relief and closed her eyes again. *Thank you, God. Thank you.*

* * *

May and Sam stood up when Gary came out to the waiting room. "Is she okay?"

"Yes, she seems okay," said Gary. "Now what happened again?"

May and Sam filled Gary in on the sketchy details that other kids from the party had told them. "We didn't see any of it," May said, looking remorseful. "We were busy with the fireworks when it happened."

"May!" called Mrs. Hicks, running into the ER waiting room. "Are you okay? What about Chloe? Where's Chloe?"

"She's here, Mom," said May. "She's doing okay."

Mrs. Hicks gasped. "She wasn't in the car, was she? I saw the crash. I was rocking Louie, and I saw a car go down our road. I think it was some sort of SUV. It was going at least 80 or 100. And then I heard the sound, and saw the flames. I was the one who called the ambulance."

From down the hall, they heard the tip tap of high heels and the sound of sobs.

Harding and Alice De Veen looked bereaved.

Gary extended his arm on the back of Harding De Veen's shoulder.

"He's gone," said Harding. "Our Tyler is gone."

Everyone listened with compassion.

"His life had such purpose . . . such promise," said Harding, "and now it's gone. He's gone."

Gary and Harding De Veen stepped to the side.

Alice silently brought her hand to her face, covering her eyes and sobbed.

May gasped.

Chloe's diamond ring was on Alice's thumb!

"Mrs. D.," said May, quietly. "That's Chloe's ring."

Alice let her hand down by her side. Through her tears, anger flared. "This was *not* that little brat's ring. This is a family heirloom of ours." Alice turned and called to her husband, "Harding, we're leaving," she said, walking toward the exit.

* * *

For the next week, Jefferson High School had grief counselors on hand to talk with students.

A large community campaign was waged against drunk driving, highlighting all of the negative consequences that result from teens taking risks. How teen lives are at stake. How alcohol is addictive and affects a person's mind and body. How parents must warn their kids, because a future generation is at risk.

℞

Chapter 26

In late April, Chloe asked Namby for a Wednesday off so she could cheer for May and Sam at the track meet. She missed working with May, but track season would be over soon.

Chloe climbed the bleachers and sat next to Mr. & Mrs. Hicks, the proud parents of the "new, promising sprinter on the Jefferson High School Track team."

Mr. Hicks smiled and nodded at her.

"Hi, Timmy. Hi, Tommy," Chloe said. Chloe squeezed a tiny fat roll on Baby Louie's stomach. "How are you, buddy?"

"It's so nice of you to come watch our May," said Mrs. Hicks. She pulled a newspaper out of the diaper bag next to her. She flipped to the center page and folded it back. "Look, May won the *Dodge Sentinel* Spring Photography contest. I bought an extra copy, so you can have this one."

"Are you sure? Thanks, Mrs. Hicks."

Mrs. Hicks looked straight at Chloe. "I don't think you even realize what your friendship has done for May." Mrs. Hicks was getting choked up. "You've helped her find her way and walk with the Lord, Chloe. Thank you,"

"She's done that for me, too. She's my best friend." Chloe looked down at May's photograph.

It was of a fragile petal pink tulip.

"It's beautiful," Chloe said, tucking the newspaper into her purse.

After the meet Chloe walked down to the fence where May and Sam were standing. She patted May on the back. "Hey, great job, guys."

"Thanks," said Sam. He turned to May. "So you're riding home with Chloe? I'll call you later tonight," he said, trotting toward the boys' locker room.

May smiled at Chloe. "So have you decided?"

"Not really."

"Chloe, trust me," said May. "Sam isn't gonna fix you up with a loser."

"I know," said Chloe. "But, prom night? That's not really the best night for a blind date, is it?" *What if I don't know what to say to this guy? I can't eat toasted marshmallows at the prom!* "Besides, technically, you're supposed to be a junior or senior, and I'm only a sophomore."

"I know, but I get to invite you, since I'm the chair of the committee. That was the deal. I told them I'd do most of the work, but only if my best friend could come," said May. She looked Chloe in the eye, begging. "Come on, Chloe. You know this is my dream. I'm going to prom! And I'm going with Sam, my dream guy. I want you there, too." May pulled a picture from a magazine out of her pocket.

"Look, my dress kind of looks like this. I spent a whole Anjou paycheck on it."

"That will look really good on you," said Chloe, studying it and then handing it back.

"And this one would look great on you!" said May, handing her another picture. "I could even go and get it for you. Well, you'd have to pay for it. Uh, actually, I already bought it, because they only had one more in your size, and I figured I could always return it if you said no. But I know you'll say yes, won't you, Chloe?"

"You already bought my dress? How much did it cost me?" Chloe laughed.

"I got you a great deal!" said May. "It was 30% off." May began to look excited. "Please, Chloe."

"Well, how does Sam even know this guy?"

"Through Fellowship of Christian Athletes. He goes to a different high school in town. Sam says he's really nice." May waited with anticipation. "So, can I tell him yes?"

"I guess."

Before Chloe could get the full word out, May was running toward the locker room. "I'll meet you at your car in a few."

As Chloe waited in her bug, she glanced at May's winning pink tulip again. Her eyes landed on a public announcement that read:

"Seeking the individual who fathered a child with Lily S. Hunt on or around Thanksgiving timeframe last year. Claim parental rights by May 2."

* * *

"For the accuser of our brothers, who accuses them before our God day and night, has been hurled down . . . He is filled with fury, because he knows that his time is short." Revelation 12:10-12

"And you say this ring of yours was valuable?" said the investigator.

"Yes. It was priceless," said Chloe.

"Are you sure this boy didn't *ask* if he could see your ring?"

"No. He stole it," said Chloe.

"Well, did you *say* you would go into the closet with him?"

"No! His friends shoved me in there."

"Miss Hudson, had you been drinking?"

"No. I told you, Ty De Veen had been drinking."

"What you were wearing?"

"Jeans, a V-neck white sweater, and a jean jacket."

"And did you wear tennis shoes, in case you *needed* to run?

"No. I wore pink sandals with sequins."

"With sequins? Oh, I see. And what was the purpose of these sequins?"

"Look. My friend saw my diamond ring on Alice De Veen's hand."

"Don't change the subject, Miss Hudson. Alice De Veen would never break the law, and she has rights."

"Well, don't I have rights, too?"

The investigator snarled and glared at Chloe. "Well, if you ask me, people who wear sequins are just asking for it."

* * *

Gary

Gary pulled open the glass door of Glisten's Jewelers and walked in, heading straight for the diamond case.

"Well, good afternoon. Welcome to Glisten's. What can I do for you today?"

"I've got my eye on that one right there," said Gary, pressing his finger on top of the glass case. "The one that looks like a football."

"Oh, sure." The jeweler took a set of keys from his pocket and opened the case. He set the diamond on a piece of black velvet for Gary to peruse. "You've been in here before, haven't you?"

"Just once," said Gary. "Came in with my niece last fall," he said, not lifting his eyes.

"That's right. Your niece had that rock," said the jeweler.

Gary looked up.

The jeweler had a weird look on his face. "I wanted to get a hold of you guys, but I didn't know how. I didn't know your names and anything about you."

"Why? What did you want?"

"Well, a couple of months ago, a gentleman came in with that ring and wanted to sell it."

Gary's eyes got big. "Are you sure it was her ring?"

"I'd know that diamond anywhere. That's a one-of-a-kind because of its internal clarity."

Gary looked excited. "She lost that ring around then. So do you have it? Did you buy it?"

The jeweler looked nervous. "Yep. I bought it--gave the guy $50,000 for it."

"*Fifty* grand!" Gary said, in disbelief.

"Worth every penny. I resold it overseas for $60,000," said the jeweler, with a slight sense of pride.

Gary stared at him. "You mean to tell me, you recognized my niece's ring, and you didn't call the police when some jerk tried to sell you hot merchandise?"

The jeweler began to hem and haw. "Well, it could have been one that just looked like your niece's. And the guy selling it wasn't some kid from the hood. He was distinguished looking. He said it was a family heirloom, and that he and his wife were getting divorced, and he was changing jobs."

"What's his name?" said Gary, bluntly.

"I'm not at liberty to give you that."

Gary waited to see if a change of mind might happen, but it didn't. "Then I'm not at liberty to buy this from you, either," he said, pushing the diamond on the black velvet square toward the jeweler, before walking out.

* * *

On Mother's Day, Chloe's phone buzzed with a text from Lily, who was going on her third month of bed rest.

HEY GIRL. HAPPY M DAY! MARG WAS JUST HERE. BABY D IS KICKING A LOT NOW! A GRT FAMILY FROM D.C. IS ADOPTING HIM. BABY DUE AUG. 8. I WANT TO SEE PICS OF YOUR PROM DRESS.

* * *

Chloe's finger couldn't take being naked any longer. After no one responded to her "lost and found" ad in the paper, and the police dissed her story about Alice De Veen, Chloe obliged. She bought herself a new pearl ring, similar to May's.

Her finger felt hugged again.

As prom approached, Chloe's feet got cold. The thought of spending six to seven hours with some strange guy, she didn't even know sounded like torture. And what kind of a mother names her son

Smitty? Weird. This guy has to have some co-club member from a different school get him a date?

Chloe visualized a capital L on a Smitty forehead.

Then, one night, as she was driving home from work, Chloe had an enlightening little revelation about 'ol Smitty.

Around Mid-May, the Purity Ball Association of Dodge put up a billboard that said, "Prom . . . Don't let one night change your future."

If Smitty thinks I'm changing his future on prom night, he's wrong! Chloe thought. *The first thing I'm going to say to Smitty is, "How do you like my ring? It's a p-u-r-i-t-y ring. You do know what purity means, don't you? That means I won't be changing your future tonight, Bub!"*

* * *

May planned prom night, like some girls plan weddings. About a week before the big night she gave Chloe a detailed schedule of the big day. Running first thing in the morning. Mani's and pedi's at 10:00. Up-dos at 11:00. Home by lunchtime for R & R and to get ready. Sam and Smitty would pick them up at May's at 4:00. Then pictures, dinner reservations at 5:00 and on to "Midnight in Paris" at the Monument Hotel in downtown Dodge.

Chloe sat still in the salon chair, watching her hair be transformed into a black messy nest, shimmering with glitter. She looked down at her French manicure and admired how it looked with her new pearl ring.

May sat in the chair next to her, beaming. How many times had she dreamed of today?

But not because of *prom*, per se. It was because of Sam.

Sam truly admired May. Since the beginning, he had focused on *one* thing: developing a close friendship with her. Finding out her likes and dislikes and hopes and dreams. Sam brought out the best in May, in every way, including spiritual things. He would text May Bible verses, which May, and Chloe, too, found *so* romantic.

"We are going to have such a blast tonight," May said. Her long nails were being painted a shimmery white that matched her bright white *déjà vu* heart.

The girl working on Chloe's up-do said, "How does that look?"

"Great. Thank you," said Chloe. She leaned forward and grasped her purse. As she reached in to pull out a tip, her phone rang. She laid a five on the counter, and said "Thank you." Heading for the front lobby, she clicked the send button on her cell. "Hello?"

"Child, it's Marg. I'm calling about Lily. She just went into labor."

A wave of panic went through Chloe. "Already?"

"They're doing an emergency C-section. I'm going over there right now. You want me to pick you up?"

Chloe's heart pounded. "Yes. Definitely," said Chloe. "I'll be home in twenty minutes."

Chloe explained the situation to May. "May, I'm so sorry."

May looked like a groom left at the alter. "Let's go," she said. "I understand, Chloe. Lily needs you right now."

They paid the salon clerk and left quickly. Once in Chloe's bug, May pulled out her cell phone and called Sam. "Sam, Chloe just had an emergency. She can't go tonight. Tell Smitty we're really sorry."

May was quiet, listening to Sam.

"Evan? I thought you said his name was Smitty?"

Evan? Chloe looked over at May, who was shaking her head in disbelief.

"Evan Smith from Cedarville is Smitty?" she said, her face glowing.

No! No way. Oh, why did Lily's baby have to come today?

"Well, tell him she's really sorry. And to *please* call her."

* * *

Hospitals smell weird.

Chloe's anxiety level rose as she watched each floor number in the elevator light up. Would Lily be okay? Would her baby?

Our Father, we ask You in Jesus' name to protect Joshua, Chloe prayed. *Who is Joshua?* she thought.

The doors of the elevator flew open.

Marg and Chloe walked to the nurses' station. "Is Lily Hunt still in surgery?" Marg asked.

"She's in recovery right now," said the nurse.

"Is Lily okay? And what about the child?" Marg asked.

The nurse looked at Marg and Chloe's skin. "I'm sorry. I'm only allowed to give details to family members."

"Well, we're friends of Carol Hunt. Could you tell her we're here?"

The nurse perked up. "You're friends of the Hunts? Of George and Carol Hunt?"

"Yes, Child," said Marg.

"I'll let them know you're here. Why don't you take a seat over there," she said, pointing to an area with chairs.

Our Father, we ask You in Jesus' name to protect Joshua, Chloe prayed. Chloe looked around. *Did I just hear this in my spirit? God, who is Joshua?*

"Marg, do you think Lily will be okay?"

Marg looked concerned but smiled. "I do, Child. Lily has the Great Physician now. He rescued her. Now He can begin to heal her."

Like Mom. And me. "Lily accepted Christ?" said Chloe.

"Yes, Child," said Marg. "She told me yesterday. Said she'd been reading God's love letter to her ever since Valentine's Day."

Chloe felt tingles inside of her. *Valentine's Day is when I gave her a Bible.*

"But her little one is goin' to need lots of prayer. Bein' a premie, he's going to have a lot of physical obstacles to overcome. His adoptive parents are going to have a lot of challenges."

Our Father, we ask You in Jesus' name to protect Joshua, Chloe prayed. "Do you think Joshua will be okay?" said Chloe.

"Who is Joshua, Child?"

* * *

A thirty-something couple passed Chloe as she approached Lily's hospital room.

Chloe tapped lightly on the door. She took a quick whiff of the bouquet she bought for Lily at the hospital gift shop.

Lily's parents met her in the doorway, greeting her. "I'm George Hunt, Lily's dad," a man said, extending his hand. "Nice to meet you, Chloe."

"Only a few minutes, okay? She needs to rest," said Carol.

Lily smiled faintly at Chloe from her bed. "Thanks, Chloe. How did you know I love white roses?"

Chloe set the bouquet on the nightstand next to her trying not to stare, but she couldn't help it.

Lily looked like herself, but she also looked like a different person.

In the center of Lily's *déjà vu* heart, a mass of bright white shone brilliantly, extending to the edges where a thin layer of black and peekadilly remained. On the outside of Lily's body, her beautiful sparkly gold band had disappeared, leaving only a thin outline of dust.

"Did you see him, Chloe?" said Lily, emotional. "He's so tiny."

"No, I haven't got to see him yet," said Chloe.

"That couple just here? That's Mimi and Scott Clark. They're adopting him." Lily pressed her lips together and smiled faintly. "They let me pick out his name, Chloe." Lily teared up and whispered, "I named him Joshua."

Joshua!

"From the Bible you gave me." Lily folded back the sheet to show Chloe she had it next to her. "Chloe, I read it cover to cover."

"Really? Even Leviticus?"

Lily nodded. "Chloe, thank you."

"For introducing you to Marg?"

"No," said Lily. "Well, that too." Lily looked Chloe in the eye. "Thank you for caring about me, and thank you for introducing me to Jesus. I fell in love with Him, Chloe."

Fall in love with Him . . . .

"I started in John and then read the whole New Testament. At first I thought it was kind of boring, but then I started to be drawn to it. And when you're on bed rest, you have nothing but time on your hands." Lily's eyes brightened. "Then I couldn't put it down. Every time I read it, I felt more and more hope--like my mess wasn't too big for Him to figure out. I mean, if Jesus could go through all the torture and pain of the cross, and then be raised from the dead by the power of the Holy Spirit, isn't there hope He could do a miracle for me, too?"

"Marg always says that every baby *is* a miracle," said Chloe.

"Joshua is a miracle," said Lily. "The doctors said he's incredibly healthy for being so premature. And . . . they don't think he got my STD either." Lily's eyes flooded with gratitude. "Chloe, you're part of the miracle, too," she said, smiling and getting choked up again.

"Lily, you're the one who went through everything--the bed rest, Ty, the De Veen's . . . the childbirth."

Lily paused. "Chloe, if you hadn't cared about me, Joshua wouldn't be here," she said, "and neither would I."

Chloe felt a surge of purpose pulsate through her body. *Really?* She stared at the vase of white roses, recalling her mother's wedding, while trying to absorb the thought.

"Dear," said a nurse, entering the room, "Lily really needs to rest. Maybe you could come back later."

Chloe touched her hand to Lily's. "See ya," she whispered. "I'm going to go see Joshua now." She smiled at her friend.

“Thanks for coming, Chloe.” Lily smiled. “And hey, I like your up-do,” she whispered.

“The NICU is down the hallway to the right,” said the nurse, as Chloe stepped toward the door.

She went down the hall, turned the corner, and stopped abruptly.

There, in front of a large rectangular window, stood Dr. Harding De Veen in a suit, staring in.

Marg walked up behind Chloe and rubbed her shoulder. “Child, it’s gettin’ late. Let’s get you home.”

“That’s him,” whispered Chloe. “That’s Ty’s dad. He’s an a---”

“I know, Child,” Marg interrupted. “I feel sorry for him.”

“You do?”

“Child, I’ve been praying for him for *years*. The Enemy has been using him as a pawn, deceivin’ him into thinking he was helping girls. But I think God is workin’ on him now.”

“Why do you say that?” said Chloe.

“Last week he stopped by the H & H Center and left an envelope with a donation and a note that said, ‘This is for the work you are doing.’”

“So, he’s sorry?” said Chloe.

“I don’t know, Child. I just know there isn’t a crime that God won’t forgive, or any sin that He can’t heal. And that’s been my prayer for him.”

“How much was the donation for?” said Chloe.

“Fifty thousand,” said Marg.

℞

Chapter 27

At 3:45 p.m. after school on Monday, May and Chloe sat in the Anjou break room waiting for their shift to begin. May was just about to share detail #529 of Prom Night, when a thought dawned on her. "Did Smitty call you yesterday?"

"No," said Chloe, popping a chocolate pear in her mouth. "And it's fine. If he calls, he calls. I'm done worrying about it."

Marg sauntered into the break room with her jacket and purse in tow. She pulled a stack of white cards from her purse and gave one to each of them. "You all are officially invited," she said, brimming.

"Is this your 50th Wedding Anniversary Party?" asked Chloe, smiling.

"It sure is. Elmer and I can't wait. Our kids are flying in from all over."

Chloe got a warm feeling inside, watching Marg's excitement. She opened the envelope and scanned her invitation.

Scan . . . Scan. . . Scan . . . Stop! No way. A surge of excitement went through her as she zeroed in on the location of the party: At the home of Evan Smith, Sr., 11502 County Line Road, Cedarville, IN.

Smitty's address!

"Just let me know if you need directions," said Marg.

Nope. I got his address from the phone book and drove past his house the day I got my license! "This family goes to your church?" she asked nonchalantly.

"Oh, yes. The Smiths are the nicest folks. Nice kids, too," said Marg. "They've been going on mission trips to Nicaragua for years to help my Donovan with his orphanage down there." Marg pulled another invitation from the stack and handed it to Chloe. "Almost forgot one for your uncle. I reckon he'll be comin' with Candice?"

"I don't know," said Chloe, concerned. "I think something happened between them last night."

"I wonder. She wasn't at work today," said Marg.

* * *

Chloe pulled her bug up to Gary's barn, idled the engine, and jumped out to slide the door open. When she got back in, she heard her cell phone ring. She rummaged through her purse, her heart skipping a beat. She watched the numbers float across the screen and didn't recognize them. She turned her car engine off, took a deep breath, and cleared her throat. "Hello?" she said.

"Hi, Chloe. This is Evan Smith."

Oh, the sweet sound of those words! Evan Smith! Chloe soaked them in, replaying them in her mind. How long had she dreamt of a sweet serenade like that from Letter Jacket Boy, AKA Smitty, AKA Evan Smith?

"Hello? Are you there?" said Evan.

"Oh, sorry. Yes, Hi. How are you?"

"I'm fine. I've recovered from being stood up from my prom date this weekend," Evan said with a laugh.

"I'm really sorry about that."

"I know. Sam explained it to me," he said. "How is your friend and her baby?"

"She's doing okay. And the baby is doing surprisingly well."

Then, a chit-chat sandwich with one awkward pause in the middle.

I need a marshmallow. God, please help me know what to say.

And then . . . an hour-long, interesting conversation that reminded Chloe of a tennis game. Lots of open-ended questions that spawned more conversation. They talked about Anjou, Evan's upcoming graduation, and his plans to go to Wheaton College and then med school, and Marg and Elmer's upcoming party. Every question made her heart smile, as if she was the only girl in the world whom Evan Smith wanted to learn about. And throughout the conversation, it was evident that he knew her Best Friend. Not in a preachy-sort-of-way, but strong and grounded, and clearly in love.

Okay, God. I'll take this one, Chloe prayed.

CHLOE, LET ME WRITE YOUR LOVE STORY.

All right. But would you mind grabbing your pen right now, because this is one holy hunk I could see myself with!

* * *

Evan, Sr. and June Smith began hosting family New Year's Eve parties in their small ranch home when their oldest child, Grace, was born. Five years later they built a larger, two-story brick home to accommodate their growing family and added June's "dream barn" soon after that. Maybe that was how their only son, Evan, came to love basketball? The barn was two stories high with a living area and a loft on one end and a half-size basketball court on the other.

The barn had something for all ages. One area looked like a play area at a fast food restaurant, with a jungle-gym, slides and a ball pit. Another "teen" area had a ping pong table, a juke box, a retro Pac-man game, and a 15-foot-long, solid oak table with matching oak shelves and two booths. The shelves were dotted with virtually every classic board game from the past three decades.

The Smith New Year's Party was an "event" in every sense of the word. June Smith loved to bake gourmet desserts and had taught her daughters well. Right after Christmas each year the whole family worked together preparing for the party. Evan, Sr. and his son were in charge of stringing twinkle lights around the perimeter of the barn and setting up the bonfire area outside. The Smith women prepared a gourmet dessert smorgasbord with a "dry" beverage area consisting of hot spiced cider, gourmet coffees, hot chocolate, and sparkling grape juice.

At least a hundred guests attended annually. These consisted of the Smith's extended family, church family and three other families that the Smith's joined for mission trips to Nicaragua every spring break.

Tonight, the Smith barn was the setting for a 50th wedding anniversary celebration: the family's pastor and his wife, Elmer and Marg Workman.

A rush of thrill went through Chloe as she pinched herself. Was she really here? Had she ever looked forward to an evening more? Evan had picked her up earlier this evening and brought her a single white rose, the most perfect that Chloe had ever seen. She inhaled its scent and then placed it in one of Mom's crystal vases. After a Mexican dinner out, Evan and Chloe arrived at the Smith Barn, where party preparations were in full buzz.

"Well, don't you make a fine lookin' couple," said Marg, smiling. She hugged Chloe and then Evan. Marg looked beautiful. She wore a fitted ivory-lace dress that sort of made her look like a giant white heart. Her bright white *déjà vu* heart shone brilliantly from her chest.

Chloe looked at Marg, admiring.

"Child, you have to come meet my children." Marg turned toward the open barn, scanning. "Donovan," she bellowed. "Come here and meet one of my special friends."

Evan turned to Chloe. "You're gonna like this guy," he said. "He would do the craziest things . . . the kids at the orphanage love him."

For the next hour Chloe met all of Marg's family, Evan's parents, and lots of girls of all ages whom Marg had apparently helped throughout the years. And Marg's elderly mom, who was about ninety years old.

Chloe thought of her own mom, and wished she was there. *I love you, God,* she prayed.

I LOVE YOU, CHLOE.

God, thank you for Marg. Thank you for my mom. Thank you for this new friendship with Evan. And, Father, thank you for being my Creator, my Savior and Great Physician, my Closest Companion, Provider and Protector, and the Lover of my Soul.

More guests arrived as the night went on. Marg and Elmer flitted about, visiting with each person.

Evan, too. He introduced Chloe to several people, when he wasn't helping his mom with party details like re-filling the ice buckets or opening more bottles of sparkling grape juice. Several cute girls from Evan's church were quite outgoing to him. He reciprocated politeness, but in his own subtle and gentle way made it clear that he was with Chloe tonight.

Chloe took a sip from her shiny clear goblet. She peered at the wall of photos dating back at least a decade. Each frame showed the same four families standing in front of Donovan's orphanage. Every year was represented except one.

Chloe's heart bubbled as she picked out Evan's face in each one. The first frame showed Evan as a skinny little blond boy with a big space between his two front teeth, holding his mom's hand. A few photos later, a boy-like Evan had teeth covered with silver. Around age 14 or so, Evan's stick-boy body turned man-like, as it was today.

Excitement raced through Chloe as she felt a hand touch her shoulder. She turned, her eyes connecting with Evan's.

"Here, I brought you a refill," he said, handing her another goblet of sparkling grape juice.

"Thank you," she said, then turned her gaze to the wall of photos. "What a cool thing to do on spring break."

"Those are some of the best memories of my life," said Evan. His hand remained on her shoulder, rubbing her sweater lightly with his index finger.

Chloe's heart beat faster. How could such a subtle gesture of affection be so exciting? She basked in the moment, trying to remain relaxed--not making any sudden movements--so this moment of touch wouldn't end prematurely. "Which was your favorite trip?" she asked.

Evan responded with details about lots of the trips, saying he couldn't pick a favorite.

Chloe zeroed in on one of the photos, puzzled.

All three of the other families looked back at her, except for Evan's family. "Why aren't you guys in this picture?"

A look spread across Evan's face that Chloe had never seen. It was a sad look, laced with a hint of healed grief. "That was the year we lost Kathryn." Evan rubbed Chloe's shoulder with his full hand and then pulled it away. He pointed to a girl in one of the other photos. "This is her. She was a year older than me. She died of cancer."

Cancer. Just like Mom. A familiar pang of grief bit Chloe. Does that ever go away when you lose a loved one?

"She was my best friend. I was only eight."

The two stood silently, each in thought.

"You know what it's like, don't you? To lose somebody you love to cancer?"

"Yes," said Chloe. "Did you get mad at God?"

Evan paused. "Yes. I remember going out to our pond the day after it happened . . . Katie and I used to build sand castles on the beach . . . I yelled at God for a long time. I just kept asking Him why and cried and cried."

Chloe listened intently.

"And, ironically, that was the moment I knew God. I heard Him speak to me. Not out loud, but I knew for sure that He said, 'I know.' And I felt this incredible sense of hope that I still can't describe today. Isn't that weird? That I never knew hope until I experienced death? I accepted Christ as my Savior at that moment. And ever since that day I've wanted to become an oncologist, so I can maybe share that hope with other people who get cancer."

"So that's why you're doing pre-med at Wheaton next year?"

"Yes. I've prayed a lot about what God's plan and purpose is for my life. I wasn't sure if basketball was supposed to be in the mix, but I don't think it is. Anyway, it's Wheaton, and then med school." Evan paused and looked at Chloe with a hopeful, yet bewildered, expression. "And someday, I want to get married and have six or seven kids."

Six kids? Chloe put another big fat checkmark on her Mr. Right list.

"Do you want kids someday when you get married?" Evan asked.

Panic poked Chloe. *What if I don't ever get my period? What if Evan is my Mr. Right, and I can't ever give him children?* Chloe disguised a choke with a cough. "Yes. I've always wanted a family. That's what I dreamed about, the whole time I was growing up." Chloe looked around the barn, catching a glimpse of Evan's parents. "You have such an awesome family."

He smiled at her. "I do. Don't I?"

The way he just said "I do" was so beautiful.

He locked eyes with her for a split second. "Gary sounds like he's been a great family, too. Is he coming tonight?"

Gary is my family. He's become like a dad to me. Chloe smiled at her thought, then swallowed a touch of sadness. "I hope we see him tonight, but I don't know if he'll make it. He's really down and out lately."

"Really? He seemed okay when I met him."

"Well, he's a pretty good actor," said Chloe. "But he's really hurting. He was really serious with this gal who worked at Anjou--Marg knows her. Her name is Candice. Anyway, a few weeks ago, Gary surprised Candice with a ring, and asked her to marry him. Initially, she said yes, and then a few days later, she wrote him a note and called if off. Then she moved back to her hometown on the west coast the very same week."

"Did she tell him why?" said Evan.

Because her dad's addiction to porn ruined her family, and she swore she would never marry a guy who ever had that problem. "I guess their first session of pre-marital counseling didn't go too well." *Poor Gary.*

Tap, tap, tap. The sound of someone tapping on a microphone interrupted the moment of awkwardness. "Testing, one, two, three," said Evan's sister, Sue. "I'd like to propose a toast to our good friends, Marg and Elmer. Would you please raise your glasses in honor of 50 years of walking with the Lord and serving Him together!"

Evan held his glass in the air toward Chloe and clinked hers.

They both took a sip.

Evan raised his glass toward hers again. "And to new friends," he said, smiling.

To new friends? How about to finding my soul mate? Or, to Chloe, the girl of my dreams, whom I can't live without? Chloe took another sip and smiled back.

CHLOE, LET ME WRITE YOUR LOVE STORY.

Chloe remained firmly planted on Cloud Nine during the next part of the celebration.

Marg and Elmer each gave a little speech about one another, talking about how God had truly blessed their marriage. Elmer's associate pastor led them in a renewal of their vows, and then said, "Elmer, you may kiss your bride."

Marg and Elmer kissed long and tenderly, reminding Chloe of her first glimpse of them in the Anjou Shoppe lobby.

And then he invited all the married people to share a kiss as a moment of renewal.

Chloe and Evan looked at each other.

Awkward.

Chloe's heart pounded fast. She looked at Evan with a longing in her eyes. *Kiss me, Kiss me, Evan Smith!*

Evan looked back into her eyes. He reached his hand to the top of her arm and caressed it, as he smiled.

His bright white heart accented his teeth and the glisten in his eyes.

He locked his gaze on Chloe for several seconds.

The noise around them was like a fireworks display, yet silence hung between them.

"Chloe," Evan said. "I really like you . . . I'm praying about you." He took her hand and gently straightened the pearl ring on her finger. "I need to tell you this."

Silence.

"What is it?" she asked softly.

"Well, I would love to kiss you right now . . . ."

Me, too! So plant one on me!

"But, I can't." Evan hesitated. "You see, I've made this commitment to God to save myself for marriage . . . for the woman He picks out for me."

It's just a kiss!

Evan traced the veins on top of Chloe's hands with his index finger. "And for me, that means saving my first kiss for my wedding day."

A smack of admiration kissed Chloe's disappointment.

"Because I know myself, and I think if I kissed, I'd want more," said Evan.

Me, too. Chloe gave him a half-smile back. "I get it." She took her glass in her hand again and raised it in the air. "To new friends," she said.

* * *

. . . Forty seven years later . . .

Epilogue

"And when before the throne I stand in Him complete, 'Jesus died my soul to save,' My lips shall still repeat. Jesus paid it all, All to Him I owe, Sin had left a crimson stain--He washed it white as snow." Elvina Hall, 1865

MY DEAR CHLOE, YOUR SINS ARE COVERED WITH MY SON'S BLOOD, AND YOU ARE CLOTHED WITH RIGHTEOUSNESS. COME INTO MY PRESENCE, MY GOOD AND FAITHFUL SERVANT!

And I looked, and I saw a rainbow around the throne! And I saw *colors* that I had never seen before. But nowhere was dust, veranda, peekadilly or black. The streets were made of smooth gold, and He was Bright White--so bright that I could barely look upon Him. Worthy is the Lamb!

And Mom was there, and my brother. And others who said, "Thank you for serving the Lord. Because of you, I met the Savior."

And Jesus said to me, *"CHLOE, I LOVE YOU, AND NOW WE'LL BE TOGETHER FOREVER, UNTIL THE END OF THE AGE."*

And He gave me my secret name, known only to me and to Him.

* * *

Gary poured himself a cup of coffee, shuffled to the kitchen table and sat. He took a bite of the blueberry coffee cake that Bev Hicks had brought over last week. He lit a cigarette, took a few puffs, and rested it in the ashtray. He opened the *Dodge Sentinel* to the obituary page. *It was nice of May to write this for me.*

Dr. Evan Smith II, 65, and his wife Chloe (Hudson) Smith, 63, died Friday in a tragic plane crash en route to Nicaragua on a medical mission trip.

Inspirational to many, Evan and Chloe were devoted to God, their family, serving others, and sharing the good news of Christ.

Born in Cedarville, IN, Evan was the son of the late Evan, Sr. and June Smith. He was a graduate of Cedarville High School, Wheaton College, and the Indiana University School of Medicine, Indianapolis. Dr. Smith ran a successful oncology practice in Dodge for 25 years. He and his wife then served as missionaries to Nicaragua for 10 years.

Chloe was preceded in death by a sibling in utero, and her mother, Lisa Hudson of Dodge, IN, and Encinitas, California. She was a graduate of Jefferson High School and Hillsdale College in Hillsdale, Michigan. She was a devoted wife, mother, and cookie baker, and the Executive Director for the Hope and Help Center of Dodge for 25 years. Currently serving a second term, Senator

Chloe Hudson sponsored many successful bills, including one to defund The Kinsey Institute For Research in Sex, Gender, and Reproduction, located on the Bloomington campus of Indiana University.

The Smiths are survived by six children and eleven grandchildren. Evan Smith III (Greta) of Cedarville, Lisa (Kevin) Kross of Cedarville, Ramirez (Elizabeth) Smith of Cedarville, Salvadore (Juana) Smith of Managua, Nicaragua, Maria Smith of Indianapolis, and Sanchez Smith of Managua, Nicaragua. Evan is survived by sisters Sarah (Smith) Ellston, and Grace (Smith) Adler. Chloe is survived by her uncle, Gary Hudson, of Dodge.

The Smiths were laid to rest in the Hudson Family Cemetery, a remote, century-old cemetery maintained by Dodge County.

Memorials to the Hope and Help Center of Dodge and to Donovan's Orphanage in Nicaragua.

Gary heard a car pulling up the lane, and then a car door slam. He smashed the butt of his cigarette in the ashtray and looked out the kitchen window.

An attractive woman in her sixties, whom Gary did not recognize, was coming to the door.

He looked at the dirty dishes in the sink, deciding to meet her at the door. He walked onto to the porch and opened the screen door, just as she was getting ready to knock.

She blushed slightly. "Hello," she said. "I'm Lily Jones. I was a friend of Chloe's from high school. I'm very sorry for your loss."

"Thank you," said Gary. "Do you want to come in?"

"No, I can't right now," she said. "But, I was wondering if you could tell me where Chloe is buried. I have some flowers, some white roses, I wanted to put on her grave."

"Our family cemetery is tucked back in a woods, about a mile from here. I can drive you, if you'd like," Gary said, his face blushing.

"Thank you," said Lily. "Let me get the bouquet from my car."

Gary opened the door of his pick-up truck, and Lily slid inside.

"I really wanted to be at the funeral," she said, "but I was out of the country. Was it nice?"

"Yes. Very nice. It was sort of like a wedding. That's how my sister's was a long time ago, too."

In the four minutes that it took Gary to drive Lily to the Hudson Family Cemetery, Lily shared that her husband had passed away several years ago, and they had no children. She would be moving from Illinois back to Dodge in the coming weeks to help her mom settle into the Dodge Nursing Home.

"Well, if you need a pick-up truck for your move, I'd be happy to help you," said Gary.

Lily smiled. "I'd like that."

Gary slowed the truck to a stop by a small wooden cross. "The cemetery is just down that path," he said, motioning. "Would you like me to walk you there?"

"No," said Lily. "I really just want to go alone."

She got out of the truck and followed the path.

The freshly dug earth led her to Chloe.

Lily stared at the pearlescent tombstone briefly, closed her eyes and prayed. She gently placed the bouquet at the base of the stone and read its inscription:

Chloe Rahab Smith
Loving wife and mother
Joyfully wed to Jesus

Revelation 19:7 Let us rejoice and be glad and give him glory! For the wedding of the Lamb has come, and his bride has made herself ready.

Lily knelt and whispered a story to Chloe--about a premature baby who grew up and became a medical researcher. How Dr. Joshua Clark was being nominated for the Nobel Prize in Physiology and Medicine for his significant medical discoveries, leading to the cure of breast cancer.

"Chloe, he thanked me for giving him life," said Lily, emotional. "And that would not have happened, if it wasn't for you. Rest in Peace, my dear sister."

THE END

Note from author

Dear Friend ~

Thank you for reading *The Color of Pure.* I hope the Great Physician touched your heart as you read, as much as He touched mine as I wrote. Please allow me the privilege of connecting with you by visiting **www.colorofpure.com.**

Blessings,
L.J. Bleed

Endnotes

1. Lagerberg, Clint and Nordeman, Nichole. 2007. "Heal the Wound." Recorded by Point of Grace on *How You Live*. CD. Nashville, TN: WordEntertainment.

2. Boberg, Carl G. (1886.) *O Store Gud.* (Gustav Johnson, Trans.) Public Domain.

3. Coalition on Abortion/Breast Cancer. http://www.abortionbreastcancer.org/

4. *Maafa 21: Black Genocide in 21st Century America.* Online Movie. Life Dynamics, 2009. http://www.maafa21.com

5. Baby Safe Haven. http://safehaven.tv/

Additional References

Anderson, Neil T. *Victory Over the Darkness, Realizing the Power of Your Identity in Christ.* Ventura: Regal Books from Gospel Light, 2000. http//www.ficm.org/

Grossman, Miriam. *You're Teaching My Child What? A Physician Exposes the Lies of Sex Education and How They Harm Your Child.* Washington, D.C.: Regnery, 2009. http://www.miriamgrossmanmd.com/

Johnson, Abby, with Cindy Lambert. *Unplanned: The Dramatic True Story of a Former Planned Parenthood Leader's Eye-Opening Journey Across the Life Line.* Colorado Springs: Tyndale and Focus on the Family, 2010. http://www.unplannedthebook.com

Ludy, Eric and Leslie. *When God Writes Your Love Story.* Colorado Springs: Multnomah Books, 2010. http://ellerslie.com

The Holy Bible, New International Version. Grand Rapids: Zondervan, 1986. (Also see copyright page.)

Warren, Rick. *The Purpose Driven Life: What on Earth am I Here for?* Grand Rapids: Zondervan, 2002.http://www.purposedriven.com/

S.D.G.

21340637R00217

Made in the USA
Lexington, KY
08 March 2013